RETROSPECTA 44
Yale School of Architecture
2020–21

Contents

Contents

Preface

This year's vicissitudes of curricular hybridity forced upon us a necessary reorientation of the medium we communicate and design with, and a renegotiation of the space we inhabit while we work. Our methods and our material worlds were pushed through the lens of remoteness, and so too were the ideas that followed. As a publication that stands to react and reflect upon the beats of the previous year, two moves were absolutely critical in order to address this fulcrum of architectural education: a virtual extension of Retrospecta, increasing the autonomy and authorship of the student work in a year where projects were developed through incredibly diverse and idiosyncratic means; and a smaller book size that emphasizes a reappraisal of the physical act of reading, a more critical format lending to internal cross-content dialogue, and an heightened importance of the book as an artifact. This volume of Retrospecta sets out to reclaim the solace of solitude by renewing a lost intimacy between story, student, and school, revisiting the reader's relationship to the book as a physical object.

Retrospecta is a narrative endeavour as much as it is a glossy billboard sitting on the highway of architectural academia; it is not only a catalogue, but also a story. The book demands careful sequencing, image rhythm, approachable text, and meaningful adjacencies. In its essence, the smaller size and thicker book is meant to be picked up, held, read, transported, flipped, and reread. Its relationship with the reader renews a humanistic quality missing in our everyday lives during this time spent collectively apart. In its existence as a physical and memorial object, it consoles the individual.

Retrospecta is a virtual endeavour. The proliferation of digital media—GIFs, soundscores, Zoom, latent space walks, animations, VR experiences, photogrammetry, websites—are far from emerging. These are legitimate modes of representation that make up the integral components of design and storytelling. While the virtual format of reviews flattened the hierarchy between pin-ups and finals, it also lent itself to highly curated and documented virtual content; hybridity became a catalyst for a necessary evolution of the Retrospecta format, one that offers an extended and accurate representation of the authorship of each project within the book. Rather than mirroring the print, the website's foremost iteration aspires to compliment the book by celebrating the liminal material—overflow, process work, and extraneous matter. Foundational work throughout the semester points to the polished work in the book, a dialogue between digital and analog that speaks to the veracity of the work being produced at YSoA.

While Retrospecta 44 responds to the cataclysm at the turn of the century through its hybrid format, it also responds to the space-time fog that virtual school, masked encounters, block scheduling, and continual policy changes created. Reading inward from both covers, the book is free of a "correct" orientation and chronology. It takes advantage of the smaller format of the print as conversation between course content transcends seminar labels and chronological distinction. Dovetailing seminar types and weaving core and advanced studios throughout the book offers a more editorial reflection of the great equalizer of virtuality. Complementary, contrasting, or conflicting readings of architectural discourse ruminating across YSoA become more legible as seminars—like those under the Technology and Practice study area—sit beside Design and Visualization courses. Simultaneously, Core and Advanced Studios—siloed in any other context—are similarly interspersed, producing non-linear readings of work across curricular programs and highlighting larger issues being tackled at different stages throughout programs. The object-oriented aspirations of the book converge with its editorial convictions as the dual-covered narrative leads to the book's proverbial end: the middle. The dedicated research chapter at the center of the book emphasizes the school's various tracks and the concepts being investigated across their respective research components. Ideas generated on site, through publication, symposia, lectures, and exhibitions define the ways that the YSoA plugs into a larger academic discourse and sociopolitical climate.

In contemplating the chaos of the past year, a reappraisal has never felt so necessary. The precarity that characterized architectural education in 2020–2021 blurred the ragged edges between work and home; school was everywhere and nowhere, at once. The communal student body lost its form, ceding importance to the individual. Despite the shortcomings of our moment—be it human health, the environment, or social calamity—the legacy of the school as a pluralistic, sensitive, and critical body, remained represented in the work produced over the past year. Thus Retrospecta's onus as both a reflection and projection of the Yale School of Architecture is cemented at *yaleretrospecta.org* and in the 44th volume—a celebration of the individual, an act of reclaiming remoteness.

—Claudia Ansorena, Bobby Ka Ming Chun, Christopher Pin, Saba Salekfard

Images have context, contexts produce stories, and stories have images. This cycle is inherent in the relationship between playfulness and placefulness; between canonical form and colonial form, in regionally bounded and parafictionally constructed domestic space. Through Indigeneous housing and domestic ritual, hybridity and classical continuity, *Advanced Studios* brush against *Core 1 Studios* as they both interface with appropriation.

ONE

ARCHITECTURAL DESIGN I

Core 1 studio addresses the content—historical, cultural, and political—inherent to key architectural methods. Architecture is fundamentally mediated and the projects explore the differences between specific media sequentially, from perspective and image to orthographic drawing and plan. Students were asked to begin each project with an act of appropriation, observation, and engagement with the world rather than a process of pure introspection or isolated intuition. Initial explorations of a particular culture and potential audience were grounded in the discipline of architecture in relation to precedent. Site and program were only considered afterwards and defined in response to each student's initial approach to space and form. [1101A]

FACULTY

STUDENTS

Brennan Buck, Coordinator

Uzayr Agha, *Charis Armstrong*, *Yong Choi*, Jerry Chow, Youssef Denial, Nathaniel Elmer, Harry Hooper, Qian Huang, Shi Li, Madeleine Reid, Ethnie Xu

Nikole Bouchard

Ethan Chiang, Bobby Ka Ming Chun, Benjamin Derlan, Signe Ferguson, *Josh Greene*, Tiana Kimball, Ying Luo, Ingrid Pelletier, Ryan Matthew Reyes, *Noah Sannes*, Caitlin Yu

Miroslava Brooks

Janice Chu, Elizabeth Cornfeld, Benjamin Fann, Clare Fentress, Ciara Kosior, *Sam Landay*, *Christopher Pin*, Joseph Reich, Katherine Salata, Huy Truong, Kevin Wong

Jaffer Kolb

Jonathan Chu, *Kyle Coxe*, Grant Dokken, *Maya Gamble*, Tim Hawkins, Sara Mountford, Faith Pang, Abby Reed, Calvin Rogers, Corinna Siu, Grace Zajdel

Michael Szivos

Ana Batlle, William Beck, *Ariel Bintang*, Sosa Erhabor, Zach Felder, *Chloe Hou*, Gina Jiang, Seung Hyun Kim, Haonan Li, Cole Summersell, Kai Wu

LOST COMMONS

A contemporary house is more often considered a product than a living space. The domestic environment has been gradually normalized into the limiting formulations of a single-family house and individual apartment. Areas of reproductive labor have been packaged into separate rooms and hidden from the public eye, while social activities are outsourced outside of the house. There is an urgent need to reclaim the commons of the house and invent a new paradigm for their architectural expression. How can we recreate a domestic space that accommodates all ways of life? How can architecture open new channels by reinventing spaces that can determine changes? How do we build the housing of our times? [1113B]

FACULTY   Tatiana Bilbao, Karolina Czeczek

STUDENTS   Vicky Achnani, *Guillermo Acosta Navarrete*, Claudia Ansorena, Paul Freudenburg, Samar Halloum, Vignesh Harikrishnan, *Liang Hu*, Sydney Maubert, *Naomi Jemima Ng*, *Saba Salekfard*

JURY   Emily Abruzzo, Pier Vittorio Aureli, Adam Frampton, Fabrizio Gallanti, Maria Shéhérazade Giudici, Dolores Hayden, Elisa Iturbe, Isabel Martínez Abascal, Ethel Baraona Pohl, Anna Puigjaner, Hilary Sample, Rudy Weissenberg

DE-COLONIZING INDIGENOUS HOUSING

Housing for the Indigenous Peoples of the US and Canada has been an instrument of colonization since the governments of these two countries decided to assimilate the native population, stripping them of their culture. It continues to be something that limits educational, economic, and cultural advancement. This studio explores the ways housing for Indigenous people have fostered colonization and proposes a means of dismantling that colonization. The studio looks beyond the housing unit, studying how housing can be aggregated in a non-colonial manner. Tools of colonization like property lines and building codes are irrelevant on sovereign Indigenous land. They are intended to make Indigenous people "like everyone else." The studio does not abandon things like life safety; rather, the issue of life safety is explored through an Indigenous lens where the benefit to the whole is as important as an individual freedom. [1116B]

FACULTY   Chris Cornelius, Aaron Tobey

STUDENTS   Ives Brown, Jiaming Gu, Alicia Jones, *Ruike Liu*, *Ben Thompson*, Hongyu Wang, *Max Wirsing*, Shelby Wright, Young Joon Yun, Sasha Zwiebel

JURY   Tamarah Begay, K. Jake Chakasim, Wanda Dalla Costa, Daniel D'Oca, Keller Easterling, Jacob Mans, Lola Sheppard, Patrick Stewart

THIRDSPACE

Drawing from the writings of postcolonial theorists Homi K. Bhabha and Gayatri Spivak, as well as the critical geographer Edward W. Soja, the studio explores the concepts of thirdspace, hybridity, and liminality. Focus is placed on "the emergence of the interstice—the overlap and displacement of domains of difference," that, according to Bhabha, can begin to destabilize the binary dialectics that reinforce the duality of colonizer and colonized. This challenge to binary dialectics can also serve to undermine dominant hierarchies within architecture, such as part-to-whole, perception-conception, figure-ground, etc. [1101A]

FACULTY   Peter Eisenman, Elisa Iturbe

STUDENTS   *Guillermo Acosta Navarrete*, *Martin Carrillo Bueno*, *Bobby Cheng*, Bingyu He, Rishab Jain, *Taiga Taba*, *Alper Turan*, *Max Wirsing*, Yuyi Zhou

JURY   Miroslava Brooks, Preston Scott Cohen, Cynthia Davidson, Kurt Forster, Caroline O'Donnell, Nicolai Ouroussoff, Anthony Vidler

ART, CULTURE, AND THE NEIGHBORHOOD

The studio engages in a dialogue about how architects consider the long, rich history of architecture in generating new building designs—exploring the notions of the "Classical" and the "Modern," two outsized architectural descriptors whose tension provides a deep reservoir of lessons, references, and inspiration that can lead architects to unusual insights— enabling a more sophisticated synthesis of the many visual, social, environmental, and cultural influences that give places identity and meaning. [1117B]

FACULTY   Melissa DelVecchio, Ana María Durán Calisto

STUDENTS   Ife Adepegba, Daniella Calma, Bobby Cheng, *Ashton Harrell*,
            Bingyu He, Hyun Jae Jung, *Nicole Ratajczak*, Scott Simpson,
            Alper Turan, Yuyi Zhou

JURY   Johnny Cruz, Adrian Fehrmann, Mark Foster Gage,
            Anya Grant, John Grove, Miriam Kelly, Elizabeth Moule,
            Demetri Porphyrios, Jeffery Povero, Annabelle Selldorf,
            Robert A.M. Stern

Jerry Chow

Clare Fentress

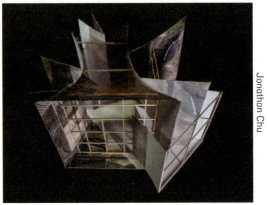

Jonathan Chu

Joseph Reich

Katherine Salata

Tiana Kimball

Caitlin Yu

Harry Hooper

Core Studio

Madeleine Reid

Janice Chu

Kyle Coxe

Maya Gamble

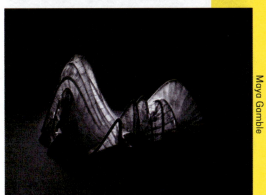

Benjamin Fann

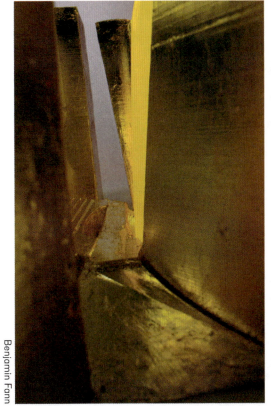

Gina Jiang

Core Studio

Architectural Design I · Image-Objects

Cole Summersell

Sam Landay

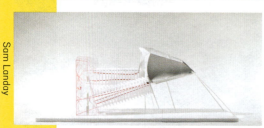

Christopher Pin

Bobby Ka Ming Chun

Charis Armstrong

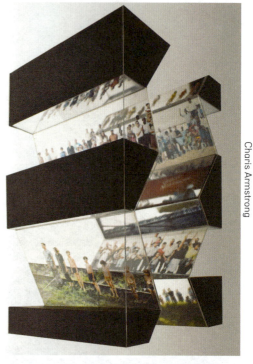

Seung Hyun Kim

Ethan Chiang

Architectural Design I · Image-Objects

Core Studio

Ingrid Pelletier

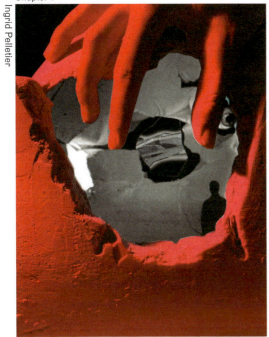

Benjamin Derlan

Josh Greene

Yong Choi

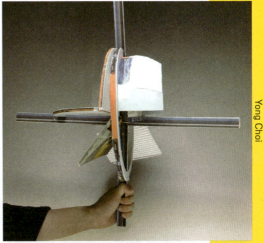

Ariel Bintang

Noah Sonnes

Chloe Hou

Ryan Matthew Reyes

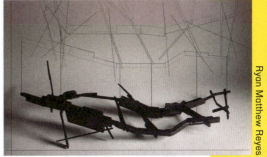

MULANJE TRADITIONAL MEDICINE & EARLY MOTHERHOOD SUPPORT CENTER
Charis Armstrong

Merging traditional medicine and early motherhood support, this center provides for the spiritual and physical needs of women and mothers within the tea-growing community of Mulanje, Malawi. This support is extended to their economic well-being through attending to childcare needs for pre-primary school children (two-to-six-year-olds), and through education in their region's Indigenous medicine traditions. Considering Mulanje's seasonal torrential rains, the plinth of the ground floor allows water to pass through the perforated steps to the east, and wash downhill to where the traditional medicine clinic would seed various medicinal plants. The orientation of a network of brick masonry arches communicates changes in programmatic function through their directional changes. These structural ribs, through light and shadow, define the meter of the large, open-air, gathering places. This presents the communal zones as dichotomic spaces which are massive yet porus, austere yet playful.

Charis Armstrong

Charis Armstrong

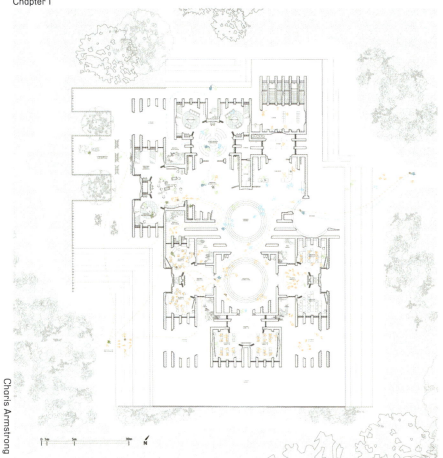

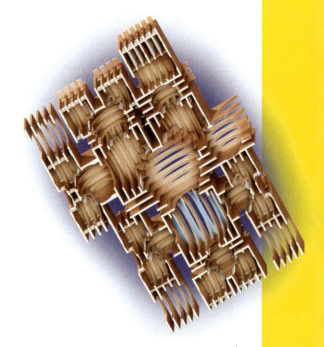

SPACE BY TIME
Yong Choi

Time and space are defined in relation to one another. Time is set in accordance with planetary motion, and countries are grouped relative to their time zones. Stonehenge is an architectural stage for the phasing of both sun and moon, a space made for/by the human recognition of such events. In contrast, the project makes one recognize and further understand the changing experiences of their specific location throughout an annual time sequence. This time sequence is not only an information and education center showing the history of this site, but also a spatial field defined by time.

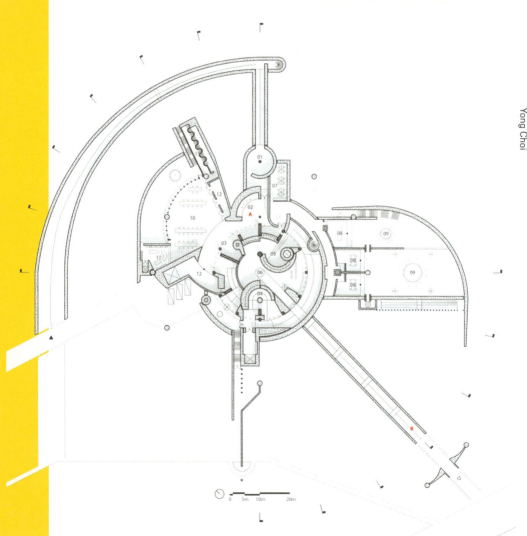

Yong Choi

Yong Choi

Naomi Jemima Ng, Liang Hu

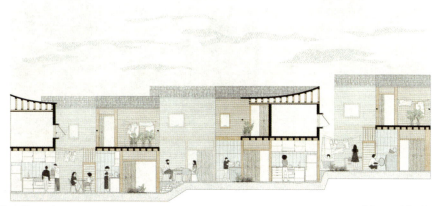

Lost Commons · Bilbao, Czeczek

Advanced Studio

LOADED CORRIDOR
Naomi Jemima Ng, Liang Hu

Gone are the days when washing machines are tucked away, when vacuum machines are quiet, when kitchens are separated from the rest of the house, and when empty corridors are quickly passed through. Say goodbye to the invisible labor, the invisible neighbor, the invisible...you.

Welcome to the Loaded Corridor! In this new mode of life, the corridor becomes the street and domestic work is no longer out of sight. One has to pass through another's kitchen, smell another's food, pry on other's gossip before entering one's private realm. Your home becomes part of the street as much as the street becomes part of your home, transforming what was once a dreaded chore for one into a form of bonding activity between your community. In the Loaded Corridor, anyone is welcome. With that said, are you ready to move from your standard double-loaded corridor into a very-loaded corridor?

Naomi Jemima Ng, Liang Hu

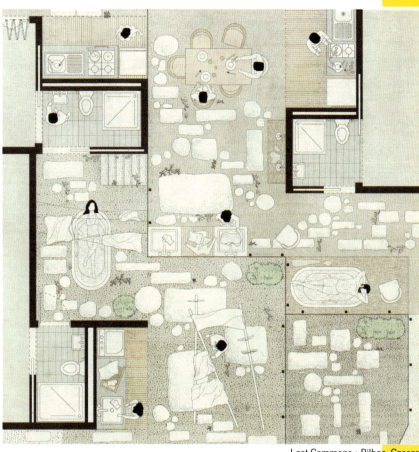

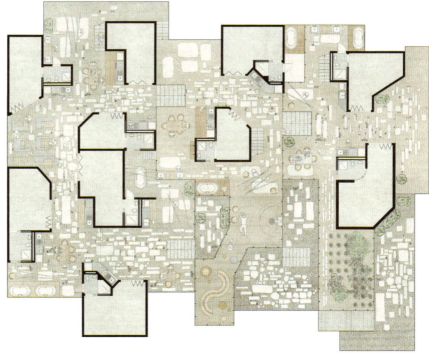

Naomi Jemima Ng, Liang Hu

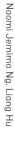

Anna Puigjaner Your project goes beyond the idea of a loaded corridor that happens in between rooms, because we are also seeing how the rooms then become corridors. You are exposing the capacity of architecture to control bodies and labour.

Lost Commons · Bilbao, Czeczek   Advanced Studio

THE REPOSITORY
OF LIVEABILITY-IES
Guillermo Acosta Navarrete

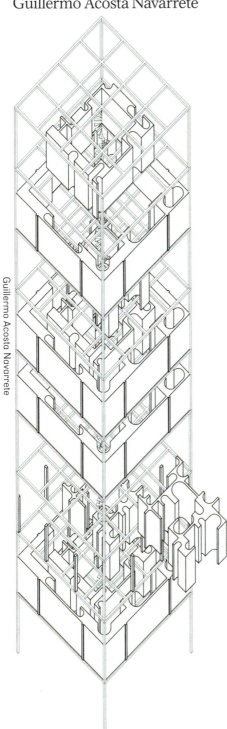

Guillermo Acosta Navarrete

This project announces eight new spaces for habitation. These idiosyncratic—yet ready-to-live-in—quarters welcome a multitude of living mannerisms, based around: Property, Hearsay, Summons, and Oneness. These traits are complimented with those of access and notions of specificity. These new pieces plea for a radical interiority within alternate forms of commonality. If you are keen on the possibilities of a field of counter-found objects reshaping your domestic life, you are invited to steward the repository. These proposed spaces for habitation are constructed according to the same 32 specific objects. They act as prescriptive building materials which shape and reconfigure each iteration.

Maria Shéhérazade Giudici In the last 40 years architect's like Sejima, Ito and many of the Italian radicals dealt with a tension in domestic objects that wanted to break free from the house. You are doing the opposite process here, molding the architecture around the objects... It's a solution that I have never seen before.

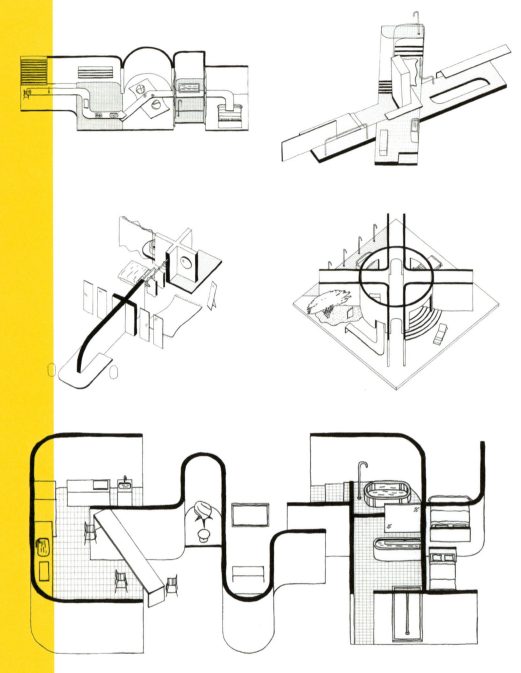

Saba Salekfard · Feldman Nominee

Pier Vittorio Aureli Your project's return to ritual allows you to deconstruct the home and create fragments that are not typological anymore— defined not by habits but through specific rituals that are singularly defined. Objects, in this case, become very important; free from human use, figures within themselves.

THE SET AND THE SPECTACLE
Saba Salekfard

The Set and the Spectacle is a proposal for domestic space based upon rituals of the home and the theatrics of everyday life. The project investigates domestic rituals and proposes it as the driver to formulate spatial conditions and form. It focuses on the reinterpretation of domestic programs as a set of characters. The proposal used techniques of screenwriting and theater to generate narratives of characters within the home, ultimately being presented as a play for the final presentation. The production's three acts focus on genres—drama, tragedy, and romance—while respective scenes address themes of privacy, spectacle, and time, alluding to the sensory elements that complete our domestic experience.

Saba Salekfard · Feldman Nominee

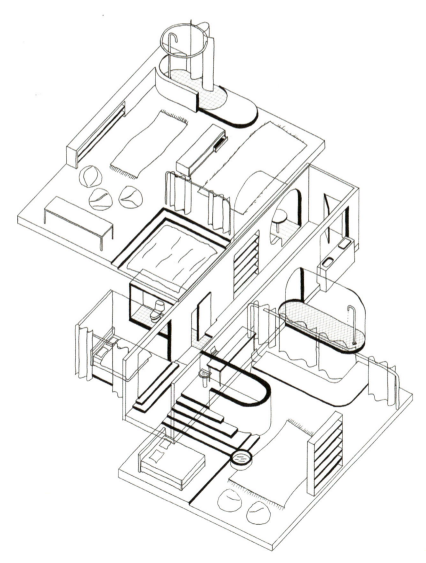

FOOD CART COMMISSARY
Noah Sannes

The proposal reimagines an underused parking lot as a continuously-occupied public destination that transforms from a cart storage facility to a play space to a market hub over the course of the day. Periods of transition between conventionally separated programs facilitate novel types of exposure, like children witnessing vendors cooking and preparing meals. Multi-use pavilions for storage, play, and shelter accommodate the diverse programmatic needs of the site. Investigations of early neural network circuit designs inform the spatial adjacencies of these freestanding structures and other critical wayfinding elements. By centralizing a portion of the city's food cart industry in Washington Heights, fresh produce can be distributed to multiple vendors at once, allowing healthier foods to be disbursed across the community as carts deploy out.

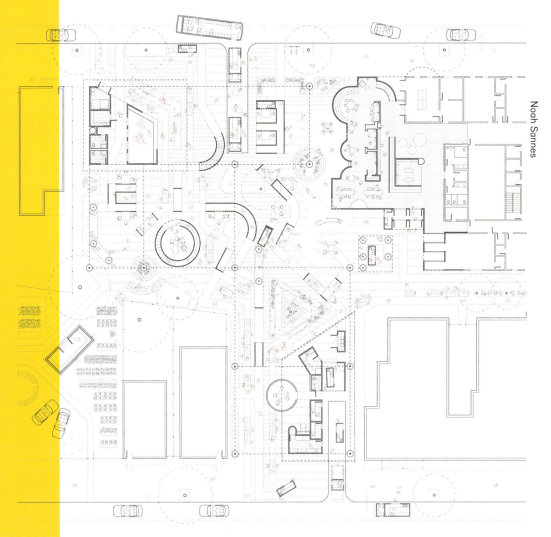

Noah Sannes

Noah Sannes

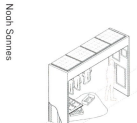

Architectural Design I · Bouchard

ABSENCE | PRESENCE
Josh Greene

This project comments on the absence of Blackness within rural America, and more specifically points towards the lack of representation within our food system. The building is erected as an architecture of reparations in the small farming community of Conrad, Iowa, where the local dirt is celebrated and spiritualized for its blackness. Drawing formally from the abstract work of Kerry James Marshall, this project is built from rammed and infilled agricultural dirt to provide spaces for the community to educate themselves on the historical disenfranchisement of people of color within the food system. By ultimately uncovering and exhibiting the power and wealth inherent in such soil, the goal is to create radical transformation in the town, and reverberations across all aspects of the food system.

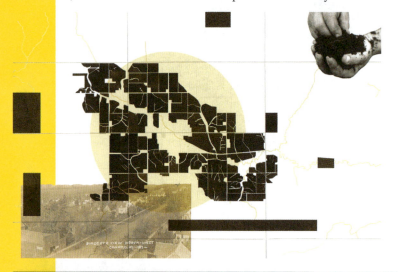

Josh Greene

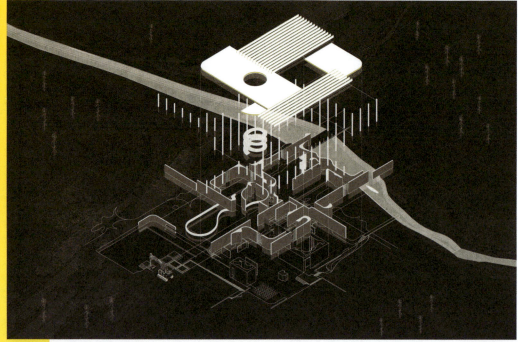

Josh Greene

LEARNING FROM SKATEBOARDING— INDIGENOUS HOUSING DESIGN
Ruike Liu

As an elder stated, "We are blessed to live under a blanket of stars." People create stories to make sense of the world, try to connect life and death with eternity, and to consider people in relation to animals and the universe. This project is an attempt to understand the culture of the Opaskwayak Cree Nation in Manitoba, Canada.

What would it be like if we don't define land by its nouns, but instead by its verbs? Skateboarding flattens the city fabric and the skatepark occupies land by the movement of people. This is a move to decolonize the existing city fabric and apply Indigeneity on the land. Using the existing skatepark as a starting point, the landscape is extended not by following the city fabric, but by following the sun's orientation and the programs on it.

Ruike Liu

Aaron Tobey The "regalia," like the paths of the skateboarding youth and the meandering elders stitch land, life, and cosmology together both on the page and on the ground, especially as they form the place of movement and inhabitation where ground and sky meet.

De-Colonizing Indigenous Housing · Cornelius, Tobey   Advanced Studio

WISAKEDJAK'S BEAR
Max Wirsing

Max Wirsing

The Opaskwayak Cree Nation (OCN), in and around The Pas, Manitoba has a need for some 880 housing units. The land that constitutes the OCN reservation has been split and fractured and drawn with lines and boundaries, separating land and people with colonial conceptions of property ownership—designations of "yours" and "mine." This project builds on a study of Indigenous epistemologies and ontologies, and riffs on the poetics of Swampy Cree cosmology and Trickster narratives in an attempt to decolonize housing in OCN. By framing storytelling as a tool of design and decolonization, Wisakedjak's Bear creates a housing scheme that unifies across colonial boundaries, stitching together the fragmented parcels of the reservation.

Jake Chakasim I'm asking myself, where is the Trickster? What is the lesson the trickster is trying to tell us right now, with the way you fragmented the bear and fragmented the land, and with the fragmentation that we continue to see today on first nation land."

Max Wirsing

Max Wirsing

Chris Cornelius We had many conversations along those lines. What becomes the trickster? What becomes the berry juice? The trickster convinced the bear to put the berry juice in it's eyes to improve it, but it actually didn't. If you're not indigenous you just see these as houses with interesting forms. Other than that, you don't tie those pieces together.

Jake Chakasim I think the third iteration was really bang on. There are interesting ties to the Cree saptuaan longhouse—the extended teepee—and how that is used. I think you really touched on that point, with the way you designed your ridge beam and through this possibility to expand and contract at the same time. You created a strong cultural piece.

Ben Thompson · Feldman Nominee

De-Colonizing Indigenous Housing · Cornelius, Tobey

Advanced Studio

THE FLOCK
Ben Thompson

Ben Thompson · Feldman Nominee

The project began with a close look at the housing stock on the Opaskwayak Cree Nation (OCN) reservation in Manitoba, home to the Swampy Cree people. The first set of operations reconnects the house to the earth which has thermal advantages and a cultural resonance with the Swampy Cree. The importance of the migrating geese is central to the Swampy Cree way of life. The form of the house to have a figural relationship to a bird in flight. The homes consist of three elements: the bermed-earth mound foundation, the rammed-earth walls, and the timber framed roof. The idea of the flock guided the conception of how these homes would form a community. Rather than master planning with rigid top-down rules, the method for how the flock comes together is defined locally in the homes.Each home is added as close to the center mass as possible and given enough space so that it can be fully added onto. The community would form as friends and family build near one another.

THROWING ARCHITECTURE
Christopher Pin

The project begins by extracting spatial strategies from found-patterns. In searching for order within the chaos of Pollock's dripped oil paintings, fields of color were analyzed and reinterpreted as poche by assigning black and white values to each field. Selective layering offers the designer endless opportunities for the eye to "catch space." A second method of analysis drew focus on the medium itself, conducted by extracting lineaments from the contrails of the paint; material becomes vector, defined by a line. These lines begin to then simultaneously escape and invade the built environment. A daycare and spiritual center is developed as these preordained strategies become architectural. They are tested on a suitable site and further developed to house the programmatic needs of the given typology.

Christopher Pin

Architectural Design I · Brooks   Core Studio

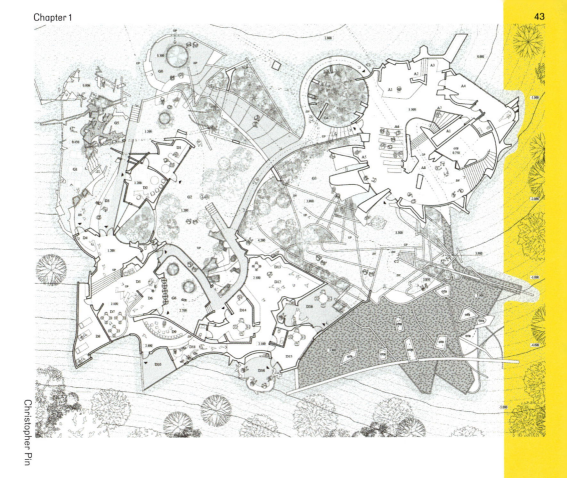

Christopher Pin

OUTER-INTERIOR, INNER-EXTERIOR
Sam Landay

Although some definitions of "line" suggest that it is merely a dimensionless connection between two points, in reality even the thinnest of lines drawn have at least a minimal amount of thickness. The idea of poche creates some ambiguity within this definition—is poche the space between two lines or is it a line in itself? Sol Lewitt's "Loopy Doopy" wall drawings, when read in an architectural manner, further cloud this distinction. One color could be interpreted as poche and the other as space; the viewer could reverse the two roles with poche now acting as space. One section of any given curve could be circumscribing the poche surrounding one space, while a different section of the same curve could be inscribing a space within another instance of poche.

Sam Landay

Sam Landay

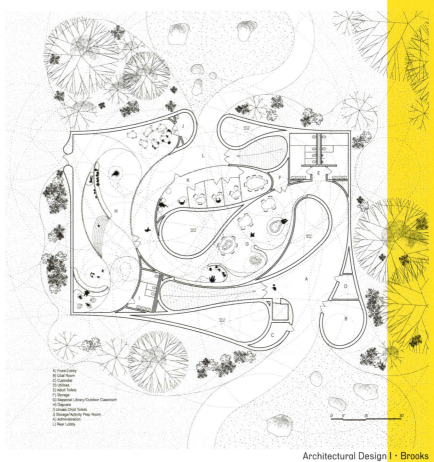

A) Front Lobby
B) Coat Room
C) Custodial
D) Utilities
E) Adult Toilets
F) Storage
G) Seasonal Library/Outdoor Classroom
H) Daycare
I) Unisex Child Toilets
J) Storage/Activity Prep Room
K) Administration
L) Rear Lobby

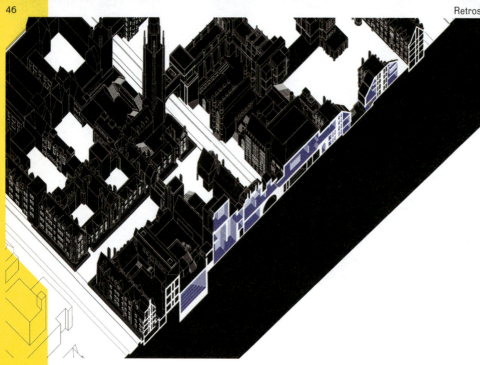

Martin Carrillo Bueno, Taiga Taba, Max Wirsing · Feldman Nominees

Thirdspace · Eisenman, Iturbe

Advanced Studio

OLD CAMPUS
Martin Carrillo Bueno,
Taiga Taba, Max Wirsing

The project formally examines the four-square organization of Yale's "Old Campus" block, and aims to critically transform its double dialectic ("either/or") nature into a "both and"—or "all-and" trialectic. Considering the dominance of the site's inward-facing, collegiate gothic frame buildings as a "colonizer" typology, this intervention aims to subvert the essence of the frame. The transformation of a closed and private form into an open public form through the introduction of a hybridized central frame creates a four-square/nine-square hybrid at an urban scale. Through a process of hybridizing adjacent quadrants, the formation of a Thirdspace emerges from their overlap. With a spatial deployment of Edward Soja's "thirding as othering," the project aims to achieve the architectural form of Thirdspace by merging the dominant natures of the dialectic quadrants, giving the central square a simultaneous reading of solid, void, frame, and figure.

Martin Carrillo Bueno, Taiga Taba, Max Wirsing · Feldman Nominees

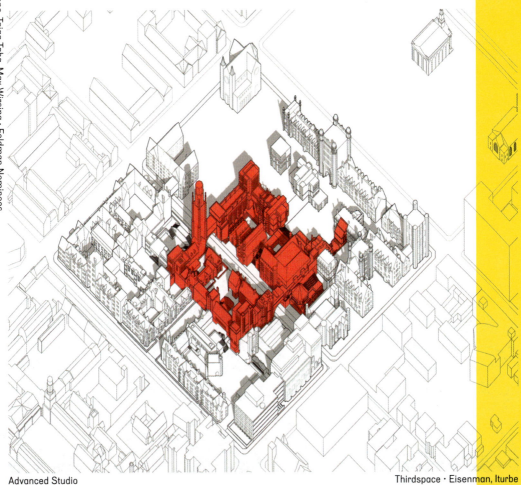

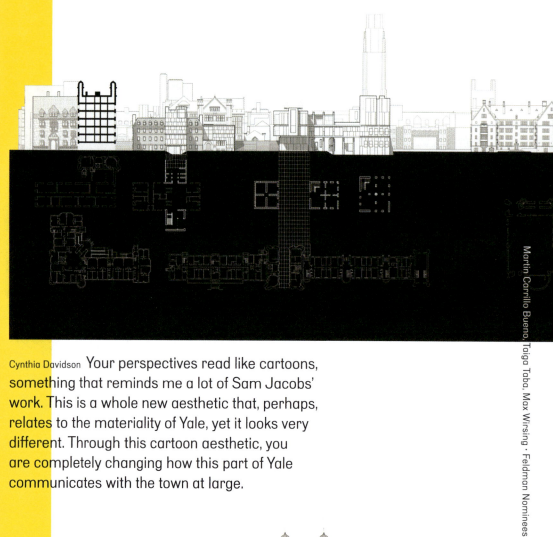

Martin Carrillo Bueno, Taiga Taba, Max Wirsing · Feldman Nominees

Cynthia Davidson Your perspectives read like cartoons, something that reminds me a lot of Sam Jacobs' work. This is a whole new aesthetic that, perhaps, relates to the materiality of Yale, yet it looks very different. Through this cartoon aesthetic, you are completely changing how this part of Yale communicates with the town at large.

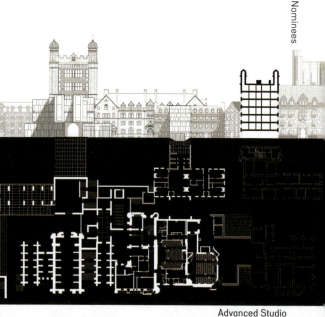

Thirdspace · Eisenman, Iturbe   Advanced Studio

THE NEW YALE SCHOOL OF DRAMA

Guillermo Acosta Navarrete,
Bobby Cheng, Alper Turan

The project, located across Yale's Old Campus and New Haven's original nine-square grid, explores the ambiguity of the postcolonial theoretical "Thirdspace" through architectural simultaneities between frame, figure, and ground. Creating a new set of performance venues for the School of Drama, the hybrid building challenges the ubiquitous courtyard system on the site while breaking the threshold between public and private. It acts as a hinge between the existing collegiate infrastructure and the city at large. While the project consists of elements with distinct formal qualities, those elements become parts of a unified scheme where their formal qualities appear ambiguous in relation to each other. By exploring post-colonial theory and hybridity, the project introduces a new spatial typology to Yale Campus.

Guillermo Acosta Navarrete, Bobby Cheng, Alper Turan

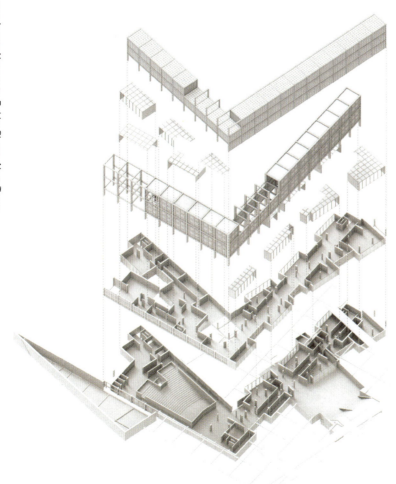

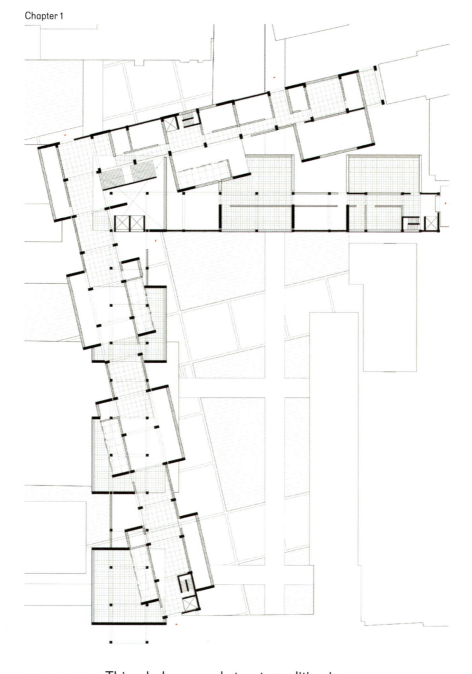

Miroslava Brooks This whole opened street condition is
something new in New Haven. Within the university
campus, I can't think of a condition where the street
opens up and creates a plaza which allows you to
enter a courtyard in such a way. To me this is the
"Third" condition, this is the hybrid condition created
with this project.

INCUBATOR FOR GROWTH
Maya Gamble

This project is located in a desert climate, where water is scarce and harnessing its potential is both challenging and critical. The building proposal integrates the programmatic elements of a meditation retreat center and a daycare through the collection, recycling, and use of the precious rainfall, both through practical elements such as underground collection cisterns and water filtration gardens, as well as through more interactive spaces like a sensory water table and an underground hot tub. Greenhouse gardens throughout the building are shared by both the retreat and daycare, linking the two programs in the spaces where the water and sunlight come to fruition. The lush interior environment provides an escape from the dry desert, and both the children and adults are immersed into the living, breathing organism.

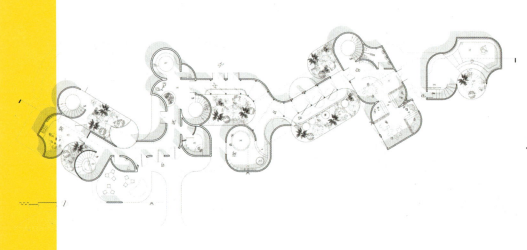

Maya Gamble

Maya Gamble

underground hot tub
kids pool
greenhouse pod

green roof and walkway
daycare classroom
soil lovers pattern play wall

quiet time pods
rainwater cistern
greenhouse herb garden

aquaponics tank
water table
rooftop garden

meditation pods
steam room and sauna
rainwater fountain wall
retreat main entry

yoga studio

living wall
greenhouse pod
deck and green roof
harvesting kitchen
solar array

filtration garden
greywater filter

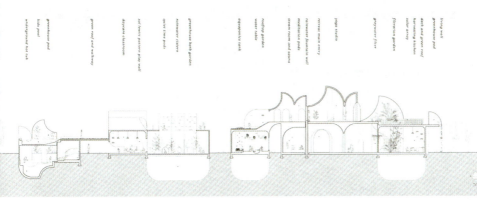

THE PLAN OF MISPRISION
Kyle Coxe

This generative satirical proposal extricates expectations for the orthodox canon of architectural typologies by rejecting, dismantling, and reconfiguring select formal precedents. An accumulated circus act of diverse plans injected with renewed function, this project offers an indistinct, collaged system of manipulated traditional forms synthesized to challenge historical programmatic use of space through wit and gentle irreverence.

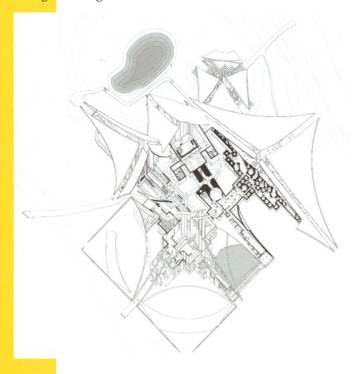

Kyle Coxe

Architectural Design I · Kolb   Core Studio

Kyle Coxe

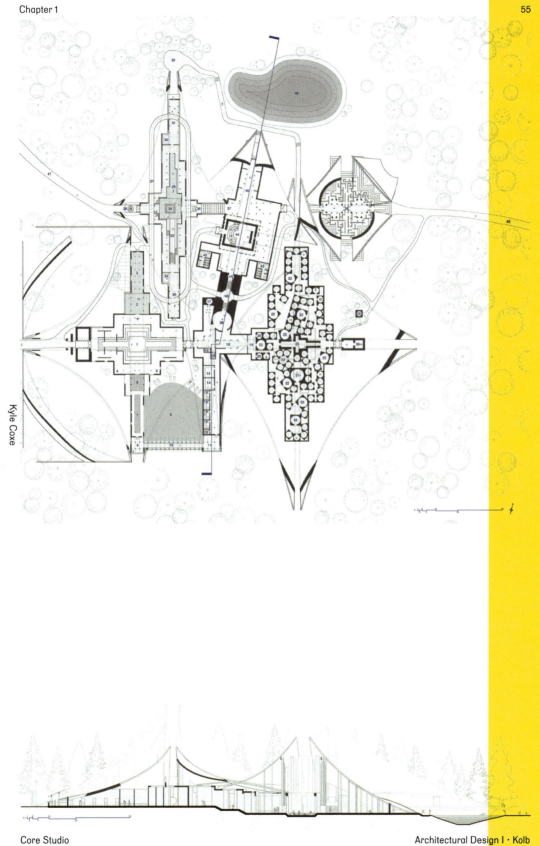

Art, Culture, and the Neighborhood · DelVecchio, Durán Calisto

THE HISPANIC SOCIETY, AUDUBON TERRACE, AND CIVIC ENGAGEMENT IN WASHINGTON HEIGHTS
Nicole Ratajczak

The inward-facing architecture of Washington Heights makes it difficult for the Hispanic Society of America's museum to engage with such a vibrant community. The museum's current facilities are too small and disconnected to properly display the full breadth of its world-class collection. Three surgical moves demonstrate the project's proposal to overcome these shortcomings: a new entrance to the museum, complimented by a welcoming landscape strategy allowing visitors to seamlessly flow in from Broadway Avenue; new space underneath the inner courtyard terrace dedicated to the museum's education program, which allows the historic terrace to be preserved; and an annex building located on the vacant lot dedicated to necessary back-of-house functions, releasing pressure from the existing space in the museum. These interventions in turn allow for the reworking of the interior layout within the historic architecture to create a cohesive gallery experience.

Nicole Ratajczak

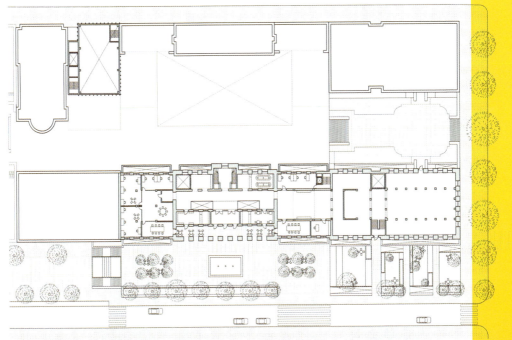

Nicole Ratajczak

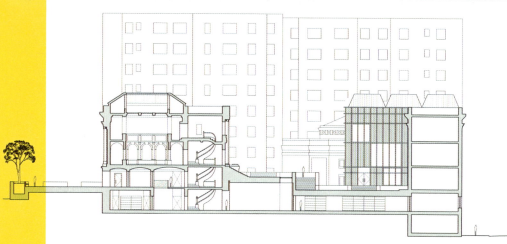

Jeffery Povero The way you planned the museum on the inside feels completely inevitable, which is one of the great things about a good classical project. Any visitor should never believe this was an intervention. You've created this big entry that looks like it should've always been there.

RE-CONNECTING
AUDUBON TERRACE
Ashton Harrell

Ashton Harrell · Feldman Nominee

The lands of the Americas have nursed many diverse peoples, cultures, and civilizations throughout time. At the Hispanic Society at Audubon Terrace, a site has been incidentally preserved as one of Manhattan's last remaining virgin lands. It is here that the museum can re-connect modern generations with the past. The unspoiled site will connect to the community of Washington Heights through a Grand Public exposition hall. Spreading from this Exposition Hall, a collection of diverse galleries will transform the subterranean terrace and connect vertically via atriums to the historic museum, library, and new learning center. Visitors will be transported to the past not only by way of the formal collections of Hispanic society, but also by the encapsulation of the virgin site and the carving of new ecological galleries beneath the terrace, culminating in a mined and transformative black box theater, able to freely morph as generations pass.

Ashton Harrell · Feldman Nominee

Mark Foster Gage I like your arching, catacomb-esque language. It's definitely not Beaux Arts but it fits within it. If you were able to cut some skylights into that space, à la Kahn's Kimbell museum, you would get this amazing natural cascading light under these beautiful guastavino arches that you've designed.

Ashton Harrell · Feldman Nominee

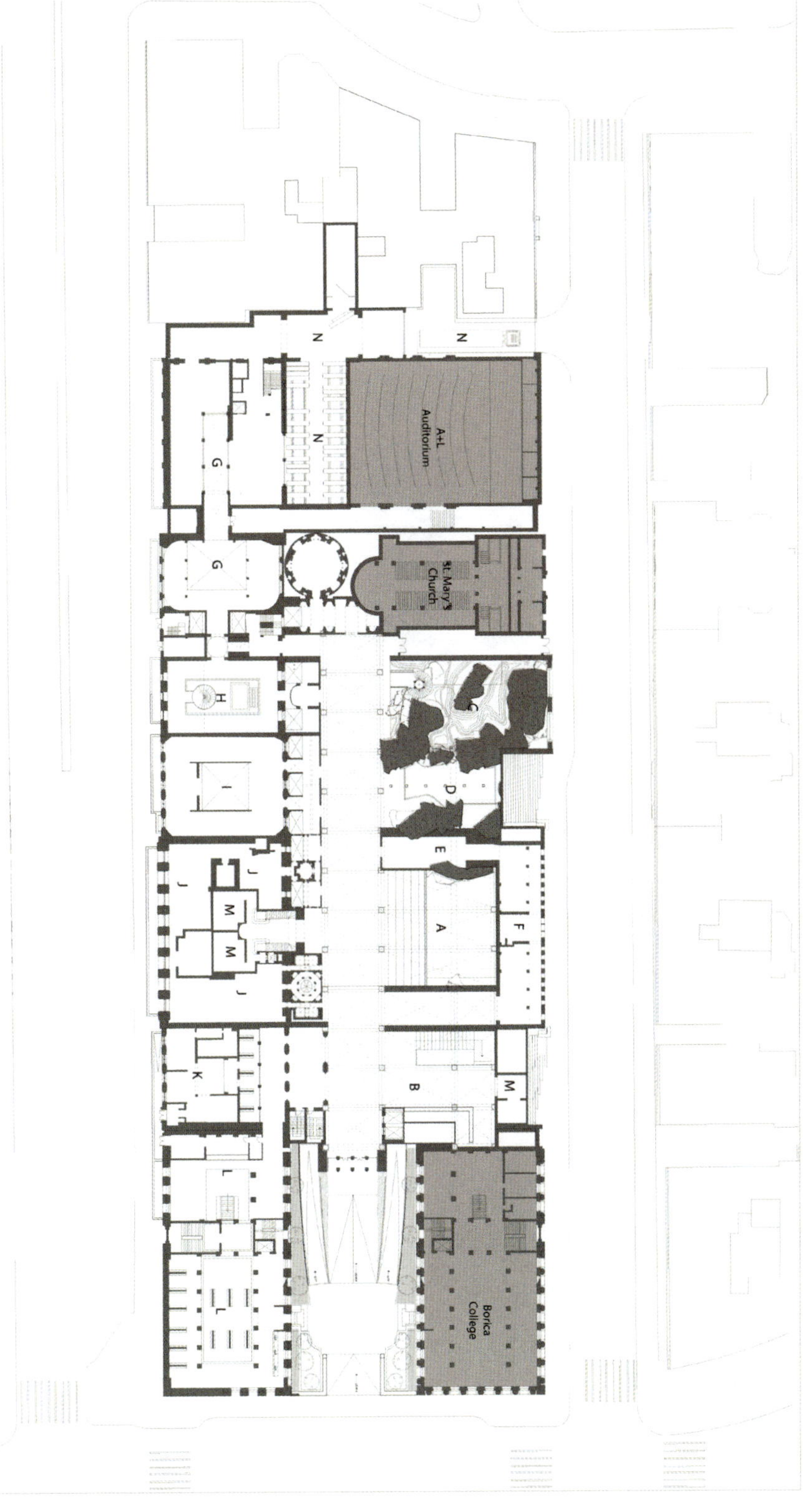

A+L
Auditorium

St. Mary's
Church

D

E

A

F

B

M

Borica
College

G

G

G

H

I

J

M

M

K

L

L

N

N

N

Art, Culture, and the Neighborhood · DelVecchio, Durán Calisto

(RE)VEIL
Chloe Hou

The plan starts with a set of wobbly lines that define the field for a cluster of buildings. After extrusion, those lines give the impression of curtains that actively break down the rigidness of the enclosure. By situating the project in a borderland and employing wire mesh not only on the undulating surfaces but also on the skins of individual buildings, the architecture begins to challenge a stereotypical conception of mesh as the demarcation of the border. Visitors are met with an optical illusion that further blurs the space's conceived limits through movement within a field of buildings, ultimately emerging from the mesh, whose presence stretches to the sky.

Chloe Hou

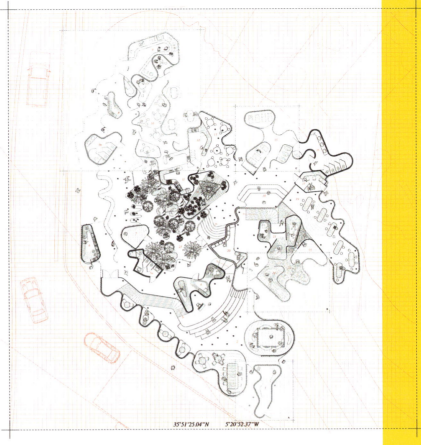

35°51'25.04"N   5°20'52.37"W

WAYS OF SEEING
Ariel Bintang

The project is about readership. Inspired by Aldo Rossi's potent interpretation of Libeskind's "Chamberwork" and "Micromegas," architecture develops through an inquiry of the oblique view, a tool used to generate multiple forms. Through the misreading of depthness in an oblique plan—a misinterpretation of the reader's obliqueness—a two dimensional drawing could be represented by various forms. The manifestation becomes an unstable object, refusing to be a product of the author's intentions.

Ariel Bintang

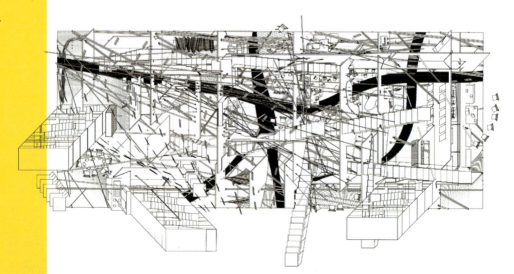

Ariel Bintang

Within the interplay of ideas and images lies a relationship between producer and production: the malleability of fundamentals and history; crafting of the architectural subject; and the latency and legibility of an underlying geopolitical climate. Situating the present within a larger spectrum of architectural discourse, *Design and Visualization* courses reveal our eye's mind, and *History and Theory* courses study our minds' eye.

Design and Visualization
History and Theory

OML

Architecture Foundations

NIKOLE BOUCHARD, MIROSLAVA BROOKS

Incoming students with limited architectural background learn the fundamentals of architectural language, ideation, creation, representation, and communication. Students are introduced to techniques and conventions used to describe the space and substance of designed objects, buildings and environments. Lessons are continuously supplemented with explorations and presentations intended to enhance students' powers of perception through close reading and critical observation to consequently cultivate a productive creative process, with an emphasis on imagination and invention. [1221A]

DESIGN AND VISUALIZATION (REQUIRED)

Modern Architecture

CRAIG BUCKLEY

Over the past century and a half, traditional fables began to yield to more scientifically conceived ideas of architecture's role in the creation of civilizations. As architecture gained importance in advancing social and industrial agendas, it also built a basis for theoretical reflection and visionary aesthetics. The course focuses on major centers of urban culture and their characteristic buildings, alternating attention to individual concepts and their impact in an increasingly interconnected culture of design. [3011A]

HISTORY AND THEORY (REQUIRED)

Formal Analysis I

PETER EISENMAN

Students develop a weekly series of texts and comparative analyses that move from the theocentric late-medieval, to the humanism and anthropocentricity of the early Renaissance, to the beginning of the Enlightenment of the late eighteenth century. Students are introduced to the seeing and reading of architecture through time. An architect must learn to see as an expert, beyond the facts of perception, different from the average user. Seeing becomes a form of close reading what is not present—the unseen. [1223A]

DESIGN AND VISUALIZATION (REQUIRED)

Renaissance & Modern II

PETER EISENMAN, KURT FORSTER

This course confronts historical knowledge with speculation about the intentions of architectural designs and the nature of their realization. Students will engage in debates between Peter Eisenman and Kurt Forster, readings of limited series of texts, and with buildings that command center stage. The course takes a broad look at the twentieth century and then organizes itself around a few key phases in the formation of architectural consciousness, moving through the postwar debates to current dilemmas. [3256B]

HISTORY AND THEORY

Designing Social Equality: The Politics of Matter

MARK FOSTER GAGE

Through the act of design, students explore ideas from contemporary thought leaders including Michelle Alexander, Ibram Kendi, Jacques Rancière, Robin DiAngelo, Steven Shaviro, Angela Davis, Justin Jennings, Stacey Abrams, the Laboria Cuboniks Xenofeminist Collective, and others. Concepts and movements addressed include, but are not limited to, the tangible, physical, and designed aspects of equality philosophy, environmental justice, colonization, anti-racism and white privilege, the geographies of voter suppression, mass incarceration, immigrant detention, virtue signaling, the contemporary status of hagiography through monuments and canon, and the relationship between protest and form. [1219A]

DESIGN AND VISUALIZATION

Body Politics: Designing Equitable Public Space

JOEL SANDERS

This course explores the design challenges triggered by an urgent social justice issue: the imperative to create safe accessible public spaces for people of different races, genders, and disabilities. The class is organized around an in depth interrogation of five building types—public restroom, museum, office, campus, and urban street—that each have marginalized or excluded persons who fall outside white, masculine, heterosexual, able-bodied norms. First, the class situates this issue in a cultural and historical context. Then, it asks students to propose alternative design strategies that allow a spectrum of different embodied people to productively mix in public space. [3290A]

HISTORY AND THEORY

After the Modern Movement: An Atlas of Postmodernism

ROBERT A.M. STERN

This course seeks to answer the questions: What was and what is postmodernism in architecture? To test the hypothesis that postmodernism was an evolution and corrective action rather than an outright repudiation of modernism, students participate in a postmodern game of imitation for the final project. Through research and formal analysis, students emulate a selected contemporary architect in the design of a facade for a hypothetical 40th-anniversary Strada Novissima redux—offering up an opportunity for students to understand their selected architect's work within the recent history of the profession. [3283B]

HISTORY AND THEORY

Spatial Concepts of Japan: Their Origins and Development in Architecture and Urbanism

YOKO KAWAI

This course origins the developments of Japanese spatial concepts and surveys how they help form contemporary architecture, ways of life, and cities of the country. Many Japanese spatial concepts, such as MA, are about creating time-space distances and relationships between objects, people, space, and experiences. These concepts go beyond the fabric of a built structure, and encompass architecture, landscape, and city. The course offers weekly lectures on specific Japanese word(s) and their respective design features, backgrounds, historical examples, and contemporary application. [3240A]

HISTORY AND THEORY

Formal Analysis II

PETER EISENMAN

This course examines two questions: what was modern and what was postmodern? Through a series of weekly texts and comparative analyses, the nature of this difference is explored with the intention of reconsidering "the modern" in a contemporary context. One half of the course is concerned with modernism from 1914–1939 and the second with postmodernism from 1968–1988. The class pursues the skill of close reading, which moves from the idealism of the modern to the criticality of the postmodern. [1225B]

DESIGN AND VISUALIZATION

The Plan

BRENNAN BUCK

Plans most clearly trace the power relations—defined by class, race, and gender—that buildings enact. The recent return of the plan as a topic of discourse and focus of architectural energy after the digital turn suggests renewed interest in the correlation of form and politics that the plan describes. This course traces the history of the plan as an index of architectural thinking. Students will be asked to define a strain of contemporary plan making, chart its historical antecedents, and speculate on its intentions and effects. [3100A]

HISTORY AND THEORY

Semiotics

FRANCESCO CASETTI

The course discusses the most relevant concepts and categories elaborated by semiotics in order to provide analytical tools for "close readings" of verbal or visual texts, cultural objects, artifacts, events, and social situations. Semiotics' foundational goal consisted in retracing how meaning emerges and circulates in connection with a variety of objects, from literary works to social rituals, from natural phenomena to artificial languages. Analytical tools are tested in class through close readings of a great variety of objects and situations, spanning from celebrities' depictions to Genesis, from social encounters to urban design. These close readings will imply the collective work of the whole class. [3267A]

HISTORY AND THEORY

Medium Design

KELLER EASTERLING

While usually focused on designing buildings, designers might also design the medium in which those buildings are suspended. Considering ground instead of figure, or field instead of object, medium design inverts some dominant cultural logics about problem-solving and offers additional aesthetic pleasures and political capacities.Benefiting from an artistic curiosity about reagents and spatial mixtures or spatial wiring, medium design suggests different organs of design or different ways to register the design imagination. Beyond buildings, master plans, declarations, laws, or standards, it deploys multipliers, switches, or time-released organs of interplay like bargains, chain reactions, ratchets. [3280A]

HISTORY AND THEORY

AI Aesthetics

BRENNAN BUCK

This course assesses the impact of artificial intelligence on design and architecture as an aesthetic rather than a purely economic question. AI has already added a series of invisible layers to how we see and create our environment. Understanding this new machine-mediated visual culture is critical to addressing its growth, finding potentials and opportunities, and identifying avenues for critique and resistance. Students will work with AI platforms such as Runway ML to develop a design proposal that takes a critical and aesthetically specific stance on the current and impending impact of AI. [1246B]

DESIGN AND VISUALIZATION

Textile Architectures

EEVA-LIISA PELKONEN

The course explores the intersection between textile arts and architecture, beginning with Gottfried Semper's inquiry into architecture's tectonic origins in textile arts. The course is organized in three parts. The first part mines different techniques, typologies, and geographies born out of that intersection and considers them in tangent with issues of colonialism, geopolitics, and labor through a broad historical and geographic scope from prehistory to the present. The second part surveys the role of textiles in twentieth-century modern architecture through case studies of collaborative projects. The third part focuses on the role textiles play in conversations about sustainability and looks into material innovation in that area. [3101A]

HISTORY AND THEORY

Textile Architectures: A Transhistorical and Global Perspective into Architectural Historiography

EEVA-LIISA PELKONEN

The course explores the intersection between textile arts and architectural historiography, with a goal of finding ways to conceive a more global and inclusive approach to architectural historiography. To be sure, textiles have been conceived around the globe for eons, and they are a ubiquitous part of dwellings, past and present. [3312B]

HISTORY AND THEORY

Architecture Foundations

Intimate Play
HARRY HOOPER

Considering the prescribed theme of "play," the project explores a line of inquiry regarding intimate play to generate architectural ideation, design, and production. The architectural discourse of intimate spaces and the subject of intimacy are limited, though architects and designers are often tasked to create forms of intimacy, safety, and control. This can be as implicit as the design of a bath house to the explicit industrial design of a sex toy. Both the sex toy as design object and the sub-theme of intimate play act as the basis for critical thinking and visual analysis; catalysts for sensitivity.

Playscape
CHLOE HOU

Points on lines and curves break free from the flatland, floating in the air or digging into the ground to create bars, pits, niches and archways. Yet, the intentional smoothness in elevations, as someone outside of the playscape might observe, disguises the awkwardness found in moments of intersections and connections. Human or animal bodies, after entering the space, need to negotiate the obstacles or corners in their ways. One visitor might find a spot comfortable and playful, which might be inconvenient in the eyes of another visitor. Wandering becomes part of the play.

Modern Architecture

Lina Bo Bardi's Modernism: A Before and After

ARIEL BINTANG

Lina Bo Bardi famously said that "the true modern architect can respond to the realities of any nation, reaching the kind of understanding that sometimes eludes architects who were born in that country." Although modern architecture since its earliest conception has been developed for western society, she claims that it has the vitalism capable of catering variances from country to country around the world. If that's the case, how did she adapt the plethora of ideas from modern architecture for a foreign society that is the opposite of its origins in terms of climate, culture and economy?

The before-after analysis of Bo Bardi as a modern architect who took function, aesthetic, and technique as her key references show there are truly universal and timeless ideas of modern architecture, like the open plan, that could uncompromisingly be applied outside of Europe.

Idealistic Origins, Uncertain Future: The Story of the Connecticut Hospice

CLARE FENTRESS

In Branford, Connecticut, just a few miles from New Haven, stands a historic building: the former Connecticut Hospice, the first purpose-built, freestanding inpatient hospice in the United States. Designed in 1974 and completed in 1980, it embodies the beliefs of a modestly visionary movement that aimed to change the way people die, and the way that the living relate to death.

Despite this building's pioneering position in the history of healthcare architecture in the United States, it has never been the subject of a comprehensive narrative treatment. This paper gathers archival documents; original interviews with the building's architect, Lo-Yi Chan, and former and current Connecticut Hospice employees; unpublished photographs; architectural, cultural, and medical history; periodical literature; current scholarship on hospice inpatient environments; and municipal records to tell the story of the Connecticut Hospice from its energetic, even utopian beginnings to its uncertain present and future.

Despite this building's pioneering position in the history of healthcare architecture in the United States, it has never been the subject of a comprehensive narrative treatment.

Formal Analysis I

Expulsion of Heliodorus
JERRY CHOW

Raphael ties his burgeoning vision of St. Peter's to the architectural and religious antecedent of the Temple.

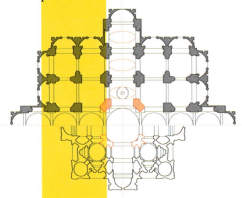

Ricetto of the Laurentian Library
CALVIN LIANG

The southerly triangular pediment, centered similar to the west and east, assumes a scalar shift bleeding into the adjacent column sections.

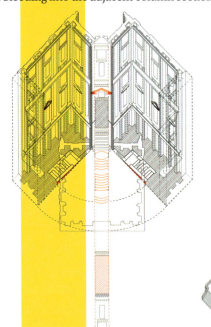

Dwelling for a Prince
QIAN HUANG

Inward protrusion of the void and outward protrusion of the solid represent languages of poche and wall, yet there exists ambiguous composite elements that combine the two.

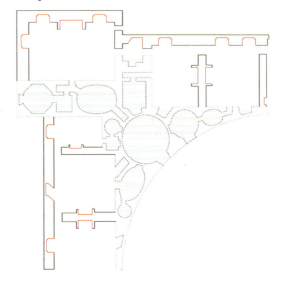

Comparing Palladian Compositional Elements
KATHERINE SALATA

Palladio displays two compositional approaches: a layering of elements, maintaining clarity of order/identity; and the intersecting of elements to achieve a unique whole.

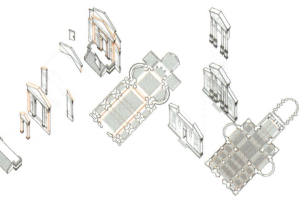

Renaissance & Modern II

From Nous and Logos to The Architectural Crisis Today

BOBBY CHENG

It is said that the Greek philosophical idea of *Nous* and *Logos* is important to the birth of Western Civilization. Generally speaking, *Nous* is represented by the expression of the free spirit while Logos is embodied in one's rationality. The dialectical relationship between Nous and Logos is critical for the following two reasons: on the one hand, it tells us that any free spirit or expression cannot exist without rationality. on the other hand, it is the spirit of *Nous* that prevents rationality becoming ossified and pushes the history of mankind forward.

I believe today's architecture, both Eastern and Western, is in a crisis. First, the crisis of Oriental architecture is because of the constant absence of both *Nous* and *Logos*. For one thing, the free spirit does not exist since architecture is always regarded as a component of a part-to-whole system. For another, rationality in the Eastern world is constantly overwhelmed by phenomenology. Second, the crisis of architecture in the West is at least caused by two major factors. On the one hand, *Logos*, the formal basis of architecture, is intentionally replaced by various social projects by architects of the new generation. On the other hand, the school of thought of OOO, based on the philosophy of Kant, is searching for the pure expression of free spirit without rationality. As Moneo points out in his *Theoretical Anxiety*, irrational as it might be at the very beginning, the process of architectural design relies on rationalization of that initial idea.

I believe today's architecture, both Eastern and Western, is in a crisis.

Thoughts on Diptych

NATALIE BROTON

Diptych in architecture comes in two forms with differing qualities: autonomous synthetic buildings, and adaptive reuse buildings. Modern additions to existing buildings are an easy target for diptych discussions as they have an inherent quality of "two-ness." New autonomous buildings have a different set of qualities and rules that are more calculated by a singular architect, where the frame becomes the most important component of the diptych. The analyses for adaptive reuse structures were focused largely on material palette, often a steel and glass structure added to an existing masonry building drawing emphasis on the difference of technologies and style between the periods of construction. This was true for the FRAC Dunkerque example, where the existing structure is opaque and heavy, and the new structure is in contrast light and translucent. The hinge point of these types of structures were celebrated, at least indirectly, as the seam between old and new. These adaptive reuse buildings foreground the quality of the "two-ness" in a diptych. In contrast, autonomous buildings, structures without any added additions, had different focuses. Oftentimes, the arguments were focused around singular elements of the structure that contained asymmetry like the differently proportioned windows on either side of a Venturi house facade or the space between two chimneys and where they fall in plan as in the Asplund summer house. Spatial juxtaposition between different rooms or sections of a building were often analysed as well. Where adaptive reuse buildings foreground "two-ness", synthetic new buildings foreground the quality and necessity of the "frame" in a diptych.

Designing Social Equality:
The Politics of Matter

Equitable Career Fair

IVES BROWN, RACHEL MULDER,
IFE ADEPEGBA

The need for equity in architecture goes beyond
the walls of Rudolph Hall. We recognize
challenges for architecture students both at
barriers of entry and exit of YSoA. A change
needs to happen. In this project, we explore
new protocols, revamping the career fair and
dismantling the inherent top-down dynamic
through prioritizing the creation of personal
connections to facilitate more equity and present
more opportunities during the hiring process.

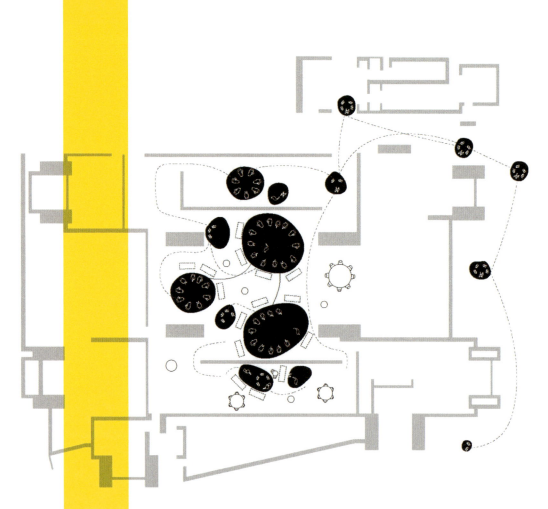

Body Politics:
Designing Equitable Public Space

Rudolph Hall:
Analytical Body Mapping

LEYI ZHANG, ALEX OLIVIER,
JANICE CHU, VICKY ACHNANI

Through analytical body mappings that compare in-person working and working from home, both in studio spaces and in the gallery, our team aims to unpack the discomfort and difficulties in accessing Rudolph Hall while participating in a hybrid-education model under the pandemic. The project's goal is to find potential opportunities for improvements through comparison studies, and to mitigate the discomfort brought on by the pandemic.

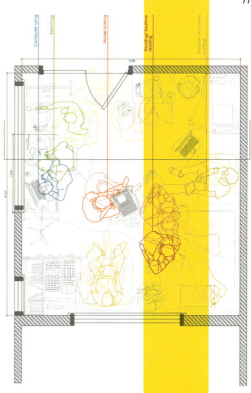

Imagery and Inclusion:
Sterling Memorial Library's
Architectural Ornament
and Artwork

NOAH SANNES, MAX WIRSING,
YUYI SHEN

Our proposal is an interpretive guide of Sterling Memorial Library's architectural ornament and imagery. With a critical eye on the use of historical erasure, our group decided, rather than proposing to physically alter the building itself, to develop an interactive online guide and an augmented reality app through a lens of diversity and inclusion.

After the Modern Movement:
An Atlas of Postmodernism

Facade In The Manner of Mark Foster Gage
CHRISTINE SONG

Mark Foster Gage is a practicing architect, theorist, and professor whose work speculates the relationship between classical architecture and digital experimentation. He speculates on contemporary architecture through philosophy and Object-Oriented-Ontology to promote new trajectories in design. In his practice, he develops and exploits digital modelling strategies, such as "kitbashing" and fractals, to develop the ideologies of OOO. This facade aims to reflect Mark Gage's experimentation with fractal design for the 40th-anniversary Strada Novissima redux.

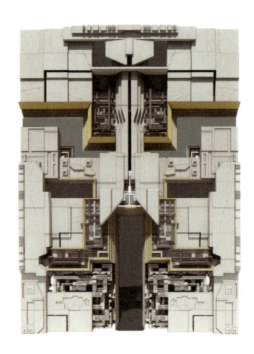

Facade In The Manner of Niall McLaughlin
BEN THOMPSON

This facade attempts to catalog the ways in which Níall McLaughlin represents the human form in his architecture. In his prayer room for Carmelite monks, each monk's chair is built into the wall and becomes a structural beam. In his facade for Olympic Village housing, the pre-cast concrete panels bear the relief of the figures on the Parthenon marbles. The elements from three projects are collaged together to synthesize a new façade that samples the different treatments of the human form.

Spatial Concepts of Japan: Their Origins and Development in Architecture and Urbanism

Emakimono 絵巻 & the visual-narrative imagination of Japanese spaces

NAOMI JEMIMA NG

This paper examines how the medium of *emakimono* 絵巻物 (traditional Japanese illustrated scrolls) visualizes imagined spaces in pre-modern Japan, and what its representation techniques say about certain conceptions and understanding of Japanese spaces. Examining how spaces are drawn, the *fukinuki yatai* technique (吹抜屋台) is discussed in relation to concepts of *hashi* (in-between) and oku (inwardness), while the *hikime kagibana* technique (引目鉤鼻) is discussed in relation to concepts of *mono no aware* (物の哀れ, pathos of things). The act of reading *emaki* is discussed in relation to the concept of *ima* (今, moving present) and Japanese philosopher Nishida Kitaro's concept of "bodymind," focusing on the integral relationship between body, space, time, and emotion. In Tadao Ando's exhibition: "The process of creation: Emaki-style sketchbooks," the paper describes how the translation of this two-dimensional medium into a physical space realizes certain aforementioned concepts but hinders others. *Emaki* is not only a storytelling medium capable of adapting to evolving socio-political contexts but also reveals a lot about the conception of Japanese spaces in pre-modern Japan.

As everyday life diffuses into art space, one truly lives in the emotional space. Space, emotion, and body become one.

Emaki is not only a storytelling medium capable of adapting to evolving socio-political contexts but also reveals a lot about the conception of Japanese spaces in pre-modern Japan.

House as a work of Art: Kazuo Shinohara's work in relation to emotion, self and body

HIUKI LAM

This paper provides an analysis of Kazuo Shinohara's work in relation to emotion, self, and body. While Modernist architects put forward the notion that houses are living machines that serve human beings, Shinohara believes that houses are where human emotions are most attached to and what people need after the war. The paper presents two houses, completed between 1964 and 1966, with opposite kinds of emotional space; House in White is a house of clarity, with a quasi-religious symbolism built around the notion of the central pillar. House of Earth is a house of darkness, with a half-buried plan developed from the "black space" concept. Investigated throughout the paper, Shinohara's "House is Art" manifesto describes house as an aesthetic experience that has the capacity to generate new and unpredicted meanings. The house is therefore a work of art that evokes emotion. Both houses in this paper offer two types of spaces: domestic space and art space. Domestic space is where the unavoidable everydayness happens. Art space's primary function is emotional. As everyday life diffuses into art space, one truly lives in the emotional space. Space, emotion, and body become one.

Formal Analysis II

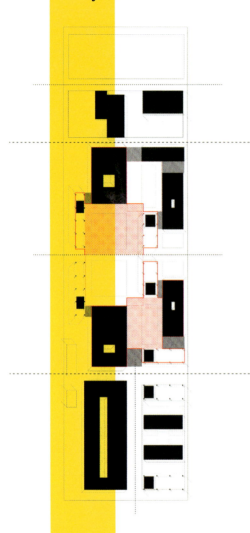

BRIAN ORSER

The worm's eye drawing of the IIT master plan shows Mies van der Rohe adapting the flowing space of his open plan concept to the much larger scale of eight city blocks. Overall the effect is of alternating inversions of figure and ground in the mirrored figures.

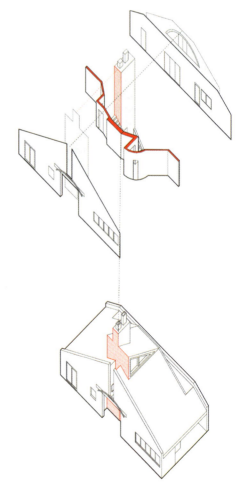

GINA JIANG

The drawing explores how the facades of the Vanna Venturi House are articulated as planes, obscuring the volumetric and dynamic quality of the internal core. The core, consisting of a folding wall and a fireplace, is highlighted in red since it manifests the most violent kind of contradiction in this design. The combinations of the three planes achieves a 'difficult whole', making the Vanna Venturi House a decorative shed that recognizes formal complexities and contradictions.

The Plan

The Striped Plan
ANGELA LUFKIN

This project investigated the emergence of
a new plan type that is characterized by the
repetition of closely consecutive wall planes.
Ultimately, it is concluded that while qualities
of the striped plan are evident in a variety of
contemporary buildings, the sacrifices made
in the transformation of the plan from an open
pavilion to enclosed structure tend to break the
reading of the type and limit its organizational
and experiential potentials.

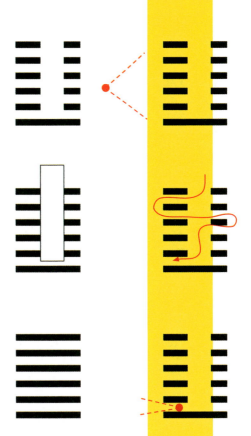

The Yin Yang Poche Plan
NATALIE BROTON

Different types of poche have emerged overtime,
sending its literal definition based on material
into a more representational interpretation. The
changes across history can be categorized into
five different typologies of poche including solid,
honeycomb, hollow, tectonic, and ying yang.
This essay tracks the history and evolution of
poche to provide a background for where yin
yang poche came from, and to determine why it
is a new trend today.

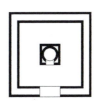

Semiotics

Calor Hogareño or The Warmth of the Home

GUILLERMO ACOSTA NAVARRETE

In architecture, the "house" has always been tied to shelter and the notion of dwelling. Yet, this condition is challenged by another: one of the collective imagining of "home" and the importance of experience and memory. One deals with function and commodification, while the other with its ideal and meaning. Yet, both are indiscriminately used to refer to the same thing: places that people inhabit in their utmost privacy. A privateness that is encouraged and privileged, one that should feel warm and cozy. But, how is this condition readable when the point of view shifts from the user to that of the beholder? Will there be a similar reading if the dwelling is evaluated from the outside and not from the inside? Can the signs and intentions of the act of 'home' be discernible without experience?

This dual condition has made it the paradoxical architecture typology par excellence. The architect's focus on its utility and profit can lead to exclusion and alienation, while its focus on significance can dwell on nostalgia and memory, stunting the ability to look forward. A house is not necessarily a home, but the supposition that something is not-a-house also does not mean that it is a home. Its connotation becomes ambiguous and the need to denote its elements becomes necessary. This relation brings a layer of subjectivity that is specific to this type of edifice. And this character is made more evident by the roots of its linguistic terms, a condition that recontextualizes 'home' in terms of warmth and "fire."

The "house" is and will always be an architecture typology that dwells with its own contradiction. It will be the place where the newest and more contemporary version of one's self will be housed, but it will also stand the test of time and remain somehow immutable. But the "home" has become something beyond architecture, something beyond the act of dwelling. The point of view of both the user and the beholder will now forever be in transit, and enclosed within emptiness. And the fire that once provided warmth to a stagnated structure will now be the spark of a moving blaze. How can we keep the metaphysical space of the new transitional dwelling warm? How much will we care for the fire inside or outside these structures? How can the architectural discourse of the "home" be evaluated if it does not have a connection to spatiality anymore? As architects, will we design "houses" or "homes"?

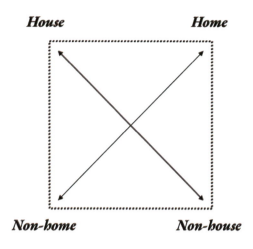

House   **Home**

Non-home   **Non-house**

Will there be a similar reading if the dwelling is evaluated from the outside and not from the inside? Can the signs and intentions of the act of "home" be discernible without experience?

Medium Design

Fluid Lands: Rural Women's Collective for Land Readjustment

JESSICA JIE ZHOU

Land, especially in the rural Chinese context, grants more than just a piece of ground and the products that it provides. It affords information, relationship, hierarchy, temperament, and everything else that determines the status of the owner in a rural collective. From the division of each family lot to their proximity to a water source, land and its associated qualities shape the geopolitics of Chinese villages. The land is never static, but the binary nature of land borders resists these alterations. Boundaries, people, and legal regulations—the dialogue among these three actors therefore determines the landscape as well as the associated power interplay in a village community.

As the negotiation of these factors demands compromises, rural Chinese women's land rights and interests are taken as casualties. Their identities are regarded as manipulable and thus rejected as needed, as the temperament of the legal structure determines that rural women's disadvantages are invisible to the community that they function within. This essay argues that the ambiguity of rural women's position within their communities calls for a reversal of the existing power dynamics; the current disadvantages of rural females can be utilized as an affordance to generate a flexible, agency-giving condition that counters the reluctance from their dependents.

Accountability and Affordance: Gender-Based Violence in Refugee Camps

CHRISTINA CHI ZHANG

In 1991, the international human rights instruments explicitly addressed the social mechanisms of violence against women. Political upheavals, civil wars and other conflicts happening around the world gave birth to many refugee camps. These camps were all set up as short-term, temporary solutions, and thus have all been forced into endless loops of responding to unforeseen situations.

The unique challenges faced by gender-based violence survivors and their helpers in refugee camps led to even more difficulties and gaps in the protection systems, "Safe Haven" being a major one of them. Implemented in many refugee camps around the world, Safe Haven is both a physical space and a network that offers temporary safety to women actively fleeing gender-based violence in refugee camps. However, with its generic response mechanism that actively avoids difficult cultural and religious conflicts and often fails to establish accountability, Safe Havens desperately need to look for new solutions that establish affordance beyond objective safety that merely ensures basic survival. Taking a close look at UNHCR documents, this paper attempts to map out the apparatus of variables involved in gender-based violence responses, and look for new affordances for Safe Havens.

Implemented in many refugee camps around the world, Safe Haven is both a physical space and a network that offers temporary safety to women actively fleeing gender-based violence in refugee camps.

AI Aesthetics

Vernacular Mining
CHRISTOPHER PIN

This project explores methods of "mining" the context of a site using artificial intelligence. The potential for latent patterns, hybrid reading, or entirely foreign ideas of "context" make one question where the line is drawn in regards to "vernacular" of a site. The process from start to finish is a symbiosis between human and machine. A dance that generates continual creative misalignment, provoking a debate surrounding authorship and authenticity as well as the meaning/meaninglessness of the context of a place.

Drawing (im)Precision
TIMOTHY WONG

Drawing (im)Precision questions what it means for machine learning (ML) to produce architectural drawings and their 3D representations. Unlike the typical architectural softwares such as Rhino or AutoCAD, ML drawings are raster-based rather than vector-based. Within this paradigm of the raster, lines become visually fuzzy, wobbly, and imprecise. Defined by their vector coordinate and truncation, the ML model can generate near infinite variations by adjusting these values. Thus, neither fully precise nor imprecise, the medium of AI drawing embodies their in-between—precisely imprecise.

Textile Architectures

RACHEL MULDER

Extraction, simply put, means removal. It connotes a power imbalance that is actualized through some type of unequal exchange, but it also conjures the plucking of some kind of essence out of its original context. This essay uses the word as a means to explore the way textiles are sourced, fabricated, and traded across time and space. The investigation spans different scales, histories, and media and identifies the complex realities manifested by extractive practices, tactile qualities of removal, and highlights both generative and oppression outcomes. While we commonly associate textiles with an additive and constructive method, here instead we highlight their complicated entanglement with extractive processes.

Weaving, Building, and Notating

PERIHAN MACDONALD

Most of the operations and patterns used in the production of bobbin lace were formed over centuries by trial and error. They were developed out of necessity, due to the difficulty in verbalizing these complex patterns and operations. However, in the process, everything but the recipe is lost. This experiment represents an attempt to notate through artifact instead of codification. It is both procedure and practice. By using color as a form of notation the structure of a basic bobbin lace stitch is diagrammed, without reducing it to a line drawing on a piece of paper. The threads are manipulated to form a textile object, but retain their individual visual identity. In this way the full process used to create it is revealed, in a way unique to the hands that created it.

Textile Architectures: A Transhistorical and Global Perspective into Architectural Historiography

Guerrilla Textiles: Aesthetics of Resistance

ALAN ALANIZ

In the years following the 1994 Zapatista Uprising, indigenous communities of the southern Mexican state of Chiapas constructed a distinctly indigenous political subject marked by the scars of generational injustice and the desire to upend the dynamics of a state and economic system that left many excluded and exploited. This paper interrogates two forms of textiles autochthonic to the mid-1990s Chiapas social justice movement—the Zapatista rebel ski mask and the work of female-led weaving collectives —and identifies them as sites of conflict where negotiations of indigenous identity, sociocultural self-determination, and relationships to the first and metropolitan third world occur. For both the Zapatista guerrilla and female weaver, these textiles symbolize a larger struggle against systemic oppression—from both an international neoliberal hegemonic order, and the coercive pressures of traditional gender roles—and act as a material practice that reifies indigenous subjectivity while reaching out and constructing networks of solidarity within and far beyond communities of southern Mexico.

By juxtaposing the material artifacts of the Zapatista ski mask and collective-produced Mayan textiles against the discourses emanating from their associated social justice movements, this paper articulates two distinct methods of indigenous resistance that unequivocally express the voices of the marginalized people of the region while foregrounding differing methods for harnessing global support and materializing political goals.

MAN-MADE: Petrochemical Development and the Material Culture of Synthetics in Iran

GABRIELLE PRINTZ

When it had brought nylon to the world market in the 1930s, the American chemical giant E. I. du Pont de Nemours & Company (DuPont) was actively propagating a vision of the world that could be improved through chemical processes and human mastery over the four elements. The technical and triumphal culture of the man-made found particular resonance in the Persian Gulf region where, in the early 1970s, DuPont set out to build the first polyester fiber plant in Iran. Focusing on the construction of the new plant, this paper examines the ambition and the reality of polyacrylic manufacturing as it was precisely and consciously situated in the late Pahlavi era of Iranian modernity and in the literal ground of the desert in Isfahan. In this analysis, two fundamental and reinforcing logics of petrochemical development come to the fore: that is (1) of the corporation, and its ability to propagate itself in new sectors and regional markets by way of capital investment, plant architecture, and the skilled human capital needed to build and operate it, and (2) something that hews closer the the material properties and material culture of plastic and polyester: the transformation of "telluric matter" into something altogether new. These were the combined forces that acted on the landscape, on labor, and on the productive (and agonistic) alignments between local, state, and multinational actors.

New metaphors continually inform architecture. Our use of the environment morphs and cultural landscapes become objects of design. Revisiting the countryside and the forest, time is considered not in tens-of-years, but hundreds-of-years; old and new architectural languages, visions of the future, and materials are negotiated in *Advanced Studios*. These stories speak to the myths, inventions, and utopias of *Core 2 Studios*.

THREE

ARCHITECTURAL DESIGN II

The second core studio, titled "Material Utopias," focuses on space and building, exploring the relationship between built intervention and environment through the medium of material. The words "material" and "utopia", were open for expansion, interpretation, and critique. Students considered the ways in which humans have occupied, altered, and inhabited their given environments over time, understanding both intention and effect. The process for the semester was observation, experimentation, speculation, and invention. Research-based material experiments, working across scales in varied contexts, reinforced project development. Using a variety of perspectives and analytic methods, students built and unbuilt possibilities. Projects were highly individual, specific responses, offering extraordinary speculations and proposed outcomes. [1012B]

Trattie Davies, Coordinator

Ariel Bintang, *Bobby Ka Ming Chun*, *Chloe Hou*, Elizabeth Cornfeld, Grace Zajdel, Grant Dokken, Josh Greene, Madeleine Reid, Signe Ferguson

Peter de Bretteville

Haonan Li, *Jonathan Chu*, Joseph Reich, Maya Gamble, Nathaniel Elmer, Qian Huang, *Ryan Matthew Reyes*, Seung Hyun Kim, Shi Li

Eeva-Liisa Pelkonen

Calvin Rogers, Ethnie Xu, Faith Pang, *Janice Chu*, Kai Wu, Kevin Wong, *Noah Sannes*, Sosa Erhabor, Zach Felder

Sunil Bald

Ben Derlan, *Charis Armstrong*, Clare Fentress, Corinna Siu, Jerry Chow, *Kyle Coxe*, Sam Landay, Tiana Kimball, Yong Choi

Joeb Moore

Ana Batlle, Benjamin Fann, Caitlin Yu, Ethan Chiang, *Gina Jiang*, *Sara Mountford*, Tim Hawkins, Ying Luo, Youssef Denial

Miriam Peterson

Abby Reed, Christopher Pin, *Cole Summersell*, Harry Hooper, Huy Truong, Ingrid Pelletier, Katherine Salata, Uzayr Agha, William Beck

THE FOREST

The boreal forest in Norway is a cultural landscape that
has influenced Nordic designers across fields; however,
designers often ignore the fact that most forests are managed
spaces and objects of design. The studio is not about wood,
nor about buildings made of wood. It is about the invention
of the forest as a cultural landscape and spatial metaphor
informing architecture. Secondarily, the studio looks into the
need for an updated set of forest representations in the
urban forests around Oslo. From myths to management to
spatial metaphors, the studio looks into the persistent yet
evolving spatial love affair to the forest in Scandinavia. [1108A]

FACULTY   Luis Callejas, Charlotte Hansson, Marta Caldeira

STUDENTS   Natalie Broton, *Stav Dror*, *Kate Fritz*, Jiaming Gu, Lillian Hou,
             Elise Limon, April Liu, *Naomi Jemima Ng*, Daoru Wang

JURY   Gro Bonesmo, Kevin Carmody, Rosetta Elkin, Andy Groarke,
             Carla Juaçaba, Marta Kuzma, Sabine Müller, Robert Pietrusko

NOT FOREVER

Our town and city centres, which have physically and socially evolved over decades, centuries or even millennia to meet the needs of their communities, are being rapidly hollowed out by changes in the way we consume products and services. To meet these changes, the countryside, once a productive landscape, now provides limitless opportunities to construct distribution or "fulfilment" centres to speedily meet the needs of this insatiable consumption. This architectural type is seemingly located, scaled and designed only by the parameters of provision. This new breed of "post-human architecture", as Rem Koolhaas calls it, is at such a scale that it no longer fits within our cities and is often conceived and delivered without regard or conscience to issues of social and physical context. More often than not it is built without the intervention of architects. The Studio proposes to challenge the preconception that such structures need only be considered as merely pragmatic or even benign in terms of their relationship to their context or purpose. By re-considering the lifespan of these buildings in terms of hundreds-of-years- rather than tens-of-years (or fewer)- refocuses value judgements about the presence of the building as a figure in the landscape and experience of material substance over time. [1104A]

FACULTY   Kevin Carmody, Andy Groarke, Gavin Hogben

STUDENTS   Shuchen Dong, Yue Geng, Mari Kroin, Ruike Liu, *Angela Lufkin*, Louisa Nolte, *Luka Pajovic*, Nicole Ratajczak, Qizhen Tang, *Hengyuan Yang*

JURY   Luis Callejas, Sofia von Ellrichshausen, Charlotte Hansson, Thomas Padmanabhan, Mauricio Pezo, Billie Tsien, Philip Ursprung

MANUFACTURING WONDERLAND

Experts predict that 90 percent of future real estate development in the near and long term will include renovation and reuse of existing structures. More so than at any time in modernity's past, future design practice will be shaped by the parameters and the design thinking distinct to adaptive reuse. Not such a bad thing, as arguably the greatest architect of the second millennium—Michelangelo—never designed a completely new building. Adaptive reuse challenges the contemporary architect in several ways. It highlights the needs to negotiate new and old architectural languages in establishing fit, to repurpose spaces through creative programming that is economically and socially regenerative of place, and to reimagine a future quite different from the one projected by the original structure. Methodologically, adaptive reuse projects are stitching operations, usually requiring lines of conceptualization and project framing different from those employed for greenfield buildings. [1115B]

FACULTY   Marlon Blackwell, Andrew Benner

STUDENTS   Natalie Broton, *Shuang Chen*, Janet Dong, Malcolm Rondell Galang, Yue Geng, Rishab Jain, Ingrid Liu, Christine Song, Shikha Thakali, Vivian Wu

JURY   Sandra Barclay, Nikole Bouchard, Maurice Cox, Jean Pierre Crousse, Ujijji Davis, Andrew Freear, Stephen Luoni, Georgeen Theodore, Billie Tsien, Tod Williams

WORKHOUSE

What is today's vision of the future living environment? If the separation of domestic and work space into discrete zones informed the ethos of modern architecture and urban planning in the twentieth century, the twenty-first century is characterized by the fluidity and flexibility of spaces and lifestyles. Co-working and co-living spaces have been at the forefront of this paradigm shift, which sees a restructuring of patterns of inhabitation, the rise of new forms of community, and the reconciliation of domestic and work environments. As lifestyles continue to transform, architecture needs to be redefined to accommodate changes in daily life. The WORKHOUSE, Life after Pandemic, will explore possibilities for the future of our environment through the research of changes happening today, specifically the merging of spaces for domesticity and for work. [1106A]

FACULTY   Hitoshi Abe, Nicholas McDermott

STUDENTS   *Ife Adepegba,* Daniella Calma, Christopher Cambio, Malcolm Rondell Galang, Alicia Jones, Qiyuan Liu, Christine Song, *Shikha Thakali,* Shelby Wright, *Vivian Wu*

JURY   Sunil Bald, Dana Cuff, Yoko Kawai, Jimenez Lai, Greg Lynn, Adi Meyerovitch, Jacob Reidel, Marc Tsurumaki, Gretchen Wilkins

LETTING SPIRITS IN
Chloe Hou

Yale Myers Forest is a space of rotational economy. Cyclical additions-to and subtractions-from the biome cause disturbances to the community of spirits living in the flora. This project asks if disturbances can open the terrain for transformative encounters between humans who work and visit the forest and spirits who are forced to move. By claiming that the room in between trees is the living room for these spirits, I propose an assemblage of artifacts—tool shed, saphouse, seed bank and various lean-tos—constructed with mycelium, for homeless spirits to dwell temporarily. The phenomenological quality of these utilitarian and ritual spaces triggers users' imaginations, enabling their capacity to recognize the spiritual within the material and the forest.

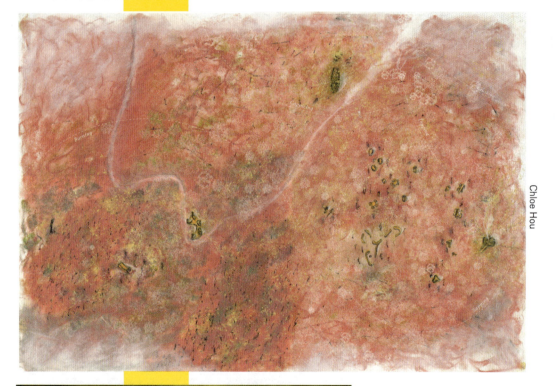

Chloe Hou

Chloe Hou

BEYOND THE GRID
Bobby Ka Ming Chun

Despite the usual depiction of the Farmington Canal as a uniform line cutting through Connecticut, it is in fact a complex weave of grids that reflects the changing material conditions across the state. This project builds on the foundational grids of the canal to create three dimensional tartans that encourage the serendipitous coexistence of different species within the cycle of food. Superimposed rectangles in the grids become opportunistic sites for material exchange in the process of production and consumption. The system grows and shrinks organically, and as time progresses, the actions of the species slowly erode the rectilinear grid.

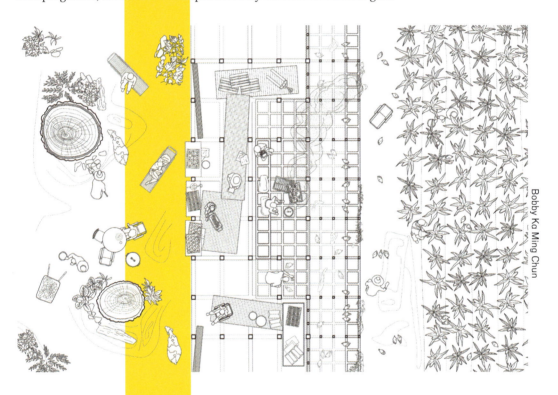

Bobby Ka Ming Chun

Architectural Design II · Davies   Core Studio

Bobby Ka Ming Chun

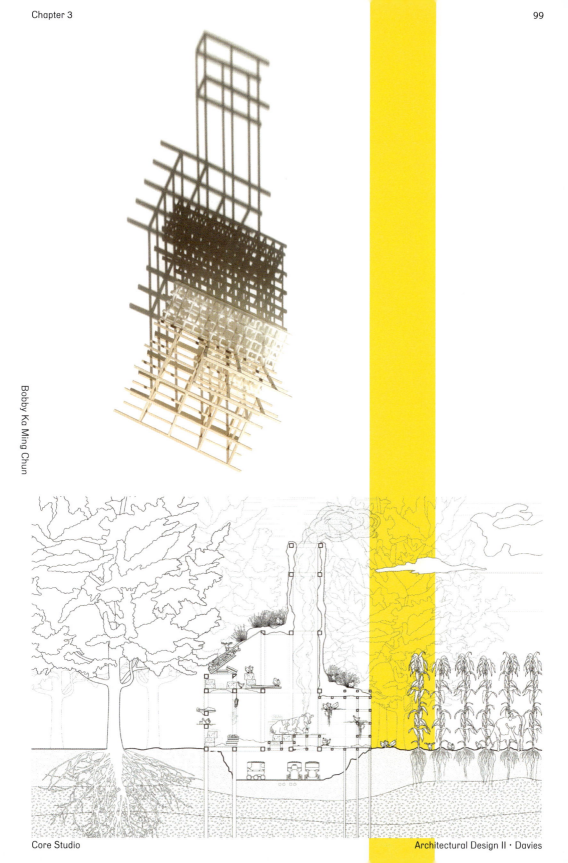

Naomi Jemima Ng

9 GATES IN THE FOREST
Naomi Jemima Ng

Architecturally, this project questions what it may be like to bring the familiar archetypal forms of the parliament back to the forest, and in doing so, how it confronts with the open landscape. Socially, this project questions how changing the spatial arrangement of the parliament may consequently change how decisions are made. Inspired by the nine gates lining the facade of the Norway parliament (the storting building) and the fragmented Icelandic "thing," this parliament primarily includes nine fragmented pieces scattered across the site. The forms derive from a mixture of geometries interpreted from the parliament in conjunction with the ruthless geometries of forest management practices. Ultimately, this project goes forwards and backwards simultaneously—forward in breaking the century old parliament archetype but also backwards in terms of bringing the assembly back into an open landscape like the Icelandic "thing."

Naomi Jemima Ng

Naomi Jemima Ng

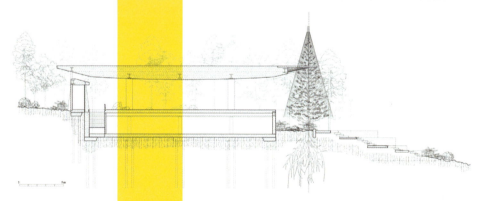

Charlotte Hansson Your project is composed of different spaces that although small, aspire to serve as civic arenas for discussion. The open air parliament challenges the idea that such a public and civic building must be centrally located. Each building has a delicate relationship to the surrounding landscape, a forest that is clearly the main protagonist.

CONFLICT IN CLEARING
Stav Dror

The Norwegian forest is a site of fantasy. A clearing within the Oslo woods is surveyed as the project's site; It is an ex-territory between narratives. The clearing's program is conflict, based on the ancient Norwegian "Thing"—a parliament conducted in landscape through arrival, negotiation, and emptying. The linear parliament structure upholds the clearing's edge while supporting the program of conflict. It remains in an almost-interior state while housing the forest's monsters—the Tiger, the Horse, and the Lion. They are reclaimed symbols from urban space, used as constructive and programmatic building parts. The trees surrounding the clearing participate as raw material for the fabrication of chairs—the project's basic moveable programmatic unit. The project's chairs are based on the sum of parliament members' actions: sit, sleep, fight.

Stav Dror · Feldman Nominee

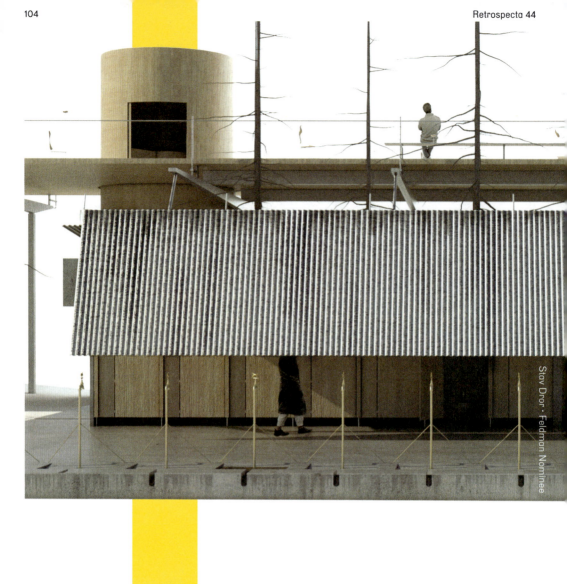

Stav Dror · Feldman Nominee

The Forest · Callejas, Hansson, Caldeira   Advanced Studio

Stav Dror · Feldman Nominee

Charlotte Hansson **You've created these artful architectural details, somewhere between abstraction and figuration. They allow the project to develop, but also to communicate other complex ideas and form a beautiful narrative in a very direct way. Your intuition takes form at different scales in an undisciplined way, which enables the building to have different levels of resolution.**

Kate Fritz

The Forest · Callejas, Hansson, Caldeira   Advanced Studio

TRIPTYCH OF THE FOREST
Kate Fritz

The project introduces three traces and cycles within the Norwegian forest, understood through the lens that the only thing permanent is the cycle of time, and within this exists scales of permanence. These three traces include the bracket (felling), the clearing (succession), and the garden (parliament). The bracket cycle is understood to be generational. Here a boy comes to plant a tree; he then visits it each summer. As his cycle advances, so does the tree, and at age 40, the tree is harvested. The clearing is a trace left by silvicultural practice and will continue to regrow through natural succession, occurring around year 150. The garden is the final trace left at the site. The introduced cycle is episodic; here, parliament commences on the first weekday of October each year to assemble the storting and then every four years for the elections, bringing an end to the parliamentary term.

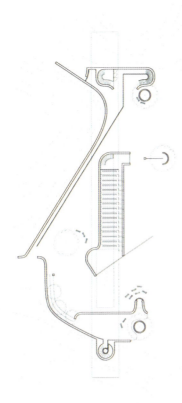

Kate Fritz

Luis Callejas There are obvious cues to the themes related to botany and the relationship that a building can establish with larger landscapes. The project's clear spatial organization is subordinate to the structure, while the main structural ideas are taken after shaping the landscape.

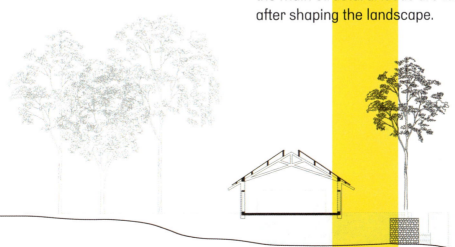

MANAGED HETEROTOPIAS: SYSTEMS OF CARE WITHIN THE YALE-MYERS FOREST
Charis Armstrong

The managed heterotopias that comprise the modern holding, within indigenous Nipmuc land—today called the Yale-Myers Forest (YMF), hosts homes, township boundaries, the bulk of Yale's of forestry education and silvicultural endeavors. Hurtling our vision into the future, this project proposes that the entirety of the forest will become a vessel for the creation of idealized controls for experimentation. The forest is divided into a square-mile grid whose divisions are defined by autonomous Outposts, each uniquely positioned to adapt the focus of their research to their surroundings. Each quadrant of the Outpost focuses on YMF's most expansive areas of study: silviculture and canopy health, trophic food webs, aquatic ecology, and the soil and microbial ecology of forests. These "petri dishes" of focused care for the forest will not return what has been lost, but they can act as a lens through which humanity may confront its inevitable ecological impact.

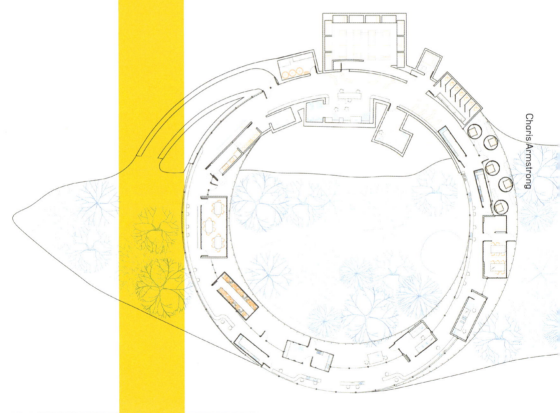

Charis Armstrong

Architectural Design II · Bald

Charis Armstrong

PROPAGATING EQUILIBRIUM
Kyle Coxe

This urban proposal doubles as a healing center for humans who have experienced trauma and offers protection for vulnerable non-human species so they may reinvigorate the site with biodiversity. Clients find solace in the versatility of mycelium as a renewable building and textile material that serves various purposes in the healing process through extensive use in occupational therapy settings. Skilled professionals harness the power of mycelium's fruiting bodies to provide psychoactive assisted therapy treatments to patients in their healing process. The concrete-infused mycelium retaining walls in the lower architectural substrate hold healing and making spaces while supporting the ephemeral upper tectonic system that consists of personalized individual dwellings.

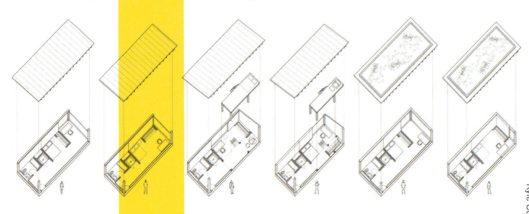

Kyle Coxe

Kyle Coxe

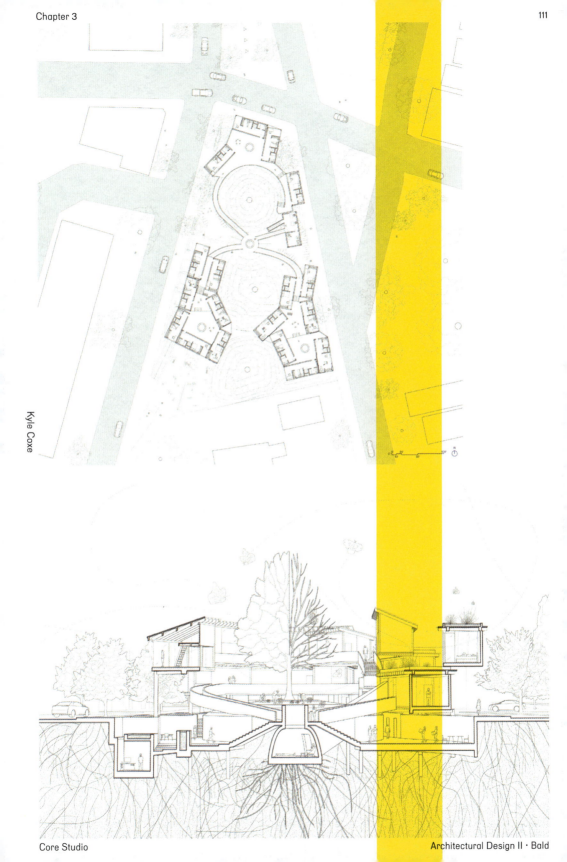

Luka Pajovic

TOPOGRAPHY OF LABOUR:
A NEW WORK-YARD FOR
THE BRITISH LIBRARY
Luka Pajovic

This project envisions a new way of structuring the British Library's main off-site storage facility over the coming two centuries. The site was first developed in the early 1940s as a Royal Ordnance Factory, retaining to this day the original grid. The British Library has occupied the site since the early 1970s, taking over most of the existing industrial buildings and repurposing them for storage. In addition to existing structures, two major new automated storage voids were constructed over the past decade. These storage spaces rely on highly energy-intensive equipment to create optimal conditions for the preservation of printed matter. Low-oxygen and low-temperature atmosphere is maintained perpetually within buildings never intended for such purposes, whilst the human-operated and institutional functions are relegated to temporary structures and the peripheries of storage voids.

Luka Pajovic

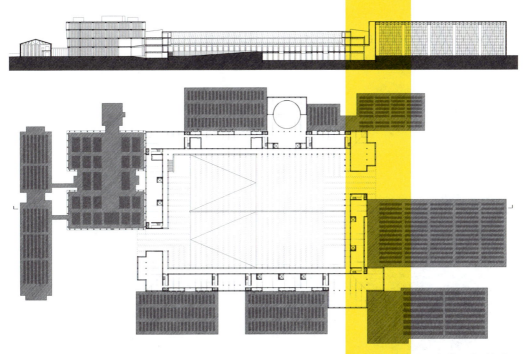

Luka Pajovic

Sofia von Ellrichshausen There is a soft nature to this project—
the section, the materials, the language of the narrative.
The uncertainty of how it will unfold over time—I think
it's quite beautiful to allow for that flexibility. It's a starting
point. What the project is about then is void, it becomes
the identity of the project; therefore the facade created
by that void is the unitary element.

Not Forever · Carmody, Groarke, Hogben   Advanced Studio

NEW SUBLIME: BRITISH LIBRARY ARCHIVE BUILDING
Hengyuan Yang

The project aims to realize the institutional resilience of the storage buildings through literary festivals during their long-lasting lifespan. In contrast to the former autonomous campus, the new site will be open to the public in the future. The storage buildings are located along the roads for efficient logistics and create a "green space" in the middle for literary festivals and leisure. The passive-sustainable archive is buried underground to meet the critical temperature and humidity requirement for book storage. As the byproduct of the excavation, the earth is used on-site to sculpt a slope landscape along the retaining wall. The lightweight roof could be accessed from the top of the slope as a reading and research space. In the future, the boxes in the landscape and events of books will facilitate each other and live over a 300-year lifespan.

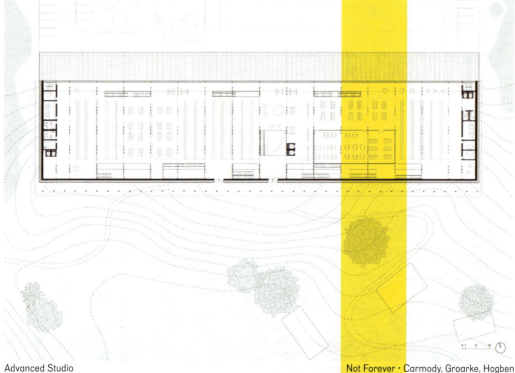

Hengyuan Yang

Hengyuan Yang

Thomas Padmanabhan Your project is almost like a land art operation. There is a beautiful contrast between the hard-edged functionalism of your buildings and the generosity and softness of the public space you're offering in between them, all which absorb and accommodate the functional requirements at the same time.

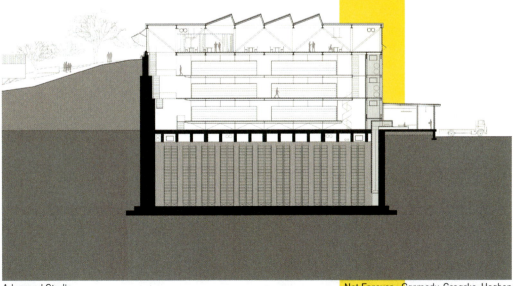

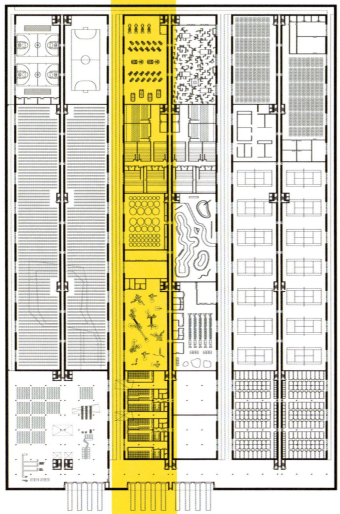

Angela Lufkin

Billie Tsien You took the most common words and put them together to make a surreal story. The idea of taking common program and using it as the basis to make something that's uncommon is the great strength of your project.

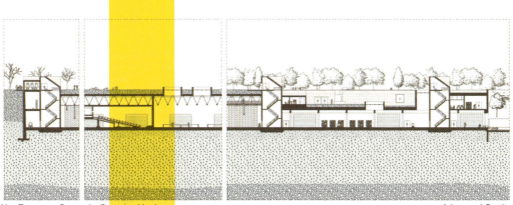

Not Forever · Carmody, Groarke, Hogben   Advanced Studio

FOREVER, FOR NOW
Angela Lufkin

With a mandate to protect one copy of every published book in perpetuity, the British Public Library (BPL) necessitates a very big box—an expansive archival space capable of holding a projected 456,557 m³ of books by the year 3000. This project meets these spatial and logistical challenges with the question of institutional resilience. How might the BPL ensure ongoing funding, attention, and space for an endeavor that will play out over many lifetimes and unpredictable generational events? By proposing an overhaul of the current site and the simultaneous intervention of the entire projected storage volume, the project envisions a new role for the BPL as real estate developer. Only filling a fraction of the total space at year zero, the books make way for a myriad of rental possibilities in the underground. In the interim, the architecture facilitates a dynamic world of public-private partnerships, creating an unexpected platform and welcome destination for a wide array of user groups.

Angela Lufkin

ALLEGORICAL ARCHITECTURE
Ryan Matthew Reyes

Human presence on earth comes to an end. This shift reveals that just as we have learnt the forest, the forest has learnt us. As the oak trees mutate in order to reclaim agency of their own afterlife, slow pulses of ethereal fibers materialize, twist and bind together as they drift over the forest floor, they ossify into boney tissue, they splinter into new ghost-like forms. Attention is given where the heart and brain of the human breach the ground, these thresholds are made liminal; from these parameters the monument is constructed. Here it becomes evident, by the craft of the ghosts, that architecture is inextricably linked to the fibers of this new material just as the leaf is to the branch, the branch to the trunk, and the trunk to the seed, from the ground where the tree's find their origin and the human finds their ancestors.

Ryan Matthew Reyes

Ryan Matthew Reyes

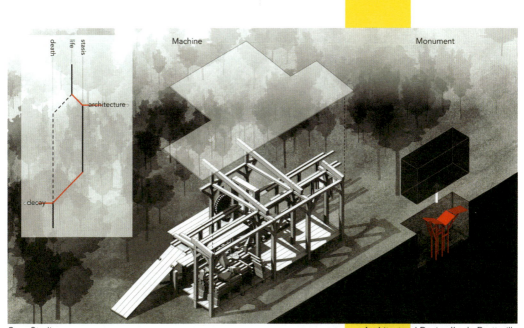

HYBRIDITY AND MODULARITY
Jonathan Chu

Passing through the town of Hamden, the Farmington Canal juxtaposes a 2.5-mile industrial strip on one side with the constructed wetland of Lake Whitney on the other. This structure is designed as a mediator, reactivating both sides of the site by introducing architectural interventions attached to the trail. Infill housing units will occupy empty parking lots, where shared gardens bleed into new green spaces that spill over from the wetland. Conversely, human activity is brought into the wetland, accompanied by local flora and fauna, through an elevated boardwalk system.

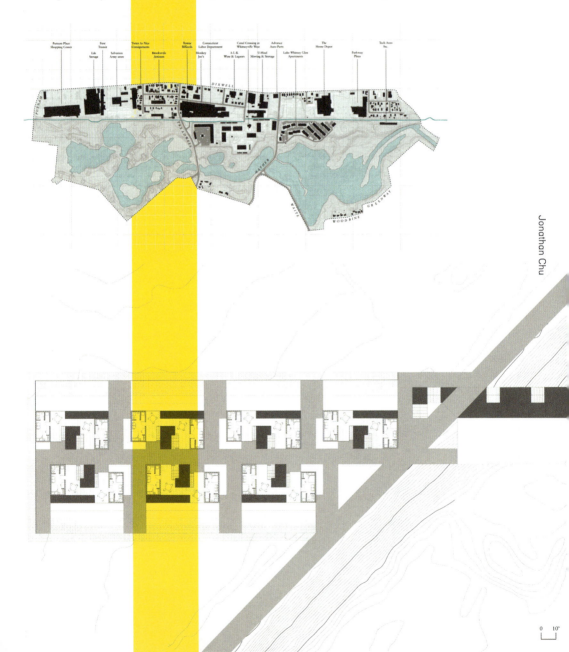

Jonathan Chu

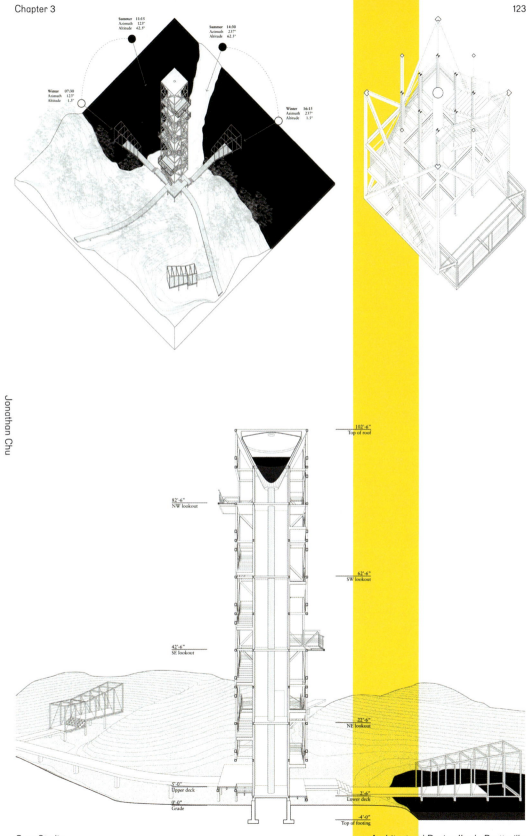

Jonathan Chu

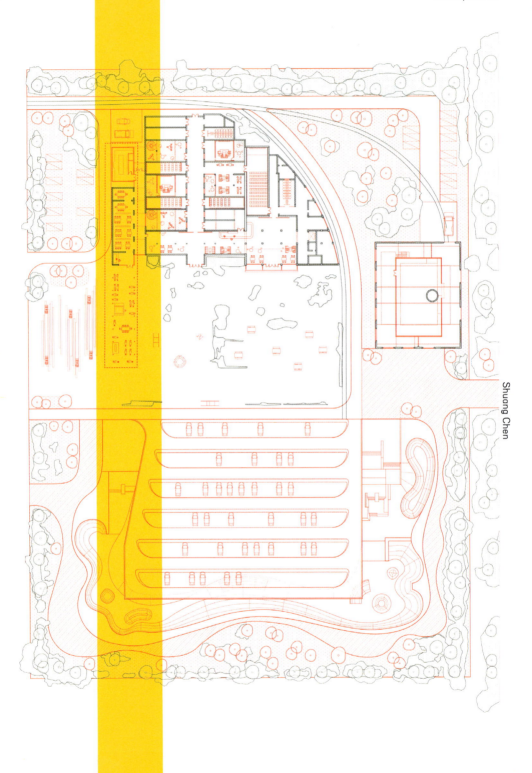

Shuang Chen

THE DRIVE-IN
Shuang Chen

Shuang Chen

The drive-in has seen a resurgence in the car culture of Detroit. Based around the event of collective movie watching, this project proposes a hybrid leisure and creative production center, offering multiple, integrated experiences across film, dining, and skateboarding. A new dining canopy hovering on the west side of the project, together with the drive-in parking and the skatepark beneath it, has zoned the site into a center plaza with programs surrounding it. Based on features of the existing building, the testing building will be small screening rooms mixed with social spaces and a garden; the engine building provides spaces for extensive screening, and a black production box will nest inside the powerplant. This project attracts film lovers, skateboarders, the local community, and Chrysler workers to meet, gather and enjoy. The Drive-In Wonderland regenerates the old continental motors, inviting people for a multi-film experience, skateboarding, gathering, and stimulating neighborhood storytelling.

Shuang Chen

Maurice Cox It's inspired site-planning: the idea of taking a parking lot and placing it on a tilted slab to create a landform and surround it with a skatepark. The project takes the most banal of functions, and realizing it's not enough to just treat the surface of the lot, instead gives it form with the tilt-up. It creates an edge to the site that it currently does not have.

ART AND SPORTS
WONDERLAND
Vivian Wu

The project proposes a wonderland of arts and sports to strengthen the Jefferson Chalmers neighborhood in Detroit, where a fledgling local art community is rising. Multi-purpose spaces and cross-programing generate new forms of play, where new ideas can emerge out of unexpected encounters. It encourages exploration and adventure for the public across all seasons. Furthermore, the project takes on the challenge to design a wonderland for all seasons. An ice ribbon, blending the exterior and interior spaces, turns into a walking trail during summer that connects and activates different parts of the site. Other interchangeable activities include rock climbing, ice climbing, basketball, and ice hockey. Landscape and multifunctional spaces also allow activities to change constantly between day and night, winter and summer. By generating numerous activities for the public, the project maximizes its impact on the Jefferson Chalmers neighborhood and city of Detroit by offering excitement and delight.

Vivian Wu · Feldman Nominee

Manufacturing Wonderland · Blackwell, Benner

Vivian Wu · Feldman Nominee

Section A-A

Section B-B
— existing
— new intervention

Vivian Wu · Feldman Nominee

Jean Pierre Crousse This is not an autonomous project—it has a relationship at the level of the city and the neighborhood. It interacts with existing activities and embraces their complexity at different times: hourly, daily, and monthly. Everything is unstable and changing—it's a project that reimagines itself along the year, the seasons, and the day.

SILENCE
Gina Jiang

The project hopes to raise awareness of digital dictatorship by materializing invisible data. The utopia is defined by a soft boundary of copper mesh and a hard boundary of magnetic rocks, a silent zone where humans are protected from data. Here, biodiversity is protected from consumption. The boundaries are interactive, deformed by magnetic forces, creating a series of lacunae. These in-between spaces allow our everyday world to undergo osmosis, resulting in the project's primary spaces. Subject to climate and cultural changes, boundaries then grow to eventually include existing buildings. The community gains a place to examine the relationships between organism and algorithm, biochemistry and data, and consciousness and intelligence.

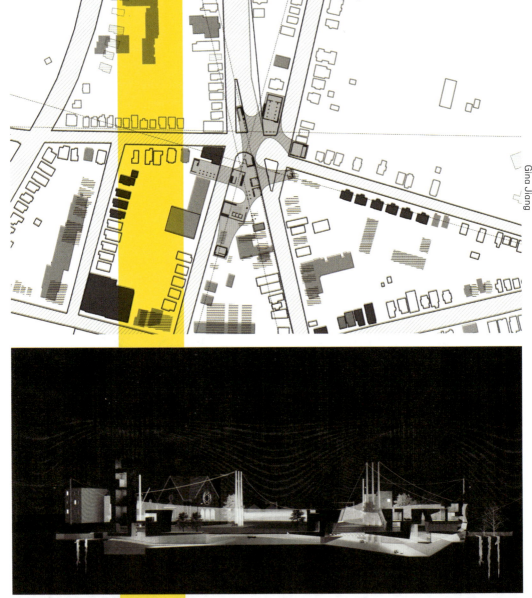

Gina Jiang

Gina Jiang

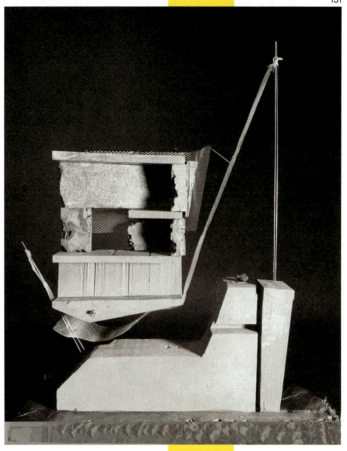

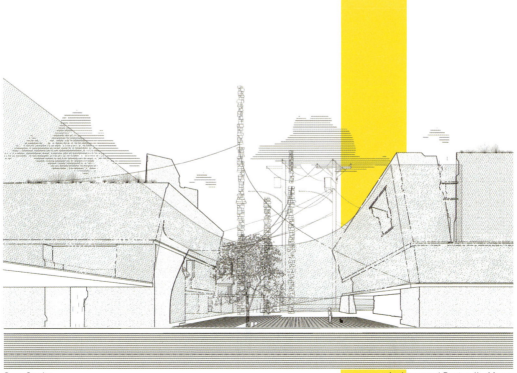

INFRASTRUCTURE
Sara Mountford

833 Dixwell Ave is a center for the pollination of materials within an urban environment. The site's locality presents an opportunity to create a new urban street that can connect parallel, yet disconnected, life lines. The project seeks to facilitate growth within human and non-human species, and utilize the possibilities presented by seven existing ecologies along the Farmington Canal. The form is changeable, an adaptable acceptance of materiality on the canal. It simultaneously self-propagates and morphs as time continues. The building starts to collapse onto the street itself, and visitors join the electricity, heating, and cooling passing through plumbing systems and structural formwork. The duality between natural and manmade phenomena dissolves, as the physicality of the building systems merge with human systems, creating a social, cultural, and environmental nexus. The building facilitates the spreading of information, the street bleeds into the facade, utopia expands further, and time passes by.

Sara Mountford

Sara Mountford

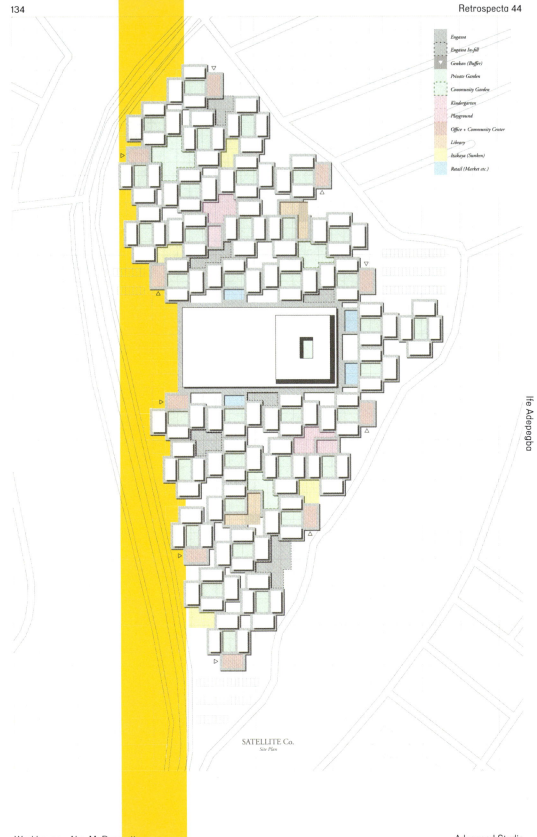

Engawa
Engawa In-fill
Genkan (Buffer)
Private Garden
Community Garden
Kindergarten
Playground
Office + Community Center
Library
Izakaya (Sunken)
Retail (Market etc.)

SATELLITE Co.
Site Plan

Ife Adepegba

SATELLITE CO.
Ife Adepegba

Satellite Co. aims to innovate upon the company town model through rethinking "management" and "ownership". By rewiring hierarchical relationships, agency is created for the salary-man, respecting their identity as a figure within a culture centered around collectivism, where ideals of stability, devotion, and community are paramount. Surrounding a central open-plan incubator space and weaving a patchwork of sorts are a series of modular residential units, composed in fours and connected by a covered *engawa*, a Japanese porch that wraps and threads through the site. Within these residential groups of fours, the commute is minimized as units are substituted for either retail spaces, offices, community centers, libraries, or kindergartens. The *engawa* forms the crux of the project, a buffer space representing a semi-interior condition serving as a bridge between home and work. The *engawa* is to be perceived as a "third space"; through its repetitiveness resides an infinite possibility of social encounters and interactions, creating ambiguity between residents and residents, residents and amenities, and residents and work-place.

Ife Adepegba

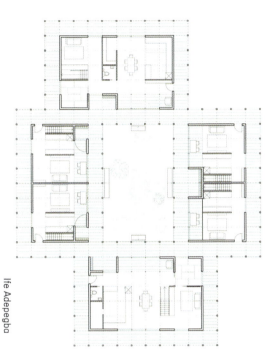

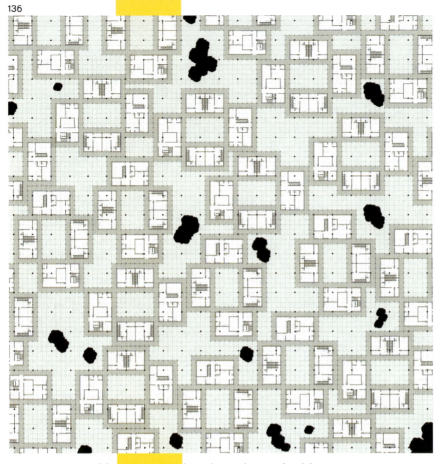

Ife Adepegba

Nicholas McDermott Your proposal ends up being highly strategic; it considers the value proposition for the contemporary corporation while using these logics to deploy a humanizing and beautifully organized plan. The architecture speaks to the individuals and families who are seeking not only a home but a community.

Workhouse · Abe, McDermott

Advanced Studio

TERRACE VILLAGE
Vivian Wu

COVID-19 has substantially affected people's mental health globally. Looking specifically into Japan, the prevalence of mental distress is a deep-rooted and increasingly severe issue, particularly in the elderly population. This has resulted in *kodokushi*—a distressing Japanese phenomenon of the elderly dying alone and remaining undiscovered for a long time. To promote physical and mental wellness in the elderly and young population, Terrace Village proposes a wellness complex where the elderly and student population live, learn, and socialize together to facilitate a supportive lifestyle and reduce loneliness. It challenges the typical organization of senior housing and student's dormitory, integrates wellness activities into everyday living and working, and bridges the elderly, students, and the larger neighborhood to reinforce a sense of community. Various age groups will contribute their varied skills to the governing and upkeep of the community, and share their expertise and free time helping each other, essentially forming an "extended family" to augment social participation and inter-generational bonding.

Vivian Wu

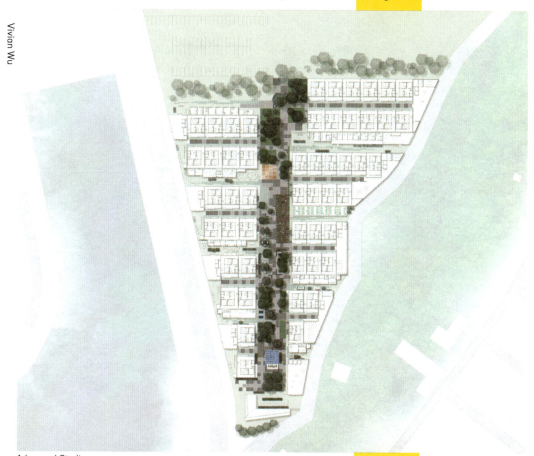

Vivian Wu

Workhouse · Abe, McDermott   Advanced Studio

Vivian Wu

Nicholas McDermott You've addressed the immediate development context of the suburban street and green space, and you're connecting it to more probing questions about how bodies of different ages might shape—and be shaped—by a post-pandemic environment.

Nicholas McDermott The looping paths are elegant in how they hold everything together and simultaneously break the larger massing into smaller relatable sections.

Shikha Thakali · Feldman Nominee

NAKANIWA COLLECTIVE
Shikha Thakali

Nakaniwa Collective is an integrated mixed-use model for intergenerational living, with wellness as its core. The project is organized and oriented around four internalized courtyards—one for student living, one for elderly living, one for intergenerational living, and one for formal communal activities such as work, study, and healthcare. The architectural design for the project is the framework for a diverse social program that aims to bridge the relationship between the ageing population of Kashiwanoha, the student population from the University of Tokyo, and the rapidly growing surrounding neighborhood. The three zones of living that come together to share communal facilities were created with the understanding that students and elderly have diverse needs. In a time where independent living is treasured yet social support networks are needed, Nakaniwa Collective provides the elderly and students a chance to live together in the same estate. The courtyard blocks are connected, yet spatially separate. They are close enough for interaction and assistance, yet far enough apart that privacy between different generations is preserved.

UTOPIA AS EXPERIENCE
Janice Chu

When a tree asks for more space on this land, do we actually listen? When we talk about nature in urban settings, we often relegate street trees as tools for shading, or urban beautification. Function, placement and growth of the "urban tree" is manipulated to serve the needs of the human. This project aims at reversing a human-centric approach to urbanized nature by allowing habitable spaces to be designed by trees. This new urban forest model creates a psycho-physical unity of man and nature, where the benefits of both human existence and tree existence are reciprocal. A minimal architectural intervention becomes a mediator, responsive to the form and growth of trees. With this approach, a tree is no longer altered, harmed, or killed when it asks for more space. In fact, when the tree designs space, human sensations can be accentuated to create new forms of meditative experiences within the city.

Janice Chu

Janice Chu

MATERIAL WASTE, PUBLIC SPACE
Noah Sannes

Our waste practices pose an existential threat to our cities and planet. Therefore, when considering a new model for a materials recovery facility, it is critical to reconsider the role of the consumer in the processes of sourcing "waste" materials, diverting recyclables from the waste stream, and celebrating these items through reuse and innovation. The proposal calls for a 700'-long historic naval warehouse to be repurposed as the site where this new model can be tested. The facility is designed to support the coalescence of consumers, materials, and previously separated building programs. Further, it is strategically organized to facilitate human and material flows between recyclable collection points, markets, innovation labs, resident apartments, galleries, and public spaces. Enhanced by wayfinding devices, the layout of the converted warehouse is intended to expose visitors to material inventories, innovations, and better recycling practices and invite them to engage in securing the afterlife of "waste" materials.

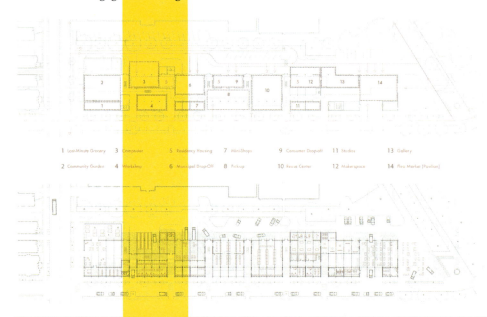

| 1 Last-Minute Grocery | 3 Composter | 5 Residency Housing | 7 Mini-Shops | 9 Consumer Drop-off | 11 Studios | 13 Gallery |
| 2 Community Garden | 4 Workshop | 6 Municipal Drop-Off | 8 Pickup | 10 Reuse Center | 12 Makerspace | 14 Flea Market (Pavilion) |

Noah Sannes

Noah Sannes

NEW HAVEN
SHARING ECONOMY

NEW HAVEN
'WASTE' ROUTES

INTRA-GRID
Abby Reed

The forest is based on reciprocities, a constant give and take, a dynamic equilibrium. Architecture is not against, but in a relationship with, the forest. Material is both found and constructed, it is a building block from a micro—to a macro—scale. Material is carbon, water, micro-organisms and soil. Material is a tree, but also its leaves, bark, vascular system and roots. The grid is also a material, constructed by humans to better understand a place. The grid makes sense of this reciprocal relationship; it allows humans to comprehend a system that is too large to take in at a glance. The grid defines the active forestry management and living processes of both the residents and forest ecosystem. The grid tracks where to plant, where to burn, where to build, and where to live.

Abby Reed

Abby Reed

UPWARD SPIRAL / COMMON DREAM
Cole Summersell

How do myths dictate the form of our built environment? How do the things we
build reveal what we believe? This project is a fantastical, allegorical interrogation of
three essential American myths: equality, unlimited growth, and meritocracy. The
structure, a kinetic manifestation of suburbia's assembly line principles, scrutinizes
these impossible truths by pushing them to their breaking points. Using the logic
of production, this suburban factory also exposes the exploitative labor flows
that undergird American single-family utopia. In this experiment, the dictates of
industrial efficiency and perfect equality turn the suburbs in on themselves; instead
of sprawl, they generate a leisure-based, non-hierarchical Tower of Babel, 1500 living
pods continuously orbit spiraling towers of common and service space. The utopians
and their subservient labor forces occupy the same site, passing by each other in
parallel, unseen worlds. Ultimately, the friction between the servants and the served,
and between the myths themselves, leads to catastrophic failure.

Cole Summersell

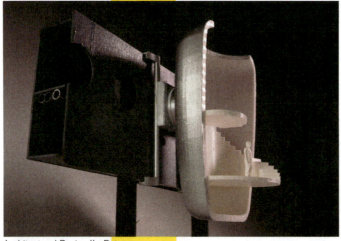

Cole Summersell

Buildings are undeniably subjects of financial and political feasibility. They undergird connections to greater networks of trade, production, and culture, which subsequently fuel new modes of regional and municipal innovation. *Technology and Practice* courses interrogate value propositions within the profession, toeing the line between ossification and conversation as *Urbanism and Landscape* courses reassess the subsequent construction and experience of the city.

Technology and Practice
Urbanism and Landscape

FOUR

Systems Integration and Development in Design

MARTIN FINIO

This course is an integrated workshop and lecture series in which students develop the technical systems of preliminary design proposals from earlier studio work. Careful advancement of structural form and detail, environmental systems, egress and accessibility, and envelope design, as well as an understanding of the constructive processes from which a building emerges, are all approached systematically. Elements of design are used not only to achieve technical and performance goals but also to reinforce and re-inform the conceptual origins of the work. [2022B]

TECHNOLOGY AND PRACTICE (REQUIRED)

Environmental Design

ANNA DYSON, NAOMI KEENA

This course examines the fundamental scientific principles governing the thermal, luminous, and acoustic environments of buildings, and introduces students to the methods and technologies for creating and controlling the interior environment. The overarching premise of the course is that the understanding and application of the physical principles by the architect must respond to and address the larger issues surrounding energy and the environment at multiple scales and in domains beyond a single building. [2021A]

TECHNOLOGY AND PRACTICE (REQUIRED)

Architectural Practice and Management

PHILLIP BERNSTEIN, JOHN APICELLA

This course provides an understanding of the fundamentals of the structure and organization of the profession and the mechanisms and systems within which it works, as well as the organization, management, and execution of architectural projects. Students explore the role and function of the architect, the legal environment, models of practice and office operations, fees and compensation, project delivery models and technology, and project management in the context of the evolution of architectural practice in the delivery of buildings. [2031A]

TECHNOLOGY AND PRACTICE (REQUIRED)

Exploring New Value in Design Practice

PHILLIP BERNSTEIN, BRITTANY OLIVARI

Intense market competition in the building sector places sole focus on differentiation by design quality. The subsequent lack of innovation in project delivery and business models results in a profession that is grossly underpaid and marginally profitable. This course redesigns the value proposition of architecture practice, explores strategies used by better-compensated adjacent professions and markets, and investigates methods by which architects can deliver—and be paid for—the value they bring to the building industry. [2230B]

TECHNOLOGY AND PRACTICE

Introduction to Planning and Development

ALEXANDER GARVIN

This course demonstrates the ways in which financial and political feasibility determine the design of buildings and the character of the built environment. Students propose projects and then adjust them to the conflicting interests of financial institutions, real estate developers, civic organizations, community groups, public officials, and the widest variety of participants in the planning process. Subjects covered include housing, commercial development, zoning, historic preservation, parks and public open space, suburban subdivisions, and comprehensive plans. [4242A]

URBANISM AND LANDSCAPE

Urban Difference and Change

JUSTIN GARRETT MOORE

Be it disinvestment, disaster, or gentrification, change is an essential indicator of difference in urban environments. Cities must consider the intersection between climate change and growing income inequality with politics, culture, gender equality and identity, immigration, and technology. This course explores how cities embody the legacies and derivatives of colonialism and modernism, and how we might find agency in the past, present, and future of urban contexts. Anti-racist and decolonial frameworks like cultural heritage, environmental conservation, and social equity and inclusion start to challenge dominant narratives and unjust past and present conditions. [4247A]

URBANISM AND LANDSCAPE

Fighting Slavery in the Building Supply Chain

PHILLIP BERNSTEIN, LUIS C. DEBACA

This course operationalizes recent statutory and regulatory changes in the United States, the United Kingdom, and Australia that extend enforcement of laws against forced and child labor into company supply chains. Drawing on law, business, and sustainability practices, we seek to incorporate an anti-slavery ethos into the architectural design process for the first time. Multidisciplinary teams of students from across Yale's professional and graduate schools "slavery-proof" a particular input or process in projects that the architecture students are working on in their studio classes. [2242A]

TECHNOLOGY AND PRACTICE

Advanced Building Envelopes

ANNA DYSON, MOHAMED ALY ETMAN

This course is geared towards graduate students in Architecture who already have an advanced background in bioclimatic analysis and design and who wish to pursue an area of design research in conjunction with their studio projects. It provides an overview of emerging critical theory and technology in the areas of environmental and energy systems. Students are asked to consider a variety of fundamentally novel ways of redirecting energy and water flows, towards the fulfillment of various social mandates to transform the relationship between the built environment and extended ecosystems. [2018A]

TECHNOLOGY AND PRACTICE

Skin Deep: Envelope As Potential Energy

MARTIN FINIO

Just as our bodies give us a false sense of ourselves as distinct from the external world, so do building facades. This course is an argument for eliminating such distinctions in buildings. We put so much emphasis on the facade as the identity of a building; the expression, the form, and the composition of a building. This course makes an argument against this approach; against caring what the building looks like in favor of how the building situates itself within the abundant energy flows of the earth—not thwarting them, but engaging with them. [2209B]

TECHNOLOGY AND PRACTICE

Port Cities

ALAN PLATTUS

Historically, port cities around the world have played a crucial role as the nodes of connection and exchange for both local and vast global networks of production, trade, culture, and power. Since the industrial revolution, rapid development of new technologies of transport and communication has challenged the planners and developers of these cities to both adapt and innovate. This course considers the changing and persistent patterns, functions, and images of port cities, particularly in the context of their regional and global networks, researching, analyzing, and mapping the architectural and spatial manifestations of those systems. [4220B]

URBANISM AND LANDSCAPE

Regenerative Building: Horse Island

ALAN ORGANSCHI

The Regenerative Building seminar explores design and building techniques that seek to reduce environmental impacts across the building lifecycle and promote metabolic, non-mechanistic approaches to the production of the built environment. By engaging renewable material supply chains and energy systems that minimize destruction and promote eco-systemic health of source landscapes, regenerative techniques in building attempt to avoid the conventions of our current linear, extractive systems of resource consumption. A sequence of short lectures, focused readings, and associated research questions challenge students from the disciplines of design and environmental management to posit and test means to mitigate the significant ecological and climatic impacts of those building sector activities. [2229B]

TECHNOLOGY AND PRACTICE ⸱

Urban Landscape and Geographies of Justice

ELIHU RUBIN

What explains the socioeconomic and ecological patterns in a city? This course introduces students to ideas in the history and theory of urban planning; the production of urban environments; and concepts in environmental justice to understand the challenges that face contemporary cities. Using New Haven as a case study, the class explores the ways in which structural inequalities are inscribed and reproduced in urban landscapes. The course builds up a sequence of historical-geographic layers and conceptual frameworks with the goal of unpacking the legacies of planning and urban development decision-making on contemporary social and environmental conditions. [4249B]

URBANISM AND LANDSCAPE

Introduction to Urban Studies

ELIHU RUBIN

This course provides an introduction to key topics, research methods, and practices in urban studies—an interdisciplinary field of inquiry and action rooted in the experience of cities. As physical artifacts, the advent of large cities have reflected rapid industrialization and advanced capitalism. They are inseparable from the organization of economic life; the flourishing of cultures; and the formation of identities. They are also places where power is concentrated and inequalities are (re)produced. Debates around equity are filtered through urban environments, where struggles over jobs, housing, education, mobility, public health, and public safety are front and center. [4246A]

URBANISM AND LANDSCAPE

Systems Integration and Development in Design

What Can Be Common

JESSICA JIE ZHOU, MEGHNA MUDALIAR, TAKU SAMEJIMA

The roofline forms a series of saw-tooth roofs oriented 30 degrees toward south, while expressing the unitized character of the building. Considering the modular nature of the project, a Variable Refrigerant Flow (VRF) system was adopted for the heating/cooling mechanism that allows for a flexible distribution of outdoor units throughout the building. The system was combined with Dedicated Outdoor Air System (DOAS) that supplements the varying ventilation needs for each of the indoor rooms and programs.

Architectural Designer: Joshua Tan

Meandering Me

JACK RUSK, WENZHU SHENTU, TIMOTHY WONG

A properly-sized steel structural frame hidden within the building's walls and floors provides a 20'×40' bay that is able to accommodate the wide range of programs present within. The building's ventilation is provided by two rooftop Dedicated Outdoor Air Systems (DOAS) with electric heat recovery and a ceiling return plenum to further temper ducted supply air. Heating and cooling needs are provided through a Variable Refrigerant Flow (VRF) system driven by cold-climate air source heat pumps.

Architectural Designer: Christina Chi Zhang

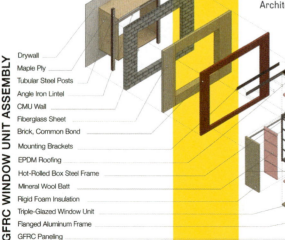

GFRC WINDOW UNIT ASSEMBLY

Drywall
Maple Ply
Tubular Steel Posts
Angle Iron Lintel
CMU Wall
Fiberglass Sheet
Brick, Common Bond
Mounting Brackets
EPDM Roofing
Hot-Rolled Box Steel Frame
Mineral Wool Batt
Rigid Foam Insulation
Triple-Glazed Window Unit
Flanged Aluminum Frame
GFRC Paneling

Environmental Design

Three Landscapes

KATIE COLFORD

This project is conceived as a set of landscapes that change over time. The southern facade is offset from the building by an exterior steel mesh, which hosts deciduous vines. This new garden landscape generates a diverse microbiome while also sequestering carbon dioxide and toxins at the scale of the local ecosystem. At the scale of the building, the use of plant matter supports passive cooling, diffuses daylight, and draws the exterior air stream into the interior.

Assemblage Energy

GUSTAV NIELSEN

The environmental design approach for the proposed Youth Arts Center on Grand Avenue in Fairhaven, Connecticut, focuses on the synergies between heat, air, and light within the building. The energy concept distinguishes between envelope dominated spaces and internal-load dominated spaces within the building, and seeks to leverage energy exchanges between them. Initial design decisionsv allow heat, light, and air to enter the building through the building envelope from where the energy is preserved, reused, and shared internally through a series of strategies.

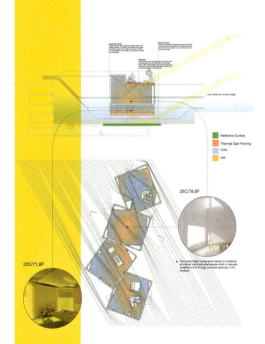

Architectural Practice and Management

Integrated Project Delivery: Fab Five

ASHTON HARRELL, SZE WAI JUSTIN KONG, ALIX PAUCHET, NICOLE RATAJCZAK, SHIKHA THAKALI

This proposal builds off of the following mission statement: It is our goal to integrate sustainability with technological innovation while maintaining profitability. Sustainability and innovation do not have to be at odds. Through this integrated, collaborative model, technology plays a central role in reaching our clients' environmental goals, without compromising schedule, budget or quality. Our firm's mission is to revolutionize how sustainability is tackled in the building industry, and to support leading tech companies with workspaces specifically tailored to their needs. We aspire to be the leaders of custom-created work environments that simultaneously enable the innovative work of rising tech companies and ensure these companies' commitment to a minimal footprint on local and global contexts. We believe in the potential for technology to help us adapt to climate change, find alternative sources of energy, and improve our wellbeing; we also believe that our role as architects does not simply lie in environmental stewardship, but in facilitating such innovations in sustainability. We propose that sustainability and innovation do not have to be at odds. Instead, with FabFive's integrated, collaborative model, technology plays a central role in reaching our clients' environmental goals, without compromising on schedule, budget or quality.

RFP for Architectural Services for ENERGIST World Headquarters

NIEMA JAFARI, ARACELI LOPEZ, NAOMI JEMIMA NG, ALEX OLIVIER, BEN THOMPSON

This simulation created an Internal Project Report for an RFP which specified a 67,000 square foot campus to contain offices, research and development departments, and an international showroom for Energist World Headquarters. The project would involve the adaptive reuse of the Gilbert and Bennet Wire Mill facility in Redding, Connecticut. The proposal emphasized our firm's familiarity with the adaptive reuse process in several previous projects we had completed along the Northeast Corridor along with our unique Design-Build approach and delicately calibrated fee allowing for contingencies.Our scope included a Pre-Design phase consisting of a programmatic and feasibility study, followed by a Basic Services Architectural and Engineering package. We employed our firm's tried and true Delivery Method of Design-Build, partnering closely with a builder, with which we've done several adaptive reuse projects with. We find the Design-Build process indispensable for adaptive reuse as irregularities in these charming and sometimes eccentric old buildings require our designers to be present in the field and design-on-the-fly, collaborating with our builder-partners on efficient design solutions. Our Design-Build model also responds to the main project drivers we identify for speed and quality. Our method allowed for high-quality work and the occupancy to be completed well before Energist's Grand Opening Deadline.

Exploring New Value
in Design Practice

CostCloud

NAOMI JEMIMA NG, QIZHEN TANG,
STELLA XU

CostCloud is a cost estimation software based
on realtime data from a data-trust, enabling
more accurate, transparent, and efficient cost
estimation in early design phases for architects
and developers. Our vision is to promote a more
efficient and transparent building industry, and
our mission is to help projects avoid mistakes by
achieving better cost estimation at an early stage.

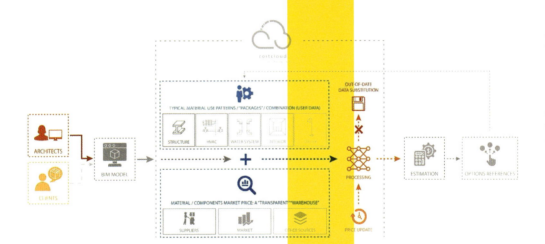

Introduction to Planning and Development

Together, Forward

JOSHUA TAN, SAM LANDAY, ANDRES
LIN-SHIU (SOM), CHARLES GRESS (SOM),
LUCAS HOLTER (UNDERGRAD)

This zoning proposal for an equitable community in Long Island City prioritizes the development of affordable housing, incentivizing mixed-use and transit-oriented development, and an employment-based perspective highlighting a good jobs strategy, critical to long-term community development. Zoning strategies include: Incentive Zoning for affordable housing to allow commercial and residential developers to achieve additional development capacity when they construct or preserve affordable housing; Commercial Activity Zoning to focus on pedestrian retail; Transit Oriented Development to rezone areas next to transit corridors for mixed use; Limiting Single Family Zoning to increase housing density; Industrial Expansion in Commercial Areas to protect jobs while providing affordable housing; Industrial Densification and Preservation to preserve the industrial space by FAR increases; and Industrial Business Zones that are restricted to industrial uses to protect the mix of industrial and commercial uses.

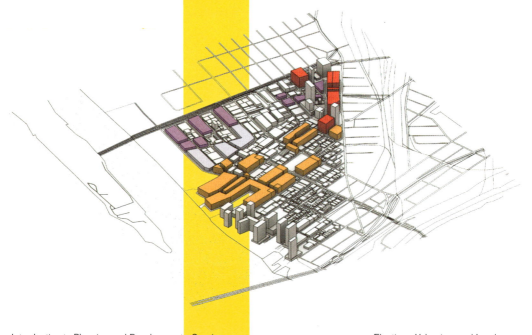

Urban Difference and Change

J. C. Nichols and the Kansas City Suburbs

HANNAH MAYER BAYDOUN, KYLE COXE, MEREESE PELTIER (MORGAN STATE UNIVERSITY)

J. C. Nichols' suburban developments and influence in Kansas City in the early years of the twentieth century established a precedent for suburbs in the United States as we know them today. Nichols envisioned a picturesque, idyllic suburbia maintained through deed restrictions and enforced through community organizations that developed into today's Home Owners' Association. These restrictions included minimum home cost, home lot line placement, design constraints, and most notoriously, banning non-white races from entry into these suburbs. The racist agenda of these deed restrictions has perpetuated throughout the twentieth century and its effects are seen today in racial divides in our cities.

Farm to Table

INGRID PELLETIER, DAVID OWE (MORGAN STATE UNIVERSITY), HAMDI ALOTAIBI (MORGAN STATE UNIVERSITY)

Throughout the country, small grassroots organizations like Plantation Park Heights and the Urban Seed Kitchen in Baltimore, MD are forming to tackle food insecurity. The urban farm includes 14 city-owned vacant lots that provide local farmers markets to surrounding communities through sustainable methods. The project sought to understand the current food desert crisis and study ways communities have started to address these issues in sustainable and locally-based ways.

Fighting Slavery in the Building Supply Chain

LBR—A Non-profit Banking System for Migrant Workers

ABRAHAM MORA-VALLE, IFE ADEPEGBA

LBR focuses exclusively on how labor is tracked and compensated throughout transnational construction projects through the implementation of a blockchain system. Workers at the lower end of the supply chain are often victims of delayed payment for their services and labor; through application of a system akin to a cryptocurrency, adequate compensation for their labor, despite operating outside of the confines of a central banking system, would be made possible.

The Cost of [Sugarcane]

JANICE CHU, NATALIE BROTON

The word "museum" is understood as an institution that cares for a collection of artifacts and other objects of artistic, cultural, historical, or scientific importance. It's primary purpose is to educate on the context of an event or collection of objects that have some significance. Similarly, the word "monument" also has references to the past. Our project reimagines the typologies of "memorial" and "museum" as something which educates on the present in order to provoke change.

Advanced Building Envelopes

A Scaling Study of Trophic Flow in Anthropogenic Biome

ANJIANG XU

In a scaling view of the anthropogenic biome (also known as, human biome), this collective research proposes to study the feasibility and potential benefits of integrating societal food systems with ecological food webs. Humans as the dominant predator in the ecosystem, play all the trophic roles in the societal food system, at once, showing how manipulating trophic flows and their settings could play a more organic role and contribute to the restoration of ecological habitat.

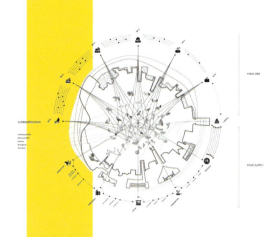

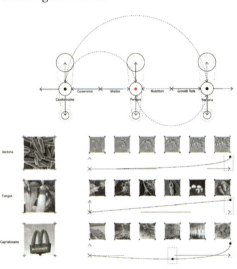

Fungi Mycoremediation

YANG TIAN

Mycoremediation's goal should not be to purify water contamination, but to understand and use this process to self-heal and self-reconstruct a local ecosystem. As mycelium runs onto the site where nearby soils and mushroom bodies decay, other species will become attracted and come to the site to work together in building their colonies. This whole process should not be a stand-alone one, but instead be integrated into a system with existing human-made structures.

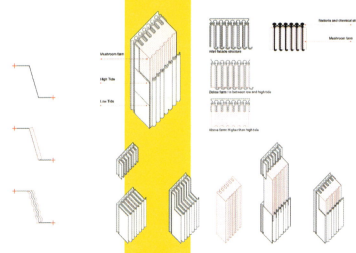

Skin Deep: Envelope As Potential Energy

Living and Breathing: A New Curtain Wall

ARACELI LOPEZ, SASHA ZWIEBEL

This project adapts the double-glazed facade of the Jerome L. Greene Science Center at Columbia University, designed by Renzo Piano. The proposed designed adds vegetation and operability through a thickened gap between the glazing in order to passively mediate light, ventilation, air quality, and moisture across interior and exterior spaces. There are two modules, each functioning as a self-sufficient system that collects rainwater to irrigate the plants, modulates light through a sliding shade, and allows for natural ventilation.

House Pet

ANGELA LUFKIN, LOUISA NOLTE,

SAM GOLINI

The proposal consists of a water collection facade of reciprocal care that is situated between high tech and low tech. You care for it, and it cares for you. It aims to return to rituals of water collection through a facade that harvests, filters, and heats rainwater for everyday use.

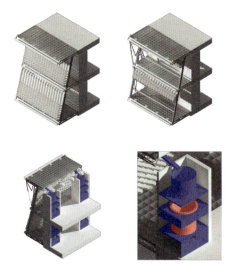

Port Cities

Maritime Tea Trade and The Shaping of Tea Industrial Landscape in Fuzhou Port

LILLIAN HOU

This essay first looks at the big picture of maritime tea trading, then zooms in to a specific place—Fuzhou—for a more detailed case study on how tea trade influenced the spatial development of Fuzhou as a port city. Experiencing decline after the 1890s, the tea industry had and still has permanent imprints on the spatial organization and cultural landscape of Fuzhou during its modernization process that can be categorized into four aspects. First, in the financial aspect, the original Hang provided a deep base for the modern financial institutions and tea exports brought more capital circulation to the local area. Second, in terms of culture and education, the emergence of church schools played an important role in supporting the establishment and development of modern education mechanisms in Fuzhou. Third, in terms of the international shipping industry, the gradual flourishing of tea also promoted the development of maritime transportation technology and the overall improvement of maritime shipping technology in China. Finally, in terms of spatial organization, the location of the center was transferred and its coverage expanded. Attention needs to be placed on the steady improvement of internal forces in order to ensure the sustainable development of the city.

Port Cities & Agrarian Land

MEGHNA MUDALIAR

The penetration of the Indian textile market and its full integration into the Indian Ocean maritime trade was a critical process of the British Raj expansion during the seventeenth century. On the island of Bombay, where no urban center had previously existed, the new base of the English East India Company was formed. The company subsequently encouraged Native settlers and merchants to migrate to the port to increase trade for both parties. However, as the port rapidly developed towards the needs of the Empire, the chief responsibility of the Native population was to serve the company as a continuous source of labour and knowledge, proving indispensable to the British Raj. The purpose of this paper is to discuss Bombay as the ideal colonial port city with pre-colonial global linkages in the world economy and existing working trade routes that were later expanded to serve its colonizers. It investigates Bombay's vitality with respect to the British East India Company, focusing on the emergence of the textile mill as a product of colonial urbanization in Mumbai. Finally, it describes the long-term effects of agrarian and capitalist urbanism that have led to India's failed infrastructure and inherited way of nation-building post-independence.

Will there be a similar reading if the dwelling is evaluated from the outside and not from the inside? Can the signs and intentions of the act of "home" be discernible without experience?

Regenerative Building: Horse Island

The Circular Economy of Ag-Waste

ASHTON HARRELL

This proposal is aimed at the abundant tonnage of ag-waste produced during agricultural sample crop production. Large masses of rice husks, wheat, and oat straw all have potential as sources for building material. These sources, like other biomass, act as carbon sequesters, absorbing carbon dioxide from the atmosphere as it grows and carbon storage when it's harvested and used in a building. The proposal focuses on agricultural production predominantly in Asian countries because it is here that the global population, along with agricultural and construction sectors, is expected to grow most rapidly. It is also in this region that rice crop-residue burning and field-flooding is most commonplace. Rice, in particular, as well as wheat and barley, are the main crops grown and exported from Asia. These crops produce agricultural waste material with a cell structure favorable for building products such as insulation, cementitious brick, laminated wood products, and manufactured paneling. This would allow builders to actually remove CO_2 from the atmosphere and sequester it in the locally built environments. Consequently, establishing a specific "Ag Waste-to-Building Material" philosophy in a regional economy with a crop-dominant agricultural sector could close the loop in the life cycle of viable crops.

Towards an Architecture of Waste

KATHERINE SALATA

Increased urbanization and the demand for new built infrastructure is rapidly depleting Earth's stock of nonrenewable construction material, while the environmental and social cost of the extraction process is now beginning to challenge its economic value. By rejecting established practices of raw material extraction and waste production, this exploration favors a new theory of design centered around the regenerative potential of a circular economy. The proposal couples the abundant accumulation of waste with the growing need for new sources of construction material. By assuming the role of modern day bricoleurs, makers and designers can invert the direction of waste flow and return it to a place of functional value within our larger society.

The paper first studies existing conditions through multiple lenses, including an impact analysis of current practices and a study of waste evaluation in both historic context and contemporary circular design principles. Conclusions drawn from the contextual analysis and synopsis of material theorists are integrated into an outlined proposal for organizing waste artifacts into hierarchical categories based on their potential to satisfy functional objectives, allow for tectonic manipulation, or disassemble into compositional elements. Through this process of analysis and categorization, designers can creatively and efficiently integrate diverse sources of waste into the construction of new built projects.

By assuming the role of modern day bricoleur, makers and designers can invert the direction of waste flow and return it to a place of functional value within our larger society.

Urban Landscape and Geographies of Justice

Community Engagement
JANELLE SCHMIDT, KEVIN STEFFES

This project began with an interest in the community engagement process within the City of New Haven. It centers around understanding how much of a voice and impact residents of New Haven neighborhoods have through Community Management Teams (CMT). Ultimately, the research is presented as a tool for students, residents, and all community members to find and join their CMT, attend monthly meetings, and bolster their voices within their community.

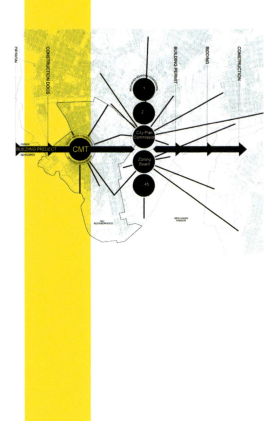

Public Preparedness for Climate Hazards in Coastal Connecticut
ALIX PAUCHET, SASHA ZWIEBEL

This project examines public preparedness for climate hazards along the Connecticut's coast at regional, coastal, and municipal scales in three policy-facing and one public-facing printed posters. New Haven is used as a case study in the final poster, "Preparing the Public," to illustrate the threat of flooding on a city-wide scale, and to provide residents with digestible information on current mitigation preparations.

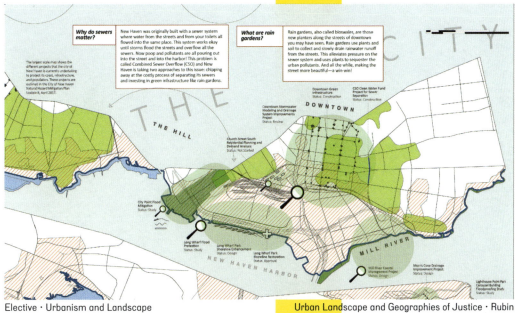

Introduction to Urban Studies

Layers of The Mill River

ABBY REED

Cities cannot be disassociated from their rivers. The project's intent is not to re-invent the Mill River Trail, but to bring further awareness to it. Photography and mapping helped reveal the various layers of the trail. These layers uncovered diverse user groups of the adjacent urban spaces, speculated how these groups would interact with the trail, and envisioned what types of signage would invite them to explore the trail.

layers of the mill river

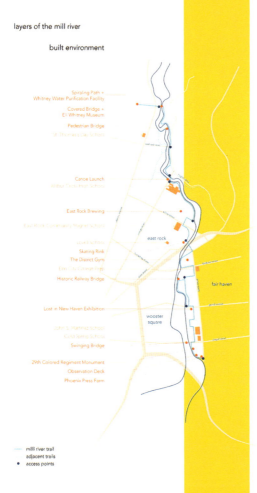

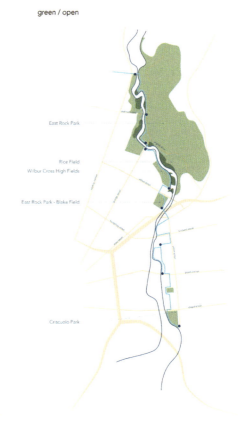

Architectural research uncovers the formwork of geographic, economic, political, and temporal boundaries: from design-build to discourse, from techniques of local construction to techniques of social production. Policy, prejudice, infrastructure, material, energy, ventilation—the scale and visibility of this "formwork" is abundantly foggy. M Arch I, M Arch II, MED, and PhD *Research* overlap through aspirations to foreground the invisible.

FIVE

MArch I: Jim Vlock Building Project

Building Project I
Building Project II

FACULTY
Adam Hopfner
Martha Foss
Alexander Kruhly
Beka Sturges

JURY
Margaret Middleton
Rudy Zimmermann
Ben Ledbetter
Carl Rodenhizer
Leslie Radcliffe
Deborah Berke
Trattie Davies
Peter de Bretteville
Eeva-Liisa Pelkonen
Miriam Peterson
Adam Hopfner
Martha Foss
Alexander Kruhly
Beka Sturges

This past semester marked the 54th consecutive year in which first-year students have embarked on a Building Project. It is a program born from student unrest in the fervor of the 1960s to discard the notion of learning as passive reception of information, and to demand an active engagement in addressing societal needs through the physical manifestation of design conceptualization.

The Building Project is compulsory for all MArch I students because the learning experience is deemed foundational to the education of the architect at Yale. The students work collectively on a research phase and are then divided into teams for a design competition. Once a scheme is selected, all students work to refine the chosen design.

The students develop full sets of documentation before going into the field for four months of construction. These documents are then put to the test, and afford learning about effective communication of design intent. Earlier studio discussions of spatial compression and release become palpable as students walk through the thresholds that they have drawn, modeled and argued over. Drawings get re-drawn, and design seeps into the build, as the build makes its presence felt in the design. The experience tints the lens through which students perceive all subsequent study.

—Adam Hopfner, Director of the Jim Vlock Building Project

MArch II: Design Research

Design Research I

FACULTY
Joel Sanders
Ana María Durán Calisto
Keller Easterling
Alan Organschi
James Tierney

Design Research II

FACULTY
Mark Foster Gage

Design Research III

FACULTY
Aniket Shahane
Sunil Bald

Design Research IV

FACULTY
Sunil Bald

The post-professional design research program is founded on the premise that architects can contribute to addressing urgent global challenges by adopting a new way of working: design research. This involves forming cross-disciplinary collaborations to explore the spatial consequences of cultural, political and environmental issues. The post-professional MArch II program equips a future generation of Yale graduates with a methodology that will prepare them to form constructive alliances with experts in allied disciplines, the outcome of which will yield viable design proposals that can be implemented on regional, local, and global scales. It consists of a sequence of three consecutive seminars that culminates in a Design Research Studio offered in the final semester of the program.

MED: Independent Research

COORDINATOR
Keller Easterling

ASSOCIATED FACULTY
Eeva-Liisa Pelkonen
Alan Plattus
Elihu Rubin

REQUIRED COURSES
Methods and Research
    Workshop
Independent Research
    Electives

The Master of Environmental Design, started in 1967, is a two-year independent research program that has long pursued activist conceptions of design. In 2020-21, MED students formed the MED Working Group on Anti-Racism. Joining forces with activists, educators, and students in and beyond the academy they convened an evolving set of conversations about the destructive whiteness of our institutional and professional practices. These conversations looked at policing, archiving and the commons. This year the Working Group will extend these conversations to consider forms of global solidarity among activists working with space. Activism was also central to the final documents submitted by the second year graduating students.

—Keller Easterling, Director of the MED Program

PhD: Independent Research

TRACKS
History and Theory of
    Architecture
Ecosystems in Architectural
    Sciences

ASSOCIATED COORDINATORS
Joan Ockman
Anna Dyson

The doctoral program in Architecture offers two tracks of study: History and Theory of Architecture, and Ecosystems in Architectural Sciences. Both tracks offer rigorous grounding in their respective fields of specialization while giving future scholars and educators a broad awareness of issues currently facing architecture in its relations with society and the world at large. The History and Theory track provides sound training in the historiography and culture of architecture and the built environment. The program aims to foster both a deep knowledge of the past and a strong spirit of critical inquiry. The Ecosystems in Architectural Sciences track provides preparation in interdisciplinary scientific inquiry in support of both academic and professional research careers, qualifying students to collaborate across disciplines and to incorporate experimental research methods within new design frameworks. Students in this track engage in research related to the behaviors of living ecosystems, emphasizing their interconnection with built environment processes

—Joan Ockman, Director of Doctoral Studies

Jim Vlock Building Project 2020: Construction

FACULTY
Adam Hopfner
Alexander Kruhly

INTERNS
Samuel David Bruce
Emily Cass
Helen Farley
Andrew Kim
Rhea Schmid

TECHNOLOGY AND PRACTICE
(REQUIRED)

[2017C]

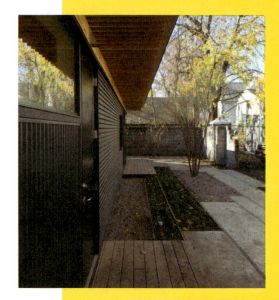

Jim Vlock Building Project 2021: Research, Analysis, Design

FACULTY
Adam Hopfner
Martha Foss
Alexander Kruhly
Beka Sturges

**TECHNOLOGY AND PRACTICE
(REQUIRED)**

[2016B]

GROUP A
Janice Chu, Elizabeth Cornfeld,
Tim Hawkins, Seung Hyun Kim,
Abby Reed, Calvin Rogers,
Ethan Chiang

The house provides a private
shelter, carving a central axis that
uses light to stitch together the
living spaces. The central atrium
highlights the vertical circulation,
while the second floor allows
space for private living.

GROUP B
Bobby Ka Ming Chun, Clare Fentress, Harry Hooper,
Sam Landay, Shi Li, Ryan Reyes, Katherine Salata

At its best, a house provides the freedom to place
oneself along a spectrum of enclosure according
to changing needs and desires. Both the house
and landscape are designed around the concept
of gradient. A predominantly private north-facing
entry gently yields to increasingly open interiors
and plantings as the inhabitant moves southward.

GROUP C
Jerry Chow, Kyle Coxe, Youssef Denial, Chloe Hou,
Tiana Kimball, Ying Luo, Joseph Reich

A home should provide mediated spaces, sequenced
and shaped to give inhabitants autonomy over
how they navigate changing interior and exterior
landscapes. Through the folding of surface and
unfolding of space, the home becomes a thickened
threshold between control and vulnerability.

GROUP D
Sosa Erhabor, Benjamin Fann, Zach Felder,
Josh Greene, Madeleine Reid, Huy Truong,
Caitlin Yu

The care of personal belongings can be a method
of survival and a way to remember who you are; a
way to preserve your history and identity against a
situation defined by insecurity. This house is imagined as a place where these belongings and stories
can rest and grow with dignity.

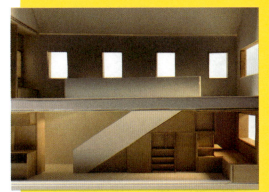

GROUP E, SELECTED DESIGN

Uzayr Agha, Charis Armstrong, Yong Choi, Maya Gamble, Noah Sannes, Cole Summersell, Grace Zajdel

A threshold is a place where transformations begin, a tool that mediates defined and flexible spaces. The house uses thresholds to comfortably accommodate the new homeowner in the near term and the needs of a growing, multi-generational family in the long term.

GROUP F

Gina Jiang, Faith Pang, William Beck, Christopher Pin, Ariel Bintang, Jonathan Chu, Ingrid Pelletier

The house grants autonomy to its inhabitants through sequenced buffer spaces; spaces that offer experiential variability, tools for cultivating a support system.

GROUP G

Ethnie Xu, Nathaniel Elmer, Sara Mountford, Ben Derlan, Corinna Siu, Kai Wu

The house is composed of humble interventions; a box, a platform, and a path. It is a seed from which its residents can grow a home; a place to put down roots and stretch up into the tree canopy.

GROUP H

Ana Batlle, Grant Dokken, Signe Ferguson, Qian Huang, Haonan Li, Kevin Wong

Sounds, views, and movement—three main actors that define neighborhood and home. The house negotiates the rhythms of West Division street with the dance of residence. Positively resonating combinations emerge; at other times potential dissonance is sidestepped with architectural nuance.

Jim Vlock Building Project 2021

324 West Division Street

The site is both the home of Building Project 2021 and a connecting element between West Division Street and Building Project 2020. Therefore, it was essential for BP21 to negotiate between the public and private realms of the house and those of its neighbors.

The eastern face of the home operates as a buffer from the public drive lane and opens into a more secluded landscape along the western edge of the site. While the peripheries of the site welcome interactions between the homeowner and their community, the front and rear entrances of BP21 prioritize privacy.

Building Project 2021's form undergoes a series of subtractions and a vertical shift that adapt a local vernacular silhouette to cultivate meaningful interactions between homeowner, home, and site. Each subtraction establishes a moment of pause, on the exterior in conversation with the site, and on the interior begins to define lived space.

Design Research I: Productive Uncertainties

FACULTY
Joel Sanders
Ana María Durán Calisto
Keller Easterling
Alan Organschi
James Tierney

HISTORY AND THEORY
(REQUIRED)

[3072A]

This seminar had a dual agenda. First, it aimed to generate a dialogue about this year's research prompt, "Productive Uncertainties" through the perspectives of four YSoA faculty—Ana Maria Duran, Keller Easterling, Alan Organschi and Joel Sanders—who each shared how they are investigating urgent cultural, political, economic and environmental challenges exacerbated by Black Lives Matter and the pandemic through their unique research agendas. Second, it acquainted students with a skill set central to the four-semester Post-Pro curriculum: the methodological tools needed to conduct Design Research. During the second half of the term, students working in cohorts, developed a Design Research proposal that drew from insights gained from the Yale faculty perspectives, and aligned with their own research interests.

STUDENT
Jiaxing Yan

This proposal aims to develop a staged process to revive community involvement in the spatial production of NYC Housing Authority superblocks. Acknowledging that prolonged disengagement between NYCHA tenants and their spaces is at the heart of the housing agency's many problems, the proposal leverages both the spatial assets of buildable land as well as the social capital of residents. Over time, this synthetic approach aims to generate an active spatial link between NYCHA residents and their shared built environment.

STUDENT
Vicky Achnani

This design research proposal investigates the use of bamboo in various building systems of low cost housing in the flood plains of Majuli, Assam, India. Chosen structural species demonstrate a constructional practice that is low in energy and subsumes less operational processes while arriving at a responsive building culture of hybrid material systems. Taking departures from the practice of permanency and redundancy, the new approach seeks lighter, more flexible building systems that can adopt and transform in new and changing conditions.

Design Research II: Emerging Schools of Thought

FACULTY
Mark Foster Gage

PRACTITIONERS INTERVIEWED
Michael Young
Ferda Kolatan
Elena Manferdini
Florencia Pita
Tom Wiscombe
Kristy Balliet
Jimenez Lai
Ellie Abrons and Adam Fure
Amina Blacksher and
　　　V. Mitch McEwen
Mark Foster Gage
Karel Klein and David Ruy

**HISTORY AND THEORY
(REQUIRED)**

[3073B]

This seminar explores the role of new schools of thought in the design of our world. No creative disciplines occur in a vacuum, and architecture is certainly no exception, relying as it does on numerous players and bodies of information ranging from professional expertise and construction knowledge to forms of social engagement and a nearly two-millennia long dialogue with new ideas—also known as architectural discourse. The intent of the course is to allow students to learn more about various schools of thought and ways of working not only through research and discussion—via class-led interviews with emerging practitioners—but through design—via the manipulation of form and its representation in formal distillation studies. The seminar culminates in a self-reflective study on the student's own mission and vision for their projected body of work, distilling a projected body of work into one brief statement.

STUDENT
Elise Limon

MISSION AND VISION STATEMENT
To further the integration of an understanding of landscape into the field of "Architecture."

° Make drawings that engage things beyond the building.

° Explore and incorporate geologic and ruinous timescales into design thinking.

° Use imagination, ambiguity, myth, and storytelling as a way to reimagine worlds through architectural materials and interventions.

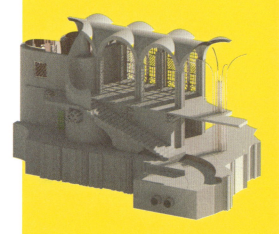

STUDENT
Vignesh Harikrishnan

MISSION AND VISION STATEMENT
To rethink architecture as a medium to democratize and celebrate the extraordinary power and beauty of everyday things.

° Weave across disciplines of art, history, and science questioning, criticizing and embracing the role of architects to cross-fertilise from one domain to other.

° Experiment with mediums, share stories and further relish the way the world looks, constantly questioning and sharing why it looks that way and what it means for people.

Design Research III: Methods Workshop

FACULTY
Aniket Shahane
Sunil Bald

**HISTORY AND THEORY
(REQUIRED)**

[3074A]

As the third, and final, of the post-professional design-research seminars, the goal of this course is two-fold: 1) to support post-professional students in the formulation and development of their individual interests and agendas as a means for future professional and/or academic trajectories; and 2) to provide the post-pros an opportunity to collaborate with the school on a student-led symposium that touches on the various themes in their individual works. Throughout the semester, guest lectures and individual advising assisted students in developing the independent work they had begun in the first two seminars into final submissions which ranged from research papers to drawing projects to design proposals. Concurrent to this individual research, students also workshopped the first post-professional symposium—a one week event in March that enabled students to prompt and lead discussions with practitioners and academics from around the world.

STUDENT
Yue Geng

As more and more permanent architecture emerged in Inner Mongolia, in tandem with over-farming and multiple socio-political factors, the grassland was transformed into a desert. The need to restore the ecology of the grassland in Inner Mongolia offers a case for a return to temporary architecture and nomadic culture in the region. This project examines the yurts at its tipping point and finds out the reason behind the critical change. It also analyzes the unchanged form and how the constant form coordinates with ecological, socio-cultural factors. This project establishes a foundation for yurts revival.

Design Research IV: Studio

ADVISORS
Eeva-Liisa Pelkonen
Sunil Bald

HISTORY AND THEORY
(REQUIRED)

[3075B]

Students meet on a weekly basis with faculty advisors to develop the Design Research Script that they developed in the Methods Workshop. The class is coordinated by the Post Pro Director who works with faculty advisors to establish shared milestone assignments, including midterm, three-quarters, and final reviews.

STUDENT
Luka Pajovic

SAILING TO BYZANTIUM:
A NEW BYZANTINE GALLERY AT THE
METROPOLITAN MUSEUM OF ART
The project proposes a new gallery for the Met's Byzantine collection. It focuses on how architectural facsimiles might be reintroduced into the museum to create a new kind of space beyond the usual "white cube" galleries, period rooms of dubious authenticity, and Kulturgeschichte displays of the sort currently found in the museum. The design employs digitally fabricated 1:1 facsimiles of Byzantine wall and vault mosaics (a la Factum Arte) to create a "sacellum" within the existing building, in which the museum's collection of Byzantine icons, liturgical artifacts and architectural fragments might be appropriately contextualised and brought to life. The purpose is to create a space that is both entirely authentic (in its relation to Byzantine precedent) and entirely (and visibly) new—both materially and architecturally; a sort of "mosaic court" in the mould of fin-de-siecle cast courts, providing a chronological and geographical overview of what Otto Demus described as the premier monumental art form of the Byzantines.

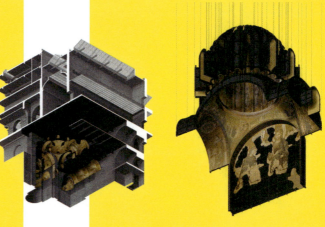

Space-Praxis: Towards a Feminist Politics of Design

STUDENT
M.C. Overholt

ADVISOR
Keller Easterling

READER
Elihu Rubin

ABSTRACT
Outside of the academy and professionalized practice, design has long been central to the production of feminist, political projects. Taking what I have termed space praxis as its central analytic, this project explores a suite of feminist interventions into the built environment—ranging from the late 1960s to present day. Formulated in response to Michel de Certeau's theory of spatial practices, space praxis collapses formerly bifurcated definitions of "tactic"/"strategy" and "theory"/"practice." It gestures towards those unruly, situated undertakings that are embedded in an ever-evolving, liberative politics. In turning outwards, away from the so-called masters of architecture, this thesis orients itself toward everyday practitioners who are grounded in the environment-worlds they seek to reorganize and re-imagine. Though few of the space-practitioners discussed in this work would consider themselves architects, their work at the margin of design meaningfully expands contemporary definitions of architecture. Indeed, they exemplify the ways in which architecture could be retooled as a mode of activist engagement. The diverse array of spaces investigated include a handful of womxn's centers in New York City, Cambridge, MA, and Los Angeles; the first feminist self-help gynecology clinic; an empty house in Oakland that was reclaimed by a group of Black mothers in 2019; and a series of pop-up block parties in Chicago.

While this project in no way operates as an encyclopedia of feminist space-praxes, it highlights an array of such projects held together in their mutual project of building feminist commons and infrastructures of care. In each project, survival is understood as a material practice, contingent on the affective relationship between bodies, space, and technologies. Though the direct object of each project's intervention varies—from the clinic, to the house, to the neighborhood— each suggests alternative ways of living, surviving, and designing outside of the built environment's hetero-patriarchal scripts.

Mapping Grounds for Reparations in Jaragua Peak

STUDENT
Laura Pappalardo

ADVISOR
Keller Easterling

READER
Ana María Durán Calisto

ABSTRACT
For the Guarani Mbya, ka'aguy (Atlantic Forest) is sacred. Yet, only 12 percent of the Atlantic Forest original coverage remains. A portion of that is in Jaraguá Peak. The Peak is also the highest point within São Paulo, located in the northwest region of the city. Anyone who lives in São Paulo knows Jaraguá Peak as a point of visual reference—the only forested area rising above dense urbanism. Two hundred years ago, São Paulo was ka'aguy. Now, the city occupies part of Guarani territory, which spans across the borders of what is now known as Paraguay, Argentina, Uruguay, and Brazil. São Paulo exists entirely within Guarani territory.

São Paulo's urban growth and the expansion of infrastructural networks (roads, power lines, and dams) have disrupted Guarani infrastructures (the presence of Atlantic Forest, the continuity of paths between Guarani villages, access to clean water). The three busiest roads in São Paulo—the first began in 1940—cut through the peak area. Since the roads opened for car use, urban growth, starting on the roads' borders, have encroached continuously on the Atlantic Forest. The São Paulo state government also transformed the peak into a state park for tourism, 60% of which overlaps Jaraguá Indigenous Land, demarcated for the Guarani. Two telecommunication towers installed at the top of the peak in the 1960s broadcast electromagnetic pollution over the Atlantic Forest and its inhabitants. Nonetheless, Guarani communities in São Paulo remake Guarani geographies every day, resisting Atlantic Forest encroachment and circumventing colonial networks. Guarani communities in the north and south of São Paulo hold a crucial infrastructural and environmental role for the entire city, increasing São Paulo's environmental security by recovering degraded soils and recuperating Atlantic Forest areas.

This project maps the history of infrastructural expansion in Jaraguá Peak. It represents the history of each infrastructural layer (roads, telecommunication towers, and power lines) in sectional maps that expose long-term changes on the ground. Each map accompanies a set of case studies that received reparations for infrastructural harm. Maps and case studies are organized in appendix-tools, which can serve as detachable documents from the larger body of the thesis. Each appendix-tool (infrastructural reparations cases for reference, activist mapping, and public engagement strategies) aspires to contribute to Guarani activism.

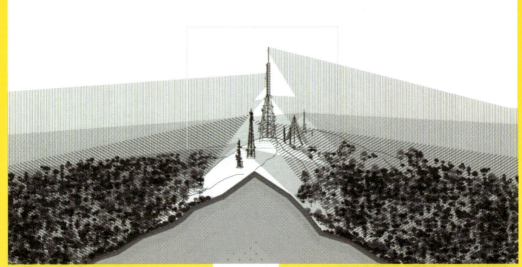

PhD Independent Research
Architectures of the Humanitarian Front, 1915–1930

STUDENT
Theodossis Issaias

TRACK
History and Theory

COURSES TAUGHT
Advanced Design Studio:
No Normal

ADVISOR AND READER
Eeva-Liisa Pelkonen

ABSTRACT

PART I: "THE RED CROSS SERVES HUMANITY"

During a period of unprecedented territorial and political insecurity around the First World War, the American Red Cross (ARC) launched a flurry of civilian relief operations in foreign lands, entrenching representations, languages, and practices of humanitarian action which have stayed with us ever since. Contingent to the geopolitical ambitions of the US empire, the ARC developed and deployed relief protocols and procedures to address exigencies caused by environmental catastrophes and conflicts, of which displacement of peoples was deemed the most urgent. Across the globe, "earthquake stricken and homeless people"; "itinerant famine victims"; "homeless persons living in temporary camps"; "the refugees [who] throng cities and villages, homeless, shelterless, starving" became the subjects –the humans– of humanitarianism. To systematize these modes of operation, the ARC sought the knowledge and technical expertise of architects and urban planners, who, in turn, conscripted to the organization's cause. Within a short period of a decade, renowned architects of the American North East led ARC departments, mapped destruction and displacement, and managed the organization's building activity, contributing to the reconfiguration of humanitarian priorities and imperatives. The first part of dissertation focuses on material traces, plans of settlements, drawings of shelters and construction details, contracts between contractors and organizations, official reports, and publicity campaigns from the ARC archives, to provide an insight into the beliefs, asymmetries, misunderstandings, and prejudices of humanitarian actors. It charts architects' critical and problematic involvement with conflict, displacement, and relief. That is, it does not intend to celebrate this involvement and the self-reifying field of "humanitarian architecture," but to create an entry that is an integral part of the history of architecture's role in the humanitarian arena.

COLONY FOR REFUGEES AT PISA
AMERICAN RED CROSS IN ITALY
SCALE 1:1000

LEGEND
4 DIRECTION
5 DIRECTOR OF COLONY
6 ECONOMIC KITCHEN
7 SCHOOL
8 SHOP
9 WORKROOM FOR WOMEN
10 W·C· FOR WOMEN
11 W·C· FOR MEN
12 LAUNDRY
13 INFIRMARY
14 CHURCH

Chester Aldrich, Architect and Director ARC Department of Civil Affairs of the Permanent Commission in Italy. Master plan of the "American City," in Pisa, 1918. ANRCR, box 103.15, folder 4.

PhD Independent Research
An Investigation of Plant-Associated Bioremediation Processes with Respect to Urbanization, Design, Urban Air Pollution, Indoor Air Quality, and Low Microbial Diversity

STUDENT
Phoebe Mankiewicz

TRACK
Ecosystems in
Architectural Sciences

CO-AUTHOR
Christina Ciardullo

COURSES TAUGHT
Teaching Fellow for
Environmental Design

JURY
Elizabeth Henaff
Jefferson Ellinger
Drew Gentner
Mark Bradford
Jordan Peccia

ADVISOR
Anna Dyson

READERS
Krystal Pollitt
Ahu Aydogan
Elizabeth Lin
Chandrima Bhattacharya
Andreas Theodoridis
Ranjit Arpels-Josiah
Andrew Rosner
Mandi Pretorius
Mohamed Aly
Nick Novelli
Naomi Keena

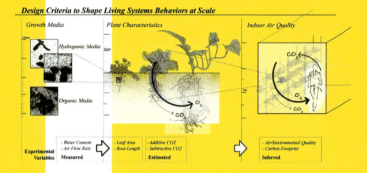

Design Criteria to Shape Living Systems Behaviors at Scale

ABSTRACT

Urbanization has contributed to systemic factors that increase energy consumption and negatively impact human health and wellbeing. Conventional Heating, Ventilation and Air Conditioning (HVAC) units designed to filter airborne pollutants and improve Indoor Air Quality (IAQ) through ventilation are often energy intensive, contribute to measured decreases in healthy levels of urban microbial diversity, and are still unable to address specific pollutants. Preliminary research has suggested that active plant-based systems may synthetically address some of these intractable problems, thereby decreasing building ventilation requirements, energy use and benefiting inhabitant health. In architecture and urban planning, despite significant demand for the inclusion of vegetation in the built environment, there are still many gaps in our understanding of fundamental bio-remediation mechanisms, leaving building design professionals without comprehensive or standard design criteria towards shaping their performance. The value of such bioremediation systems, as well as the reliability of the evidence at the scale necessary to advocate for them, is necessary to be able to design building and cities with and for living systems. Our research consists of multi-scalar experiments as part of an extensive interdisciplinary research team designed to explore biogeochemical processes inherent to plant-based indoor bioremediation systems. Although mechanical systems performance, IAQ, and human health have long been correlated, emerging fields of study such as metagenomics, combined with emerging sensing and control networks, are increasingly revolutionizing the quantity and quality of accessible data, fundamentally changing our understanding and characterization of these co-relationships, and of the intensely interdependent relationships that human beings have to living systems in general.

Students

M ARCH I, YEAR I

Uzayr Agha
Georgetown University

Charis Armstrong
University of Virginia

Ana Batlle
Savannah College of Art and Design

William Beck
University of Virginia

Ariel Bintang
University of Melbourne

Ethan Chiang
Chinese University of Hong Kong

Yong Choi
Yonsei University

Jerry Chow
Carleton University

Janice Chu
University of Hong Kong

Jonathan Chu
University of Virginia

Bobby Ka Ming Chun
University of Hong Kong

Elizabeth Cornfeld
Tufts University

Kyle Coxe
Ohio State University

Youssef Denial
University of Washington

Ben Derlan
St. Mary's College of Maryland

Grant Dokken
Montana State University

Nathaniel Elmer
Wesleyan University

Sosa Erhabor
University of Virginia

Benjamin Fann
Maryland Institute College of Art

Zach Felder
Hobart and William Smith Colleges

Clare Fentress
University of Chicago

Signe Ferguson
Brown University

Maya Gamble
Mount Holyoke College

Josh Greene
Arizona State University

Tim Hawkins
Catholic University of America

Harry Hooper
New York University

Chloe Hou
Smith College

Qian Huang
Washington University in St. Louis

Gina Jiang
University of Edinburgh

Seung Hyun Kim
Seoul National University

Tiana Kimball
Portland State University

Ciara Kosior
Rhode Island School of Design

Sam Landay
Washington University in St. Louis

Shi Li
Mount Holyoke College

Haonan Li
Pratt Institute

Ying Luo
University of Pennsylvania

Sara Mountford
Kean University

Faith Pang
Washington University in St. Louis

Ingrid Pelletier
University of Washington

Christopher Pin
Ryerson University

Abby Reed
Northeastern University

Joseph Reich
Texas A&M University

Madeleine Reid
Brown University

Ryan Matthew Reyes
Texas Tech University

Calvin Rogers
University of Minnesota Twin Cities

Katherine Salata
University of Virginia

Noah Sannes
Georgia Institute of Technology

Corinna Siu
Washington University in St. Louis

Cole Summersell
Auburn University

Huy Truong
Yale University

Kevin Wong
Parsons School of Design

Kai Wu
Yale University

Ethnie Xu
University of Sydney

Caitlin Yu
Hamilton College

Grace Zajdel
Washington University in St. Louis

M ARCH I, YEAR II

Lillian Agutu
Kean University

Brandon Brooks
Maryland Institute College of Art

Adare Brown
Washington University in St. Louis

Claudia Carle
Hobart and William Smith Colleges

Lauren Carmona
Texas Tech University

Katie Colford
Yale University

Lindsay Duddy
Case Western Reserve University

Audrey Tseng Fischer
University of Waterloo

Sam Golini
Dartmouth College

Sangji Han
Yonsei University

Jingfei He
University of Tokyo

Students

Claire Hicks
Clemson University

Chocho Hu
South China University of Technology

Audrey Hughes
University of Virginia

Suhyun Jang
Hongik University

Yushan Jiang
Tongji University

Morgan Anna Kerber
Dalhousie University

Sarah Kim
Northwestern University

Jessica Kim
University of Notre Dame

Zhanna Kitbalyan
Columbia University

Caroline Kraska
University of Virginia

Zishi Li
Yale University

Calvin Liang
Columbia University

Perihan MacDonald
Columbia University

Hannah Mayer Baydoun
University of Minnesota, Twin Cities

Paul Meuser
Rhode Island School of Design

Abraham Mora-Valle
Columbia University

Meghna Mudaliar
University of Toronto

Veronica Nicholson
Princeton University

Gustav Nielsen
Aarhus School of Architecture

Brian Orser
Pitzer College

Dominiq Oti
Leeds Beckett University

Yikai Qiao
Soochow University

Jingyuan Qiu
University of California, Los Angeles

Michelle Qu
Cornell University

Jack Rusk (MEM)
University of California, Santa Cruz

Taku Samejima
Keio University

Abby Sandler
Barnard College

Janelle Schmidt
Lawrence Technological University

Levi Shaw-Faber
Bard College

Wenzhu Shentu
Zhejiang Normal University

Jun Shi (MEM)
College of William and Mary

Diana Smiljković
University of Bath

Andrew Spiller
Ohio State University

Kevin Steffes
University of Chicago

Joshua Tan
Singapore University of Technology and Design

Hao Tang
College of Wooster

Yang Tian
University of Michigan

Rachael Tsai
University of Michigan

Tianyue Wang
University of the Arts London

Timothy Wong
University of Hong Kong

Hao Xu
Ball State University

Anjiang Xu
South China University of Technology

Tian Xu
University of Bath

Yuan Iris You
University of Pennsylvania

Calvin Yang Yue
University of Toronto

Alex Mingda Zhang
University of Illinois Urbana-Champaign

Christina Chi Zhang
Yale University

Jessica Jie Zhou
University of Toronto

M ARCH I, YEAR III

Ife Adepegba
University of Cambridge

Natalie Broton
Ball State University

Ives Brown
University of California, Los Angeles

Christopher Cambio
Hobart and William Smith Colleges

Martin Carrillo Bueno
Bennington College

Rosa Congdon
Brown University

Ruchi Dattani
New Jersey Institute of Technology

Jiachen Deng
Washington University in St. Louis

Janet Dong
University of Michigan

Xuefeng Du
Hunan University

Paul Freudenburg (MEM)
Yale University

Kate Fritz
James Madison University

Malcolm Rondell Galang
University of California, Los Angeles

Anjelica Gallegos
University of Colorado Denver

Yangwei Kevin Gao
University of Illinois Urbana-Champaign

Ian Gu
McGill University

Jiaming Gu
Southeast University Nanjing

Ashton Harrell
Ohio State University

Liang Hu
University of Melbourne

Students

Niema Jafari
University College London

Alicia Jones
University of California, Los Angeles

Hyun Jae Jung
University of Bath

Sze Wai Justin Kong
University of Hong Kong

Tyler Krebs
Ohio State University

Hiuki Lam
University of Hong Kong

Dreama Simeng Lin
College of William and Mary

April Liu
University of California, Berkeley

Qiyuan Liu
University of Hong Kong

Araceli Lopez
University of Washington

Angela Lufkin
Arizona State University

Rachel Mulder
University of Michigan

Leanne Nagata
University of California, Berkeley

Naomi Jemima Ng
University of Melbourne

Louisa Nolte
New York University

Alex Olivier
University of Florida

Alix Pauchet (MEM)
Middlebury College

Nicole Ratajczak
University of Waterloo

Scott Simpson
Yale University

Christine Song
University of Toronto

Shikha Thakali
Mount Holyoke College

Ben Thompson
College for Creative Studies

Sarah Weiss
Brown University

Max Wirsing
Carleton College

Shelby Wright
Ohio State University

Stella Xu
University of California, Los Angeles

Sean Ming Jue Yang
University of Waterloo

Yuhan Zhang
University of California, Berkeley

Leyi Zhang
University of Illinois
Urbana-Champaign

Sasha Zwiebel
Vassar College

MARCH II, YEAR I

Vicky Achnani
CEPT University

Claudia Ansorena
University of Miami

Elise Limon
Cambridge University

Bobby Cheng
Nanchang University

Stav Dror
Bezalel Academy

Samar Halloum
American University of Sharjah

Vignesh Harikrishnan
Anna University

Bingyu He
Illinois Institute of Technology

Lillian Hou
Virginia Tech

Ingrid Liu
Rhode Island School of Design

Sydney Maubert
University of Miami

Serge Saab
American University of Beirut

Saba Salekfard
California State University Pomona

Steven Sculco
New York Institute of Technology

Yuyi Shen
Pratt Institute

Taiga Taba
Waseda University

Vivian Wu
Syracuse University

Jiaxing Yan
Rice University

Young Joon Yun
Syracuse University

Yuyi Zhou
Illinois Institute of Technology

MARCH II, YEAR II

Guillermo Acosta Navarrete
Tecnológico de Monterrey

Daniella Calma
Pratt Institute

Shuang Chen
Hefei University of Technology

Rebecca Commissaris
Rhode Island School of Design

Elaine ZiYi Cui
University of Southern California

Shuchen Dong
Tsinghua University

Yue Geng
Tianjin University

Gabriel Gutierrez Huerta
University of Tennessee, Knoxville

Rishab Jain
Southern California Institute
of Architecture

Gordon Yuhao Jiang
Rhode Island School of Design

Srinivas Narayan Karthikeyan
CEPT University

Mari Kroin
Pratt Institute

Ruike Liu
Wuhan University

Luka Pajovic
University of Cambridge

Qizhen Tang
Tsinghua University

Students

Alper Turan
Istanbul Technical University

Hongyu Wang
Harbin Institute of Technology

Daoru Wang
North Carolina State University

Hengyuan Yang
Tsinghua University

MED

Cayce Davis
University of Tennessee, Knoxville

Tianyi Hang
Syracuse University

Alex Kim
Syracuse University

Alex Klein
Kenyon College

Devi Nayar
Visvesvaraya Technological University

M.C. Overholt
Stanford University

Laura Pappalardo
Escola da Cidade

Mila Samdub
Bard College

PHD

Alan Alaniz
University of Cincinnati

Adi Meyerovitch
University College London

I-Ting Tsai
Yale University

Iris Giannakopoulou Karamouzi
Massachusetts Institute of Technology

Gabrielle Printz
Columbia University

Christina Ciardullo
Columbia University

Nicholas Pacula
Massachusetts Institute of Technology

Jia Weng
Yale University

Ishraq Khan
Architectural Association

Phoebe Mankiewicz
Rensselaer Polytechnic Institute

Mandi Pretorius
Rensselaer Polytechnic Institute

Aaron Tobey
Rhode Island School Design

Zachariah Michielli
Southern California Institute
of Architecture

Summer Sutton
Massachusetts Institute of Technology

Gary Huafan He
Cornell University

David Turturro
Harvard University

Theodossis Issaias
Massachusetts Institute of Technology

AWARDS

Rebecca Commissaris
Leyi Zhang
William Wirt Winchester
Traveling Fellowship

Diana Smiljković
Gertraud A. Wood Traveling Fellowship

Christina Chi Zhang
Audrey Tseng Fischer
George Nelson Scholarship

Angela Lufkin
David M. Schwarz / Architectural
Services Good Times Award

Araceli Lopez
H.I. Feldman Prize

Malcolm Rondell Galang
Sasha Zwiebel
Moulton Andrus Award

Rachael Tsai
Wendy Elizabeth Blanning Prize

Leanne Nagata
Sonia Albert Schimberg Prize

Rachel Mulder
Henry Adams Medal—AIA

Anjelica Gallegos
Alpha Rho Chi Medal

Martin Carrillo Bueno
William Edward Parsons
Memorial Medal

Scott Simpson
Janet Cain Sielaff Alumni Award

Luka Pajovic
The Drawing Prize

Shikha Thakali
Gene Lewis Book Prize

M.C. Overholt
David Taylor Memorial Prize

Alix Pauchet
David M. Schwarz / Architectual
Services Summer Internship and
Traveling Fellowship

(MEM)
Joint degree program, Master
of Environmental Management,
Yale School of the Environment

Faculty

Hitoshi Abe
Norman R. Foster Visiting Professor
of Architectural Design

Emily Abruzzo
Critic

Anthony Acciavatti
Daniel Rose (1951) Visiting
Assistant Professor

Melinda Agron
Instructor

Mohamed Aly Etman
Scientific Researcher

John Apicella
Lecturer

Victoria Arbitrio
Lecturer

AJ Artemel
Lecturer

Pier Vittorio Aureli
Charles Gwathmey
Professor in Practice

Sunil Bald
Associate Dean and Professor Adjunct

Sandra Barclay
Eero Saarinen Visiting Professor

Annie Barrett
Critic

Anibal Bellomio
Lecturer

Andrew Benner
Director of Exhibitions and Critic

Deborah Berke
Dean

Phillip Bernstein
Associate Dean and Professor Adjunct

Stella Betts
Critic

Tatiana Bilbao
Norman R. Foster Visiting Professor

Marlon Blackwell
Louis I. Kahn Visiting Professor

Kent Bloomer
Professor Emeritus Adjunct

Dorian Booth
Lecturer

Nikole Bouchard
Critic

Faculty

Sara Bronin
Lecturer

Turner Brooks
William Henry Bishop Visiting
Professor and Professor Adjunct

Miroslava Brooks
Critic

Brennan Buck
Senior Critic

Craig Buckley
(Affiliated Faculty) Assistant
Professor History of Art

Can Vu Bui
Critic

Luke Bulman
Lecturer

Nathan Burnell
Instructor

Marta Caldeira
Senior Lecturer

Luis Callejas
Louis I. Kahn Visiting Assistant
Professor of Architectural Design

Sara Caples
William B. And Charlotte Shepherd
Davenport Visiting Professor

Kevin Carmody
William Henry Bishop Visiting
Professor of Architectural Design

Iñaqui Carnicero
Critic

Francesco Casetti
(Affiliated Faculty) Thomas E.
Donnelley Professor of Humanities
and Professor of Film Studies

Chris Cornelius
Louis I. Kahn Visiting
Assistant Professor

Jean Pierre Crousse
Eero Saarinen Visiting Professor

Karolina Czeczek
Critic

Esther da Costa Meyer
Visiting Professor

Trattie Davies
Critic

Peter de Bretteville
Critic

Violette de la Selle
Critic

Peggy Deamer
Professor Emerita

Luis C. deBaca
(Affiliated Faculty) Lecturer
in Law at Yale Law School

Melissa DelVecchio
Robert A.M. Stern Visiting Professor
of Classical Architecture

Kyle Dugdale
Critic

Ana María Durán Calisto
Lecturer

Anna Dyson
Hines Professor of Sustainable
Architectural Design

Keller Easterling
Enid Dwyer Professor and
Director of the MED Program

Peter Eisenman
Visiting Professor

Ariel Ekblaw
Lecturer

Alastair Elliott
Lecturer

Dov Feinmesser
Instructor

Martin Finio
Senior Critic

Kurt Forster
Visiting Professor Emeritus

Martha Foss
Critic

Bryan Fuermann
Senior Lecturer

Mark Foster Gage
Associate Professor

Alexander Garvin
Professor Adjunct

Narracci Gina
Lecturer

Kevin Gray
Lecturer

Andy Groarke
William Henry Bishop Visiting
Professor of Architectural Design

Faculty

Abby Hamlin
Edward P. Bass Distinguished
Visiting Architecture Fellow

Charlotte Hansson
Louis I. Kahn Visiting Assistant
Professor of Architectural Design

Steven Harris
Professor Adjunct

Andrei Harwell
Critic

Erleen Hatfield
Lecturer

Robert Haughney
Lecturer

Kristin Hawkins
Lecturer

Dolores Hayden
Professor Emerita of Architecture
and American Studies

Gavin Hogben
Critic

Adam Hopfner
Critic

Joyce Hsiang
Assistant Professor

Alicia Imperiale
Critic

Theodossis Issaias
PhD Student

Elisa Iturbe
Critic

John D. Jacobson
Professor Adjunct

Everardo Jefferson
William B. And Charlotte Shepherd
Davenport Visiting Professor

Larry Jones
Lecturer

Dana Karwas
Lecturer

Yoko Kawai
Lecturer

Naomi Keena
Post Doc

Beom Jun Kim
Lecturer

George Knight
Critic

Jaffer Kolb
Critic

Alexander Kruhly
Critic

Nicholas McDermott
Critic

Bimal Mendis
Assistant Professor Adjunct

Kyoung Sun Moon
Associate Professor

Joeb Moore
Critic

Justin Garrett Moore
Lecturer

Timothy Newton
Critic

Kari Nystrom
Lecturer

Joan Ockman
Vincent Scully Visiting Professor
in Architectural History

Brittany Olivari
Instructor

Cristian Oncescu
Instructor

Alan Organschi
Senior Critic

Eeva-Liisa Pelkonen
Assistant Dean and Professor

Miriam Peterson
Critic

Laura Pirie
Lecturer

Alan Plattus
Professor

Victoria Ponce de Leon
Lecturer

Daniele Profeta
Lecturer

Alexander Purves
Professor Emeritus

Craig Razza
Lecturer

Bika Rebek
Critic

Elihu Rubin
Director of Undergraduate Studies
and Associate Professor

Joel Sanders
Professor and Director of the
Post-Professional MArch Program

Deborah Saunt
Eero Saarinen Visiting Professors
of Architectural Design

Surry Schlabs
Critic

Karen Seto
(Affiliated Faculty) Frederick C.
Hixon Professor of Geography and
Urbanization Science

Aniket Shahane
Critic

Edward Stanley
Lecturer

Philip Steiner
Lecturer

Robert A.M. Stern
J.M. Hoppin Professor of Architecture

Beka Sturges
Critic

Michael Szivos
Critic

Dana Tang
Visiting Professor

Celia Toche
Lecturer

Adam Trojanowski
Lecturer

Billie Tsien
Charles Gwathmey Professor
in Practice

Marc Tsurumaki
William B. and Charlotte Shepherd
Davenport Visiting Professor of
Architectural Design

Tod Williams
Charles Gwathmey Professor
in Practice

Amy Wrzesniewski
(Affiliated Faculty) Michael H.Jordan
Professor at Yale School of Management

Julie Zink
Instructor

Retrospecta 44
2020–21

Published by the
Yale School of Architecture

EDITORS
Claudia Ansorena
Bobby Ka Ming Chun
Christopher Pin
Saba Salekfard

BOOK DESIGNERS
Mike Tully
Immanuel Yang

WEBSITE DESIGNER
Alvin Ashiatey

PRINTER
Allied Printing Services,
Manchester, CT

TYPEFACES
Lector and Normal Grotesk,
Forgotten Shapes,
Leipzig, Germany

PAPER
Accent Opaque Smooth 100lb,
Starbrite Opaque Text 50lb

DISTRIBUTOR
Actar
440 Park Avenue South
17th Floor
New York, NY 10016
actar.com

SPECIAL THANKS
Dean Deborah Berke

AJ Artemel
Phillip Bernstein
Michael Bierut
Sheila Levrant de Bretteville
Miroslava Brooks
Terence Brown
Zelma Brunson
Luke Bulman
Richard DeFlumeri
Vincent Guerrero
Larissa Hall
Rich Kaplan
Tanial Lowe
Stephan Müller
Nina Rappaport
Kate Rozen
Reymund Schröder
Rosemary Watts
Donna Wetmore
Gert Wunderlich
and the faculty, staff, and
    students of the YSoA

IMAGE CREDITS
Jacob Hoeppner, P 89; Mari
Kroin, P 71, 95, 169, 214, 324; MIT
Space Exploration Initiative, P
230; Laura Pappalardo, P 87, 234;
Christopher Pin, P 67; Jack Rusk,
P 171; Saba Salekfard, P 7, 13, 155,
167, 300, 326, 376; Noah Sannes,
P 151; Janelle Schmidt, P 294.

For more information and
copies of this book, please
write, call, or visit us at:

Yale School of Architecture
180 York Street
3rd Floor
New Haven, CT 06511

+1 203 432 2288

architecture.yale.edu
yaleretrospecta.org

©2021 Yale School of Architecture

ISBN 978-1-63840-976-2

Retrospecta 44
2020–21

Published by the
Yale School of Architecture

EDITORS
Claudia Ansorena
Bobby Ka Ming Chun
Christopher Pin
Saba Salekfard

BOOK DESIGNERS
Mike Tully
Immanuel Yang

WEBSITE DESIGNER
Alvin Ashiatey

PRINTER
Allied Printing Services,
Manchester, CT

TYPEFACES
Lector and Normal Grotesk,
Forgotten Shapes,
Leipzig, Germany

PAPER
Accent Opaque Smooth 100lb,
Starbrite Opaque Text 50lb

DISTRIBUTOR
Actar
440 Park Avenue South
17th Floor
New York, NY 10016
actar.com

SPECIAL THANKS
Dean Deborah Berke

A.J. Artemel
Phillip Bernstein
Michael Bierut
Sheila Levrant de Bretteville
Miroslava Brooks
Terence Brown
Zelma Brunson
Luke Bulman
Richard DeFlumeri
Vincent Guerrero
Larissa Hall
Rich Kaplan
Tanial Lowe
Stephan Müller
Nina Rappaport
Kate Rozen
Reymund Schröder
Rosemary Watts
Donna Wetmore
Gert Wunderlich
and the faculty, staff, and
    students of the YSoA

IMAGE CREDITS
Jacob Hoeppner, P 89; Mari
Kroin, P 71, 95, 169, 214, 324; MIT
Space Exploration Initiative, P
230; Laura Pappalardo, P 87, 234;
Christopher Pin, P 67; Jack Rusk,
P 171; Saba Salekfard, P 7, 13, 155,
167, 300, 326, 376; Noah Sannes,
P 151; Janelle Schmidt, P 294.

For more information and
copies of this book, please
write, call, or visit us at:

Yale School of Architecture
180 York Street
3rd Floor
New Haven, CT 06511

+1 203 432 2288

architecture.yale.edu
yaleretrospecta.org

ISBN 978-1-63840-976-2

Donors

2018
Anonymous
David Alston Langdon
Tess K. McNamara
Jiajian Min
Meghan S. Royster
Liyang Wang

2019
Anonymous
Brian J. Cash
Kerry D. Garikes
Jacob S. Schaffert

2020
Michelle F. Badr
Emily J. Cass
Taiming Chen
Serena Ching
Phoebe W. Harris
Baolin Shen
Jen Y. Shin

TRIBUTE GIFTS IN HONOR OF

Mary Ceclia Alcacova
Deborah L. Berke
Kent C. Bloomer
Peter Eisenman
Dylan Albert Grant
Philip Grausman
Lee Yock Hua
Elliot Lee
Hyeun J. Lee
Yifan Li
Victor I. Morary
Robert A.M. Stern
Ng Eng Teck
Stanley Tigerman
Jim Vlock

TRIBUTE GIFTS IN MEMORY OF

Alvar Aalto
Constance Adams
William H. Bailey
George R. Brunjes, Jr.
Richard W. Chapman
John E. Decell
Marciano Medina Flores
Herbert M. Hodgman
Andre F. Houston
Timothy E. Lenahan
Thomas W. Luckey
Carroll L. Meeks
Charles Moore
James E. Palmer
Cesar Pelli
Drika Purves
David S. Scheele
Sonia A. Schimberg
Vincent J. Scully
Jean Sielaff
Clinton J. Sheerr
Herman D. Spiegel
Helen C. Towle
Christopher Tunnard

Donors

1998
Anonymous
Lana Berkovich
Paul J. Boulifard
Holly M. Chacon
Thalassa Alexandra Curtis ◇
Marjorie K. Dickstein
Clifton R. Fordham
Kee-won A. Hong
Hemmant Jha
Hahn Joh
Emily Sheya Kovner
Karl A. Krueger
Paul D. Stoller
Gretchen V. Wagner
Mo R. Zell

1999
Jonathan David Bolch
Kimberly Ann Brown
Yoonhee Choi
Celia Corkery Civello
Martha Jane Foss
Adrienne James
Bruce D. Kinlin
Aaron W. Pine
Katherine E. Sutherland

2000
Benjamin Jon Bischoff ◇
Rosemarie Buchanan
Joseph Shek Yuen Fong
Ronald Michael Stelmarski

2001
Anonymous
Ghiora Aharoni
Julie Anne Fisher
Roland Sharpe Flores
Mark Foster Gage
Jaehee Kim
Adam Joseph Ruedig
Elizabeth Weeks Tilney
Juliana Chittick Tiryaki
Can M.A. Tiryaki
Laura Louise Zaytoun

2002
Sarah Marie Lavery
Kayin Tse

2003
Ioana Barac
Andrew William Benner
Marcos Diaz Gonzalez
Li-Yu Hsu

2004
Gary Britt Eversole
Anthony Andre Goldsby
Leejung Hong

Janny Hyun-Jeung Kim
James C. Nelson III

2005
Ralph Colt Bagley IV
Nora Ingrid Bergsten
Brent Allen Buck
Ruth Shinenge Gyuse
Diala Salam Hanna
Brandon F. Pace
Noah Riley
Brett Dalton Spearman
Nicholas Martin Stoutt

2006
Eron Ashley
Benay Alena Betts
Namil Byun
Angel Paolo Campos
Michael Joseph Grogan
Sean A. Khorsandi ◇
Marisa Jocelyn Kurtzman
Julia M. Leeming
David Nam
Frederick C Scharmen
Maxwell Riley Worrell

2007
Gabrielle Eve Brainard ◇
Molly W. Steenson
Adrienne E. Swiatocha Turner
Michael J. Yeung

2008
Chiemeka Anayo Ejiochi
Marc Charles Guberman ◇
Whitney M. Kraus
Yichen Lu
Rustam-Marc Mehta
Jacob I. Reidel
Leo Rowling Stevens IV ◇

2009
John Capen Brough III
Rebecca B. Winik

2010
Helen B. Bechtel
Daniel David Colvard
Nicholas Andrew Gilliland
Jacquelyn Page Wittkamp
　　　Hawkins
Jang Hyung Lee
Scott Brandon O'Daniel

2011
Kipp Colby Edick ◇
Zachary R. Heineman
Kee Hyun Lew
Brian Douglas Spring
Alexandra Fox Tailer ◇

2012
Anonymous
Amy E. DeDonato
Erin Colleen Dwyer
Kathryn L. Perez
Ian Gordon Starling
Eric Douglas Zahn

2013
Daisy Ames
Adrienne K. Brown
Alexander J. Chabla
Owen Detlor
Antonia M. Devine
Brittany B. Hayes
Edward Hsu
Amy E. Kessler
Hao Li
Altair L. Peterson ◇
Ryan Salvatore
Jeongyeap Shin
Paul C. Soper III
Katharine J.M. Storr

2014
Ali John Pierre Artemel
Mary F. Burr
Brandon D. Hall
Britton E. Rogers
Katie B. Stranix
Caroline M. VanAcker

2015
Anonymous
Elena R. Baranes
Hyeun J. Lee
Yifan Li
Laurence P.E. Lumley
Hui Zhen Ng

2016
Lisa N. Albaugh
Dorian A. Booth
Cynthia Hsu
Samantha L. Jaff
Charles A. Kane II
Nicolas Thornton Kemper
John W. Kleinschmidt

2017
Ava Amirahmadi
Garrett Hardee
Alexander O. Kruhly
Maxwell T. Mensching
Ali Naghdali
Cecily M. Ng
Georgia M. Todd ◇
Margaret Jau-ming Tsang

Donors

1984
Bruce R. Becker
Paul F. Carr, Jr.
Marti M. Cowan
Michael Coleman Duddy ◊
Teresa Ann Dwan
Douglas S. Dworsky
Mr J. Benjamin Gianni
Blair D. Kamin
Elizabeth M. Mahon
Michael L. Marshall
David Chase Martin
Sharon Matthews
Kenneth E. McKently
Scott Merrill
Jun Mitsui
Lawrence S. Ng
David L. Pearce, PhD
John R. Perkins
Ted Trussell Porter
Jennifer C. Sage
Mary E. Stockton
Marion G. Weiss

1985
Barbara K. Ball
Rasa Joana Bauza
William Robert Bingham
Robert L. Bostwick
M. Virginia Chapman
Frank R. Cheney, AIA
Lucile S. Irwin
Charles H. Loomis
Peter B. MacKeith
Chariss McAfee
Roger O. Schickedantz
R. David Thompson

1986
Margaret J. Chambers, AIA
Tim Culvahouse
Carey Feierabend
David D. Harlan, Jr.
David J. Levitt
Jeffrey P. Miles
Nicholas L. Petschek
Madeline Kay Schwartzman
J. Gilbert Strickler
John B. Tittmann

1987
Mary Buttrick Burnham
William D. Egan
R. Andrew Garthwaite
Elizabeth P. Gray
Andrew B. Knox
David G. Leary
Douglas S. Marshall
Timothy Day Mohr

Lilla J. Smith
Duncan Gregory Stroik
William L. Vandeventer

1988
Anonymous
Hans Baldauf
Cary Suzanne Bernstein
Charlotte Breed Handy
John David Butterworth
Allison Ewing
Drew H. Kepley
Ann Lisa Krsul
Thomas Fleming Marble
Oscar E. Mertz III
Nicholas Alfred Noyes
Alan W. Organschi
Elaine M. Rene-Weissman
William Taggart Ruhl
Gilbert P. Schafer III
Li Tze Wen
Robert Duncan Young

1989
Larry G. Chang
Darin C. Cook
Craig Gamble Copeland AIA
John DaSilva
Steve Dumez
Thomas J. Frechette
Kevin S. Killen
David J. Rush
Rossana H. Santos
Margaret Sherman Todd
Claire Weisz

1990
Lori B. Arrasmith Quill
Charles Bergen
William V. Fereshetian
Kristen L. Hodess
Jeffrey E. Karer
David M. Levine
Marc D. L'Italien
Peter J. Newman
Deborah R. Robinson
Mildred I. Sung
Marie B. Wilkinson
Mark A. Yoes

1991
Peter J. Brotherton
Dominic L.C. LaPierre
Joeb Moore
Alexander M. Stuart
Lindsay S. Suter
Susan E. Sutton
Kevin Wilkes
Heather H. Young

1992
Peter Kevin Blackburn
John C. Calderon
Kelly Jean Carlson-Reddig
Larry Greg Cohen
Perla Jeanne Delson
Frederick Adams Farrar II
Bruce Marshall Horton
Maitland Jones III
Douglas Neal Kozel

1993
Sari Chang
George Andrew Clemens
Richard G. Grisaru
Louise J. Harpman
Michael A. Harshman
George Thomas Kapelos
Jordan J. Levin
Gitta Robinson
Allen Douglas Ross
Evan Michael Supcoff
Katherine D. Winter

1994
Brendan Russell Coburn
Paul W. Jackson
Thomas Allen Kamm, Jr.
William J. Massey
Tania K. Min
Edward B. Samuel
Jim Tinson

1995
Carolyn Ann Foug
George Craig Knight
Johannes Marinus Knoops
Aaron Matthew Lamport
Dana Elizabeth Tang
John Christopher Woell

1996
Andrew C. Backer
Douglas C. Bothner
Ching-Hua Ho
Russell S. Katz
Michael V. Knopoff
Chung Yin J. Lau
Arthur J. Lee
David A. Thurman
Dade G. Van Der Werf
Mai-Tse Wu ◊

1997
Drew Lang
Peter Downing Mullan
Bertha A. Olmos
David Jason Pascu
Elizabeth P. Rutherfurd
William James Voulgaris ◊

Donors

1971 (Cont'd)
An-Chi H. Burow
Mazie Cox
Carlton M. Davis, Jr.
H. Rodriguez-Camilloni

1972
Marc F. Appleton
Paul B. Bailey
Edward P. Bass
Frederick Bland
Phillip Mack Caldwell
Roberta Carlson Carnwath
Heather Willson Cass
William A. Davis, Jr., Esq.
John L. Delgado, Jr.
John H. T. Dow, Jr.
Joseph A. Ford III
Coleman A. Harwell II
William H. Maxfield
David B. Peck, Jr.
Barton Phelps
Henry B. Teague, AIA
Brinkley S. Thorne
Carl H. Wies
Roger Hung Tuan Yee ◊

1973
Judith Bing
Everardo A. Jefferson
Nancy Brooks Monroe
Karen Rheinlander-Gray
Steven C. Robinson
Michael J. Stanton
J. Lawrence Thomas
Jerome J. Wagner
John W. Whipple
Robert J. Yudell

1974
Gordon M. Black
Sara E. Caples
William E. Odell ◊
Thomas C. Payne
Patrick L. Pinnell
Barbara W. Ratner
Barbara J. Resnicow
David M. Schwarz
George E. Turnbull

1975
Tullio A. Bertoli
Douglas J. Gardner
Karyn M. Gilvarg
Stephen A. Glassman, AIA
Susan E. Godshall, Esq.
Margaret R. Goglia
Keith B. Gross
Susan L.M. Keeny
Edwin R. Kimsey, Jr.

Francis C. Klein
Larry W. Richards
Elsbeth Selver-Haladay
J. David Waggonner III

1976
Shalom Baranes, FAIA
Henry H. Benedict III
Anko Chen
Stefani Danes
Henry M. Dearborn
Barbara R. Feibelman, AIA
James R. Kessler
Roy T. Lydon, Jr.
Adrienne K. Paskind
Scott Van Genderen
Eric Jay Oliner
Barbara Sundheimer-Extein

1977
James David Barnes
Louise M. Braverman
Bradley B. Cruickshank
W.J. Patrick Curley
Eric W. Epstein
Jonathan S. Kammel
James Hirsch Liberman
Kevin P. Lichten
Randall T. Mudge
Davidson Norris
Cynthia Mitchell Tauxe
Stephen M. Tolkin
Alexander C. Twining

1978
Philip H. Babb
Frederic M. Ball, Jr.
Paul W. Bierman-Lytle
Kenneth H. Colburn
Cynthia N. Hamilton
William S. Mead
L. Hawkins Mitchell
Daniel Arthur Rosenfeld
Julia Ruch

1979
Steven W. Ansel
Jack Alan Bialosky, Jr. ◊
James Leslie Bodnar
Richard H. Clarke
Jeffrey P. Feingold
Bradford W. Fiske
Patti Lee Glazer
John Charles Hall *
Michele Lewis
Richard L. McElhiney
George R. Mitchell
Thomas N. Patch

1980
Anonymous
Jacob D. Albert
Turan Duda
J. Scott Finn
G. Peyton Hall
Stephen W. Harby
Mariko Masuoka
Ann K. McCallum ◊
Julia H. Miner
William A. Paquette
Beverly Field Pierz
Joseph F. Pierz
Michael I. Zenreich

1981
Anonymous
Mark Denton
Brian E. Healy
Mitchell A. Hirsch
T. Whitcomb Iglehart
Michael G. Kostow
Jonathan Levi
Jane Murphy
Frances H. Roosevelt
Spencer Warncke
Diane L. Wilk

1982
John A. Boecker
Michael B. Burch
Domenic Carbone, Jr.
David P. Chen
Bruce H. Donnally
Kay Bea Jones
John E. Kaliski
Charles F. Lowrey, Jr.
Theodore John Mahl
Paul W. Reiss
R. Anthony Terry

1983
Maynard M. Ball
Ankie Stephen Barnes
Phillip G. Bernstein
Carol J. Burns
Stuart E. Christenson
Ignacio Dahl Rocha
John Lam
Erica H. Ling
Elisabeth N. Martin, FAIA ◊
Elizabeth Ann Murrell
Nicholas J. Rehnberg
Brent Sherwood
Robert J. Taylor
Nell W. Twining
Michael R. Winstanley

Donors

ALUMNI

1944
Leon A. Miller

1949
Theodore F. Babbitt *

1952
James A. Evans *
Donald C. Mallow

1953
Milton Klein
Julian E. Kulski

1954
Charles G. Brickbauer
Boris S. Pushkarev
Thomas R. Vreeland, Jr.

1956
Richard W. Chapman *
Walter D. Ramberg, AIA

1957
Edwin William de Cossy
Richard A. Nininger
William L. Porter

1958
James S. Dudley
Mark H. Hardenbergh ◊
Allen Moore, Jr.
Malcolm Strachan II *

1959
Bernard M. Boyle
Frank C. Chapman
Bruce W. Sielaff ◊
Carolyn H. Westerfield
Andrew C. Wheeler, AIA

1960
Larence Newman Argraves
James B. Baker
Thomas L. Bosworth
Richard S. Chafee
Bryant L. Conant
John K. Copelin ◊
Michael Gruenbaum
Raymond F. Liston *
Konrad J. Perlman

1961
Edward R. Baldwin II
Paul B. Brouard
Peter Cooke
Warren Jacob Cox
Francis W. Gencorelli
Charles T. Haddad
Lewis S. Roscoe
Yung G. Wang

1962
Richard A. Hansen
Tai Soo Kim
James Morganstern
Leonard P. Perfido
Renato Rossi-Loureiro
Meredith M. Seikel
Myles Weintraub

1963
Austin Church III
David A. Johnson
Ward Joseph Miles
F. Kempton Mooney
William A. Werner, Jr.

1964
Philip Allen
Theoharis L. David
Peter Jeremy Hoppner
Charles D. Hosford
Judith A. Lawler
Robert J. Mittelstadt *
Joan F. Stogis

1965
Thomas Hall Beeby
H. Calvin Cook
Norman E. Jackson, Jr.
Isidoro Korngold
Gary L. Michael
John I. Pearce, Jr.
Alexander Purves
Robert A.M. Stern
Leonard M. Todd, Jr.
Jeremy A. Walsh
Mason Smith

1966
Andrew Andersons
Emily Nugent Carrier
Richard C. Carroll, Jr.
James Scott Cook
Loren Ghiglione
John S. Hagmann
Donald A. Metz, Jr.
William F. Moore

1967
Anonymous
Gunter Dittmar
Charles M. Engberg
Alexander D. Garvin
Glenn H. Gregg
Chung Nung Lee
H. Fraser Mills
John W. Mullen III
Charles S. Rotenberg, AICP
Theodore Paul Streibert

1968
Frederick S. Andreae
Gail H. Cooke
Peter de Bretteville
Richard M. Donnelly *
John Fulop, Jr.
Christopher C. Glass
John Holbrook, Jr.
Erno Kolodny-Nagy
Peter C. Mayer
Peter Papademetriou
Franklin B. Satterthwaite Jr., PhD
Donald R. Spivack
Salvatore F. Vasi
John J. Vosmek, Jr.
James C. Whitney, Esq.

1969
Stephen Harris Adolphus
Albert M. Barokas
James E. Caldwell, Jr.
Samuel R. Callaway, Jr.
Robert J. Cassidy
James M. Gage
George T. Gardner
Harvey R. Geiger
Jane L. Gilbert
Edward J. Gotgart
William H. Grover
Roderick C. Johnson
Raymond J. Kaskey, Jr.
David H. Lessig
Jeffrey H. May
John H. Shoaff
Kermit D. Thompson ◊

1970
Judith L. Aronson
Richard F. Barrett
Roland F. Bedford
Paul F. Bloom
F. Andrus Burr
Richard K. Dozier
Ronald C. Filson
Brin R. Ford
Kathrin S. Moore ◊
James V. Righter
Laurence A. Rosen
Daniel V. Scully
Marilyn Swartz Lloyd
Walter C. Upton
Karen M. Votava
Jeremy Scott Wood
William L. Yuen, Esq.
F. Anthony Zunino

1971
William A. Brenner
Martin B. Buckley

Donors

The Yale School of Architecture is grateful to all those who provided financial support during the period July 1, 2020– June 30, 2021.

* Denotes deceased donors
◊ Denotes YSoA Annual Fund Volunteers

Anonymous
Nancy Alexander '79 BA, '84 MBA
Michael Corcoran Barry '09 BA
Dean Deborah L. Berke '16 MAH
Kent C. Bloomer '59 BFA, '61 MFA
Joan N. Borinstein
Mrs. George R. Brunjes
John A. Carrafiell '87 BA
Carla Cicero
Richard D. Cohen
Claire Creatore
Thomas J. Deegan-Day '89 BA
Enid Storm Dwyer *
Michael D. Fain '82 MFA
Sheryl and Jeffrey S. Flug
George Balle and M. Ian G.
    Gilchrist '72 BA
Kevin Douglas Gray '85 MBA
Nina L. Hachigian '89 BS
Judy Hart Angelo
Andrew Philip Heid '02 BA
Judith T. Hunt
James L. Iker
Adam Inselbuch
Elise Jaffe + Jeffrey Brown
Isaac Kalisvaart
Meredith J. Kane '76 BA
Andrew L. Lawton '83 BA, '92 MEM
Elizabeth Lenahan
Anne Kriken Mann
Gilbert Maurer
Margaret McCurry
Bruce McLanahan '57 BA
Susan Mead
Esther Da Costa Meyer '87 PhD
Kathryn Milano
Arthur F. Nacht '06 MFA
Helen W. Nitkin
Michael A. D. Nock '19 MBA
Brian O'Looney '90 BA
Jean Lattner Palmer
Richard B. Peiser '70 BA
Gregory Matthew Perez '11 MBA
Kathryn L. Perkins
Karen L. Pritzker
Albert B. Ratner
Audrey Ratner
William L. Rawn III '65 BA
William K. Reilly '62 BA, '94 MAH
Julie Schindler '89 BA
Brenda Shapiro
Robert V. Tauxe, MD
Billie Tsien '71 BA
Elpidio R. Villarreal, Esq. '85 JD
James Von Klemperer

Betty L. Wagner
Elizabeth A. Wegscheid
Robert Weinstein
Anne C. Weisberg
Jill Nolan Westgard
Mathew D. Wolf
Vivian Kuan and Pei-Tse Wu '89 BA
Arthur W. Zeckendorf

CORPORATIONS, FOUNDATIONS,
AND MATCHING GIFT SUPPORT

Avangrid Foundation
The Barclays Bank PLC
Barry Family Foundation
The BPB & HBB Foundation
Deborah Berke & Partners
    Architects
Earl & Brenda Shapiro
    Foundation
Elisha-Bolton Foundation
Erving and Joyce Wolf
    Foundation
The Fidelity Charitable Gift
    Fund
The Jaffe Family Foundation
The Jewish Communal Fund
JP Morgan Charitable Giving
    Fund
Kohn Pedersen Fox Associates PC
MAD Office Limited
The Maurer Family Foundation
The National Philanthropic
    Trust
The New York Community Trust
The Robert A.M. Stern Family
    Foundation
Schwab Fund for Charitable
    Giving
Seedlings Foundation
The Tang Fund
The U.S. Charitable Gift Trust
Vanguard Charitable
Willametta K. Day Foundation

Paprika! Volume 6

Student Groups

Yale NOMAS

NATIONAL ORGANIZATION OF MINORITY ARCHITECTURE STUDENTS (YALE NOMAS)

The mission of the Yale NOMAS is to champion diversity within the design profession by promoting the academic excellence, community engagement and professional development of its student members.

EQUALITY IN DESIGN (EID)

EID is a coalition of committed students from the Yale School of Architecture seeking equity within the architectural profession and the built environment.

INDIGENOUS SCHOLARS OF ARCHITECTURE, PLANNING AND DESIGN (ISAPD)

ISAPD is a collective student group focused on increasing the knowledge, consciousness, and appreciation of indigenous architecture, planning, and design at the Yale School of Architecture and the Yale community at large.

YSOA EAST

YSOA EAST

YSOA East is a student group at the Yale School of Architecture dedicated to fostering critical discourse and knowledge of Eastern architecture. The aim of the group is to consolidate and drive interest for Eastern architectural and urbanist trends.

YSOⱲ

THE CHRISTIAN FELLOWSHIP

The Christian Fellowship is a community and discussion group of Yale architecture students that meets weekly to explore the overlap of ideas relating to the Christian tradition, our work, and architecture.

THE YALE ARCHITECTURE FORUM

The Yale Architecture Forum serves as a place for discussion between PhD students from both the School of Architecture and from the History of Art Department who share an interest in architectural history and theory.

OUTLINES

OUTLINES

OutLines is a social and advocacy group, support system, and social network focusing on the exploration of LGBTQ issues within the YSOA, Yale University at large, and future professional settings.

THE ARCHITECTURE LOBBY

The Architecture Lobby is an organization of architectural workers advocating for the value of architecture in the general public and for architectural work within the discipline.

GREEN ACTION IN ARCHITECTURE

GREEN ACTION IN ARCHITECTURE

Green Action in Architecture is a student group devoted to addressing sustainability and environmental health and well-being issues within the school, as well as promoting broader discussion of environmental considerations as they pertain to architecture, generally.

M.E.D.

MED WORKING GROUP FOR ANTI-RACISM

The MED Working Group for Anti-Racism is an evolving multifaceted project founded by students from the Masters of Environmental Design program that joins forces with activists, educators and students in and beyond the academy to further an evolving set of conversations about the destructive whiteness of our institutional and professional practices.

PAPRIKA!

Paprika! is a window into emerging discourse from Yale School of Architecture and Yale School of Art. Every issue is student-curated and aims to broadcast diverse voices in the fields of art, architecture and design. Founded in 2014, Paprika! is named after the vibrant orange carpet in Rudolph Hall. Every issue of Paprika! is a newspaper broadsheet uniquely designed by students from Yale's Graphic Design program. No two issues are alike.

Paprika! Spring 2021

COORDINATING EDITORS
William Beck
Gina Jiang
Jerry Chow

In conceiving the Vol. 06 Spring Edition of *Paprika!*, the Coordinating Editors came together with a shared intent to channel this shared moment of reflection into productive conversations. Recognizing the psychological endurance required amidst the pandemic, "Now What?" embraced slowness as a guiding principle, offering editors, contributors, and readers more time to think, respond, and write—in contrast to the typically fast-paced nature of *Paprika!* with a disorienting digital array of communication modes that exhausted student discourse. "Now What?" was conceived as a haven for circumstantially scattered student voices. We felt the prevailing reflective attitude provided a prime context for us to revisit archived *Paprika!* content, allowing our readership to review *Paprika!* and re-examine its role within YSoA and beyond. Supporting this retrospection was the idea of compounding conversations across different platforms. We sought to accomplish this by experimenting with new avenues for collecting and presenting diverse voices both in and outside YSoA (e.g. polls, questionnaires, data visualization) as well as also expanding *Paprika!*'s presence to more agile media platforms to accommodate our circumstantially displaced audience. We envisioned "Now What?" as an opportunity for our readers to reflect, respond, and invent with empathy, criticality, and imagination.

P6!—ISSUE 11
From Real Estates to Possible Estates
Alex Kim

"Inherent in declaring something as 'real-world' is an implicit statement that lays claim to the real. So what models of development are declared real by the Bass Fellowship? Is designing neocolonial villas for sunburnt millionaires our reality? What does the inclusion or exclusion of particular development vehicles do to our understanding of the limits of possibility?"

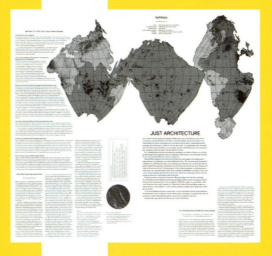

P6!—ISSUE 11
Architecture and Abolition
Ben Derlan
Merrell Hambleton

"The suggestion that a refusal to design something—refusing to give an idea physical and spatial form—might support the abolition of that thing demonstrating the power that we currently place on architecture and design thinking. But what power do architects truly have to make or unmake the criminal justice system?"

Paprika! Fall 2020

COORDINATING EDITORS
Alex Kim
Audrey Tseng Fischer
Brian Orser
Hannah Mayer Baydoun

During our tenure, we asked how *Paprika!* could respond more directly to the political contexts that came to the fore during the pandemic—profound isolation, structural racism, and institutional failure. We refigured the publication to stand in solidarity with the Black Lives Matter movement and the BIPOC members of the design community who continue to lead efforts to confront our discipline's historic shortcomings and violent complicity in the structures of racial injustice and social precarity. The proposal, for better or worse, was to take *Paprika!* seriously as a collective body and to expand the platform into a provisional ecology of media, matching the rhythm of our experience. Podcasts, newsletters, and digital publications were to be produced by a growing team of students in the Schools of Art and Architecture. In our efforts to hold space for the many overlapping identities and affordances of *Paprika!*—investigative journalism, academic testbed, and community space—we ran up against the limits of our own capacities and our audience's bandwidth. There was a tension to negotiate—our ambitions to succeed in a demanding academic institution seemed to impinge on our intentions to steward an empathetic space for community dialog. We hope future editors continue to feel empowered to refigure *Paprika!* and resonate with shifting tempos.

P6!—ISSUE 02
The Sophistry of Mapping
Rukshan Vathupola

"Therefore it is critical that we who use and mine cartography for information and 'truth' recognize that there is nothing harmless or benign about the images they contain, the information they represent, nor the greater interests that produced them. And by creating maps, it is not just a manipulation of our shared reality but a distoriation of the truths of our common past."

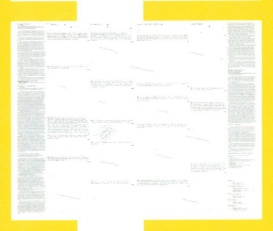

P6!—ISSUE 07
Rediscovering Rudolph
Lillian Agutu

"When Rudolph Hall opened this fall with COVID guidelines in place, I was one of the very few who ventured out to the studios. The immediate contrast between what I had known and the present stillness of the building was especially jarring; the feeling of those first weeks was of being left alone in someone else's home. Carefully treading down empty halls, careful as to not make a sound…"

HMWRK: Room

January 15, 2021–
March 15, 2021

CURATORS
Rachael Tsai
Jack Rusk
Diana Smiljković
Gustav Nielsen

DESIGNERS
Luiza Dale
Nick Massarelli

SPONSOR
Are.na

The room is an environment of screens. The room performs. The room has a "back-of-house." The room is where work life and family life converge. The room is a place for play and social life. The room of one's own is the room of all. The room is public and private. The room exists between architecture and furniture. The room is idiosyncratic. The room is real and virtual. The room is one and multiple. The room is defined by objects. The room has latent dispositions. The room is an abstraction.

Room catalogues the mutants, hybrids, and chimeras that have arisen in response to this new state of exception. This strange menagerie will be depicted in plan drawings submitted by students and practicing architects at Yale and beyond. These drawings show accidental assemblages of domestic and professional life, of productive and reproductive labor, that go beyond contemporary speculations about the interrelationship between work and domesticity. This exhibition stakes that a critical collection of these new arrangements, made by necessity more than design, are a message from the future of architectural production.

HMWRK: Pop-up Office

September 21, 2020–
October 16, 2020

CURATORS
Rachael Tsai
Jack Rusk
Diana Smiljković
Gustav Nielsen

DESIGNERS
Luiza Dale
Nick Massarelli

SPONSOR
Are.na

We now live betwixt and between, in the real and the virtual, offline and on, remotely and in person. In this new state, we can work from bed, change our camera settings, and mute without having to be silent. Our environments are customizable, not bound by reality.

Pop-Up Office was a new imagined space in the North Gallery where groups could meet in person and online. Table and chairs were arranged in the way that resembled a typical conference room, while at the same time maintaining the six-feet distance as required by social distancing regulations.

"Book a meeting in advance, arrange the space as you'd like, and work in real life and out."

This installation is part of HMWRK, an ongoing research project. More news about this project can be found online at Hmwrk.work

Reframing Brazil

May 31, 2021–
July 21, 2021

CURATORS
Leonardo Serrano Fuchs
Laura Pappalardo
Nathalie Ventura

DESIGNER
Ana Lobo

SPONSORS
The Yale MacMillan Center
Yale School of Architecture
    Exhibitions Fund
The Tsai Center for Innovative
    Thinking at Yale (Tsai City)
La Casa Cultural

INSTITUTIONAL PARTNERS
Yale School of Architecture
BRUMASTUDIO
YSoA ISAA International
Students & Alumni Association

Reframing Brazil offers an incomplete critical panorama of the logic of production and consumption that operates at local and global scales. The project proposes to visualize this underlying logic by returning to the origin of the material chain, rewinding its processes, and making visible its essential abstractions. This work contests the alienation of a building from its territories of neocolonial extraction, exposing the landscapes left behind.

It is the first research project undertaken by Brazilian architects and designers at the Yale School of Architecture. Furthermore, the exhibition is the first bilingual English-Portuguese show held at YSoA and encompasses a series of six large-scale drawings that can be contemplated both as wholes and in their detailed parts as the visitors are invited to navigate freely through a grid set in the space of the North Gallery.

Play It by Ear / Mixtape

November 1, 2020–
December 4, 2020

PLAY IT BY EAR CURATORS
Alex Kim
Brian Orser

MIXTAPE CURATORS
Brandon Brooks
Sarah Kim

This exhibition joins images with sounds to facilitate, reproduce, and collage conversations across the spatial and temporal distances which are a part of student life this semester. It aims to create a layered space for broadcasting and listening, among members of our community—for conversations about precedent and originality, agency and circumstance.

　　In this collective experiment, new relationships within architectural pedagogy are sought—by students, for students. Such interaction already takes place in the institutionalized formats of the studio, the critique, and the late hours between, but there is an opportunity in the student gallery for a lower-stakes, counter-performative conversation that remains comfortable with uncertainty, error, unoriginality, and ambiguity.

Publications

Towers in the City: Berlin, Alexanderplatz

AUTHOR
Hans Kollhoff

EDITORS
Kyle Dugdale, Kirk Henderson

PUBLISHER
Yale School of Architecture, 2021

Towers in the City takes Berlin's Alexanderplatz as an opportunity to challenge the role of the skyscraper in the contemporary urban fabric. Documenting an advanced design studio taught by Hans Kollhoff, Davenport Visiting Professor, with Kyle Dugdale, critic in architecture, the book examines the tower as the architectural expression of a long-term commitment to the city. The conclusion is that development must be driven not only by property value and architectural ingenuity but also by respect for collective memory and common humanity. The book argues that these public commitments find architectural expression in a radically different tectonic to that of contemporary patterns of development. It combines photographs of Berlin and essays by Kollhoff and Dugdale.

Kent Bloomer: Nature as Ornament

EDITORS
Sunil Bald, Gary Huafan He

DESIGNER
Luke Bulman Office

PUBLISHER
Yale School of Architecture, Yale University Press, 2021

Nature as Ornament celebrates Kent Bloomer's indispensable intellectual and pedagogical contribution to the Yale School of Architecture and the profession of architecture over the last fifty years. Bloomer's dedication to the design and thinking of ornament in architecture has influenced collaborators and students in a broad range of fields. Many have contributed to this collection of essays including— Thomas Beeby, Turner Brooks, Edward Casey, Douglas Cooper, Mari Hvattum, Guru Dev Kaur Khalsa, Emer O'Daly, Richard Prum, Willie Ruff, Stacey Sloboda, and Michael Young— exploring the diverse meaning of ornament in contemporary discourses. The book poses critical questions in order to reorient the discourse of ornament from a contentious vestige of modernity toward its active relationship to architecture, landscape, urbanism, and the sense of place.

Next Generation Tourism— Touching the Ground Lightly

AUTHORS
John Spence, Henry Squire, Patrick Bellew, Timothy Newton

EDITORS
Nina Rappaport, Rukshan Vathupola

DESIGNERS
MGMT. Design

PUBLISHER
Yale School of Architecture, 2021

Next Generation Tourism— Touching the Ground Lightly is the latest book in the Edward P. Bass Distinguished Visiting Architecture Fellowship series, focusing on the advanced studio directed by John Spence, chairman of the Karma Group; Henry Squire, of Squire and Partners, Patrick Bellew, founding director of Atelier Ten, joined by Timothy Newton, Yale critic in architecture. The professors challenged the students to research and design innovative strategies centered around ecology, sustainability, and the rise of future tourism models on the resort island of Gili Meno, Indonesia. The book includes the student building material analysis and climate research on Gili Meno, as well as interviews with Henry Squire about his architectural practice, and John Spence about eco-resorts and the tourist industry's response to the COVID-19 crisis.

Publications

Perspecta 53: Onus

EDITORS
Caroline Acheatel, Paul J.
Lorenz, Paul Rasmussen,
Alexander Stagge

DESIGNERS
Nilas Andersen, Rosa McElheny

PUBLISHER
The MIT Press, 2020

In architecture, ethics are malleable. In theory, the terms are rigid, yet the reality is elastic. While much of the built environment is ostensibly designed for an individual client's needs, architecture's effects reverberate politically, environmentally and culturally, often in unexpected ways and far beyond the limits of any parcel or project. This volume of Perspecta—the oldest student-edited architectural journal in the United States—considers the ethical questions and moral tensions that arise during the ideation, development, completion, and aftermath of the design process.

Constructs

Fall 2020

EDITOR
Nina Rappaport

DESIGNER
Manuel Miranda Practice

PUBLISHER
Yale School of Architecture, 2020

Spring 2021

EDITOR
Nina Rappaport

DESIGNERS
Hyo Kwon, Goeun Park

PUBLISHER
Yale School of Architecture, 2021

First Published in January 1999, Constructs is a bi-annual news magazine highlighting activities and events at the Yale School of Architecture. The large-format, 28-page publication features interviews with visiting professors, previews, and reviews of exhibitions, symposia, and lectures sponsored by the school, as well as faculty and alumni news. It also has feature articles on issues relevant to discussions in the design studios and on architectural events worldwide.

Two Sides of the Border: Reimagining the Region

EDITORS
Tatiana Bilbao, Nile Greenberg,
Ayesha S. Ghosh

DESIGNER
Luke Bulman Office

PHOTOGRAPHER
Iwan Baan

PUBLISHER
Lars Müller Publishers,
Yale School of Architecture, 2020

In Two Sides of the Border, Tatiana Bilbao, Norman R. Foster Visiting Professor at Yale, coordinated thirteen architecture studios across the United States and Mexico and attempted to capture the complex and dynamic region of the US–Mexican border. The work was presented at Yale's Architecture Gallery in 2018 and compiled into a book that envisions the borderland through five themes: migration, housing and cities, creative industries, local production, tourism, and territorial economies. The projects use design and architecture to address social, political, and ecological concerns along the border. Featuring essays, student projects, interviews, research, and a photography project by Iwan Baan, the book highlights the distinct qualities of this place.

Lecture Series

YSOA LECTURE SERIES

○ Everyday 2020
August 27, 2020

SPEAKERS
Deborah Berke

○ Surveillance and
Self-Determination:
The Black Workshop
October 1, 2020

SPEAKERS
Rebecca Choi

○ Dream the Combine:
Recent Work
October 8, 2020

SPEAKERS
Jennifer Newsom
Tom Carruthers

○ Embracing the Discourse:
New Horizons in
Architectural Criticism,
Brendan Gill Lecture
October 29, 2020

SPEAKERS
Kate Wagner

○ Local + Global:
Lace up your shoes
November 2, 2020

SPEAKERS
Tod Williams
Billie Tsien

○ Creative Collaboration—A
Strategy For Impactful Change
November 5, 2020

SPEAKERS
Abby Hamlin

○ What next for the city?
November 9, 2020

SPEAKERS
Deborah Saunt

○ Recent Work:
Tale of Two Museums
November 12, 2020

SPEAKERS
Walter Hood

○ Unbounded
November 19, 2020

SPEAKERS
Ronald Rael
Virginia San Fratello

○ LCLA office: Recent Work
November 30, 2020

SPEAKERS
Luis Callejas
Charlotte Hansson

○ Radical Practice
February 1, 2021

SPEAKERS
Marlon Blackwell

○ SO-IL: Recent Work
February 11, 2021

SPEAKERS
Jing Liu

○ Design is Ceremony
February 18, 2021

SPEAKERS
Chris Cornelius

○ Barozzi Veiga: Recent Work
February 25, 2021

SPEAKERS
Alberto Veiga

○ Lecture
March 25, 2021

SPEAKERS
Fiona Raby

○ Lecture
April 1, 2021

SPEAKERS
Olalekan Jeyifous

○ Lecture
April 8, 2021

SPEAKERS
Kate Orff

○ Timothy Egan Lenahan
Memorial Lecture
April 12, 2021

SPEAKERS
Justin Garrett Moore

○ George Morris Woodruff,
Class of 1857,
Memorial Lecture
April 22, 2021

SPEAKERS
Sarah Lewis

ADDITIONAL LECTURES

○ Performing Consumption
October 21, 2020

SPEAKERS
Edek Sher

○ Climate Adaptation:
America's growing struggle
to live with global warming,
Poynter Lecture
October 28, 2020

SPEAKERS
Christopher Flavelle

○ Our Days Are Like
Full Years
March 22, 2021

SPEAKERS
Deborah Berke
Nathanial Kahn
Harriet Pattison
Jock Reynolds
Billie Tsien

○ Labor or Love
April 13, 2021

SPEAKERS
Sarah Jaffe
Peggy Deamer

○ Native Astronomy and
Spatial Resonance:
Aligning with the Cosmos
April 15, 2021

SPEAKERS
Gregory Cajete

Symposia and Colloquia

*Ornament's Refracted
Cosmologies Colloquium*

ORGANIZERS
Misha Semenov,
Kassandra Leiva

○ Ornament and Ecology:
A Visual Language for
Connecting with Nature
February 7, 2020

SPEAKERS
Aaron Ellison, Alex Felson,
Stacy Levy

○ The Language of Ornament:
Rhythm, Movement,
and the Cosmos
March 7, 2021

SPEAKERS
Kent Bloomer

○ Ornament &
Neuroscience: Your
Brain on Fractals
April 14, 2021

SPEAKERS
Nikos Salingaros,
Richard Taylor

○ Making Ornament:
Past, Present, Future
April 26, 2021

SPEAKERS
Gary Huafan He,
Matt McNicholas

Yale Architecture Forum

ORGANIZERS
Iris Giannakopoulou Karamouzi,
Gabrielle Printz

○ The Residential Form
of Race
April 13, 2021

SPEAKERS
Adrienne Brown

○ Networking the Bloc:
International Relations
in Eastern European
Experimental Art of
the long-1970s
March 16, 2021

SPEAKERS
Klara Kemp-Welch

○ Life Underground:
Mines, Shelters,
and other Artificial
Environments
March 30, 2021

SPEAKERS
Eric C.H. de Bruyn

PhD Dialogues

ORGANIZERS
Iris Giannakopoulou Karamouzi,
Gabrielle Printz

○ Architecture and the
Framing of Bodies
April 29, 2021

SPEAKERS
David Turturo,
Annabel J. Wharton

Symposia and Colloquia

MED Roundtable Series

ORGANIZERS
MED Working Group
for Anti-Racism

GRAPHIC DESIGN
Mike Tully

○ POLICING
September 9, 2020

SPEAKERS
Jaime Amparo Alves,
Arissa Hall,
Philip V. McHarris,
Black Students for
Disarmament at Yale

○ ARCHIVE
September 21, 2020

SPEAKERS
Cierra Chenier, Mel Isidor,
Amrita Raja

○ COMMONS
November 11, 2020

SPEAKERS
Lauren Hudson,
Sunny Iyer, Rachel Valinsky,
Dan Taeyoung

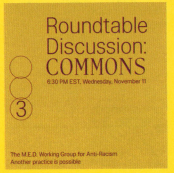

Latinx Features: Spring '21 Roundtable Series

ORGANIZERS
Araceli Lopez, Guillermo Acosta
Navarrete, Saba Salekfard,
Claudia Ansorena

GRAPHIC DESIGN
Alicia Jones

ADVISORS
Ana María Durán Calisto

Outreach

○ Agency in Architecture
February 23, 2021

SPEAKERS
Elisa Iturbe, Enrique
Walker, Adriana Chávez

MODERATORS
Guillermo Acosta Navarrete
(YSoA), Alice Fang (GSAPP),
Gabriel Gutierrez Huerta
(YSoA)

○ Women in Architecture
March 23, 2021

SPEAKERS
Tatiana Bilbao, Elisa Silva,
Mónica Ponce de León

COORDINATOR
Limy Fabiana (YSoA
alumni), Larissa Guimaraes
(Princeton SoA), Luis
Fernando Muñoz
(Princeton SoA)

○ Practice, Place,
& Partnership
April 21, 2021

SPEAKERS
Ana María Durán Calisto,
Cúre & Penabad, Estudio
Macías Peredo

MODERATORS
Claudia Ansorena (YSoA),
Rogelio Cadena (GSD),
Gabriela Dávila Rivera
(GSD)

Symposia and Colloquia

Beyond The Visible: Space, Place, and Power in Mental Health, the inaugural J. Irvin Miller Symposium

ORGANIZERS
Kate Altmann, Mariana Riobom, Gus Steyer, Jen Shin, Jackson Lindsay, Araceli Lopez

ADVISORS
Elihu Rubin, Joel Sanders, Sheril Holbrook, Jessica Helfand

○ Keynote Speech:
The Social and Ecological Aspects of the Psychology of Place
September 10, 2020

SPEAKERS
Mindy Thompson Fullilove

MODERATOR
Elihu Rubin

○ The Hospital Panel
Deconstructing "Otherness"
September 15, 2020

SPEAKERS
Kelechi Ubozoh, Christian Karisson, Jason Danziger, Martin Voss

MODERATOR
Matthew Steinfeld

○ The Home Panel
After the Asylum: Housing & Mental Health
September 17, 2020

SPEAKERS
Alison Cunningham, Earle Chambers, Sam Tsemberis

MODERATOR
Jessica Helfand

○ Architectures of
Mental Health
September 22, 2020

SPEAKERS
Christopher Payne, Hannah Hull

MODERATOR
Joel Sanders

○ The City Panel
Mental Health and the Right to the City
September 24, 2020

SPEAKERS
Bryan Lee, Molly Kaufman, Nupur Chaudhury

MODERATOR
Justin Garrett Moore

Retrofuturisms Symposium

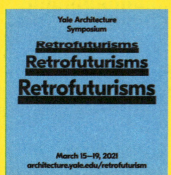

ORGANIZERS
MArch II, Class of 2021

○ Session 1
March 15, 2021

SPEAKERS
Anna Heringer

MODERATOR
Rebecca Commissaris

○ Session 2
March 16, 2021

SPEAKERS
John Lin, Xu Tiantian

MODERATORS
Srinivas Karthikeyan, Hongyu Wang

○ Session 3
March 17, 2021

SPEAKERS
Lucia Allais, Peggy Deamer

MODERATORS
Guillermo Acosta Navarrete, Luka Pajovic

○ Session 4
March 18, 2021

SPEAKERS
Neyran Turan, Clark Thenhaus

MODERATORS
Mari Kroin, Alper Turan

○ Session 5
March 19, 2021

SPEAKERS
Liam Young

MODERATOR
Gabriel Gutierrez Huerta

FIVE

Architecture is a production extending far beyond its physical parameters, further manifesting itself in conversation, conviction, and collaboration. *Outreach* describes an amniotic system of exchange, a give-and-take of ideas and resources that sustains a greater pedagogical ether through symposia, publications, exhibitions, and student groups. Free from outreach, architecture is rendered hollow.

Architectural Writing and Journalism

Love or Labor? How architectural education perpetuates the exploitation of labor in the workplace.

CLAUDIA ANSORENA

The article explores the legacy of undervalued work in the architectural profession, outlining its relationship with pedagogy and its perpetuation amongst a capital-centered profession. It questions the value of work, the fantasy of creative sacrifice, and the University's role in establishing unrealistic standards of practice. The quest for innovation envelopes the mind of the young architect-to-be. Guided by a desire to succeed whilst subsisting, the architecture student enters practice armed with myths of exceptionalism. Year by year, the myths are slowly, painfully unmasked to reveal a reality of building that is subservient to capital. How is the "innovator" able to persevere if a 9-to-5 really means a 9-to-9 and requires an inordinate amount of sustained labor at below-minimum wages for menial benefits? Blood, sweat, and tears. We are taught duress and endurance breed creation. Architectural education equips the spatially-adept fledgling with the confidence of a solitary thinker, but misses the mark in accompanying the soloist with logistical tools necessary to free themselves from capital.

How is the "innovator" able to persevere if a 9-to-5 really means a 9-to-9 and requires an inordinate amount of sustained labor at below-minimum wages for menial benefits?

Press Release: Inter-House

KATE FRITZ

"Inter-House" proposes a design that directly engages with the existing cultural heritage sites within the urban fabric of the city of Lima. In an effort to re-activate these sites frozen in time to once again be lively dwellings, markets, and gardens, the design of the site engages with three primary stakeholders: the farm, the market, and the table.

Farming within the site takes on the language of huachaques, who's canals and geometric pools become fruitful sources of nutrients for growth of reeds and grasses further used in the screen-system of the adjacent housing complex. Market spaces exist throughout the site however are focused on the ground level of the housing complexes and on platforms located at the top level of the Huacas. In an effort to maintain simplicity in elements and composition the unit of the $3' \times 6'$ table is used as the foundation for the market's surfaces. The kitchens are located at all levels of the housing complex including the ground floor where they are incorporated into the market system.Through combination and adjacencies these units begin to share and thicken walls although all while still maintaining visual connections to both the immediate huaca and larger garden systems. The kitchens become the bridge between the two.

"Inter-House" proposes a design that seeks to recognize, bridge, and re-activate these cultural heritage sites throughout Lima with the deployment of mixed-housing, markets, and farming spaces. The project minimizes the distance between field and kitchen through the continual nurturing of both field and facade. Dialogue with the huacas informs the internal organization and composition of the building while it simultaneously re-activates and brings life back to the heritage site. The project aims not to encroach upon these heritage sites, but instead return them to their natural order of accumulation and allow for continued narratives.

Graphic Inquiry

Neon Signage

NAOMI JEMIMA NG

How do we bring the shallow reading, rapid flickering, and blatant yet momentary impressions of neon signage onto a page, screen, or somewhere in between? This project is a printed book-video hybrid that experiments with ideas of clustering, framing, timing, and the constant fungibility between image and text. As neon signs in Hong Kong become obsolete, how do we bring the streetscapes of Hong Kong into our consciousness through the representation, permanence, and reach via various graphic mediums?

Burn

LEANNE NAGATA

This project is an inquiry into the short run photography magazine, *Provoke*, and some of its makers, Kōji Taki and Moriyama Daidō. I made a book of past pages and screenshots, and burned it. Here, there are multiple realities and infinite memories, both so fabricated and dreamt that they blur together.

Building Disasters

Hartford Circus Fire

BEN THOMPSON

The Hartford Circus Fire was a building disaster involving a sudden and calamitous fire that took place on July 6, 1944 at the Hartford tour stop of the Ringling Brothers and Barnum and Bailey Circus. Shortly after the main show began, the sidewall of the Big Top Tent caught fire. It took just minutes for the entire structure to be engulfed in flames due to the flammability of the tent's water-proofing membrane, which was made up of a combination of Paraffin Wax and Gasoline. Temporary chutes for the lion performance brought in through the entrance halls hindered many of the 7,000 attendees from exiting the quickly burning Big Top. The fire would claim 167 lives and seriously injure 700 more. The disaster is remembered by The Hartford Circus Memorial dedicated on July 6th, 2005 on the 61st anniversary of the fire.

The exact cause of the fire is unknown. One man claimed he did it late in his life, others say it was careless cigarette tossed into some hay, or sparks from a generator. The initial flame that caused the fire may be unknown, but what is known is the reason it spread so quickly and with such devastation—which are these two ingredients: Gasoline and paraffin wax.

Rana Plaza

NICOLE RATAJCZAK

On April 24, 2013, at 8:45am, Rana Plaza, a concrete garment manufacturing building in Bangladesh, collapsed. The disaster killed a total of 1134 people and injured another 2500. It is the single deadliest garment industry accident in modern history and a true tragedy. In an industry worth 20 billion dollars where workers earn less than 2 dollars per day, the collapse of Rana Plaza revealed the true cost of cheap and fast fashion. It was a wakeup call to the entire fashion industry and to consumers around the world.

There were several contributing factors to this disaster, many developing from the very beginning of construction. The loads placed on the Rana Plaza building far exceeded what the building could bear. Originally designed as a four-story retail and office building, four additional floors were added illegally without legitimate permits, with a ninth floor under construction at the time of collapse. Poor ground conditions led to differential settlement of the foundation, and less steel reinforcing was used within the concrete construction than was required. In addition, four large diesel generators, each weighing seven metric tons, were installed on the roof and added considerable additional loads as well as vibrations. It was the vibrations of the generators which ended up being the final tipping point which led to the progressive collapse of the building.

The Rana Plaza collapse has led to some significant victories for workers safety in Bangladesh. The undertaking of thousands of building inspections and the compliance with their findings is also ground-breaking in a country where building safety standards were rarely applied or enforced. While the victories can and should be celebrated, the fight to make sure that no more workers die in death-trap factories, both in Bangladesh and elsewhere, still has a long way to go.

Ruins and Ruination

The Big Duck Shed

CHRISTINE SONG

The Big Duck in Long Island received a lot of attention in architectural discourse due to Robert Venturi's "Decorated Shed" argument. A decorated shed occurs when ornament or signage is added onto a shed and the building then reflects its function. Approaching this argument differently, this project argues that an additional facade is not necessary—the image of the duck can become both signage and facade.

The ~~White~~ Polychromatic House

SHELBY WRIGHT

White has long been the color associated with Neoclassicism, as seen in U.S. government and civic buildings, and exemplified by "the White House." Since we now know that Classical buildings were originally polychromatic, would it be appropriate for Neoclassicism to be repainted in a similar manner? Does the color white hold such symbolic value to these buildings that they would be "ruined" if they were anything else? This project explores the White House as if it were painted in colors similar to ancient Greek temples.

Color in Architecture

Razzle Dazzle

CORINNA SIU

This collection of work covers a series of color explorations done through various oil painting studies. By using a basic set of primary paints, we mixed, matched, and experimented with contrast and tone. The painted images were then photographed and edited to best capture the true colors of the physical painted piece. The final project culminated in a three-dimensional study of a box painted in the razzle-dazzle pattern, blurring the edges of the 3-D object.

Experiments in Color

RACHAEL TSAI

Over the course of the semester we explored the use of color through a series of weekly oil painting exercises exploring form, shape, and contrast. Color was used in different combinations to blur, dissolve, emphasize, and create illusions between edges and surfaces. Beginning with a simple color wheel, primary, secondary, and tertiary colors were manipulated and paired over the course of the class to a higher degree of complexity, culminating in a three-dimensional study of dissolving edges.

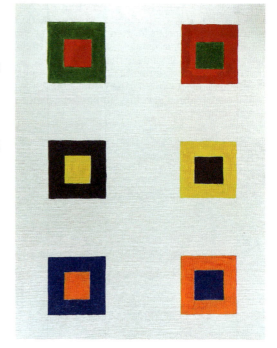

The Mechanical Eye

Prosthetic Memory
JOSEPH REICH

As our tools evolve, so do the processes through which we entangle our understanding of ourselves, the spaces that constitute our realities, and the dynamics between the self and the real that we engage as perception, memory, and the generation of meaning. Through these terms, the project manifests itself as an aligning of techno-social memories that help to constitute an understanding of the real. This offers something beyond the biological processes through which we have narrowly defined the finitude of our own realities. Such enhanced reality is a facet of the tools we accept as extensions of ourselves and allows us to embody a system of engagement inseparable from these tools, despite our ability to comprehend their presence. Beginning with the mechanism of the window, memories of Rudolph Hall were supplanted with remnants of prosthetic vision, enacting a latent process in which memory transforms a foreign amalgam into something uncannily familiar.

Supertemporal Space
YOUNG JOON YUN

Even though the hard wave of development played a key role in creating a new urban infrastructure in Korea, accommodating 10 million people within 50 years, spatially condensing developments through a fixed grid deleted the historical and cultural value of existing infrastructure. This research rejects the conventional urban framework's absolute geometries and utilizes a diverse and ever-changing typology in virtual tourism. By the action of overlapping the digital vision upon the physical site, the site's existing frameworks can sustain longer without deconstruction.

Composition and Form

Directional Modularity

QIYUAN LIU

This course is composed of four individual
projects, exploring programmatic organization,
sectional language, structural system, and
facade configurations. All these sectional studies
are trying to explore how space can be divided
without traditional vertical partitions. What if
the boundaries between different spaces are
softened and merged with other surfaces? This
project explores the making of a complicated
and flexible structural system with a very
simple module.

The Section

LIANG HU

This project explores formal and spatial
strategies through sectional models and
drawings. It explores the potential connections
between different levels and possibilities for
intricate moments between spaces.

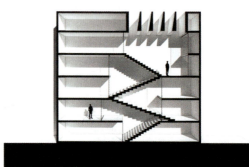

Technology and Design of Tall Buildings

Vertical Habitat

SHUCHEN DONG, ELAINE ZIYI CUI

Situated along the waterfront of the former
Chicago Spire, the project is a mixed-used, mile-
high tower that is composed of stacked city
blocks interwoven by green landscapes, artificial
waterscapes, and roads. Four main elements—
park, water, roads, and city blocks—are considered
essential and translated vertically into the design.
The project is both socially and environmentally
sustainable and intends to provide its own
self-sustaining microclimate.

Urban Voids

YOUNG JOON YUN, LILLIAN HOU,

VIVIAN WU

Tall buildings are mini-cities; therefore, their
design scheme should not be a single form,
but rather, an interdisciplinary gesture with
political, social, economic, and cultural
ideologies. Thus our design concept carves out
a series of voids within the building to create
orchestrated forms that encompass collaborative
narration of the city. The prototype for this idea
is developed to exist at the center of Midtown
New York City—a gigantic, social intervention
space where the city can play, work, and
educate together.

Design Computation

The Color Loom
TIANYUE WANG

The project explores the concept of slit-scan—a photography technique—with a digital approach. By scanning physical objects placed on a rotating platform, the project reconfigures the pixels and creates novel images of the physical image-object.

House Music
SAM GOLINI, GUILLERMO ACOSTA
NAVARRETE

House Music was developed as a way to vocalize harmonies, tempos, and rhythms of built form. The project began as a means to convert visual information in architecture into audible sound. Looking into ways of decoding the information embedded in architecture, we created a platform that reads video and converts it into music, using three different notes across three octaves and a synthesized bass drum.

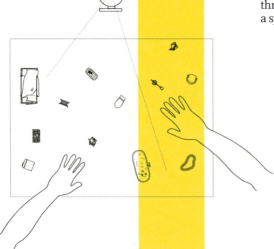

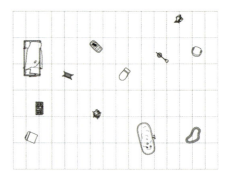

Drawing Projects

Living with Decay
RACHEL MULDER

Inspired by the hermetic conditions experienced during a year of lock down, this semester-long drawing studied the decomposition of rotting vegetables: the same rotting vegetables. Through many experiments of materials and drawing techniques, each study drew in closer to discover a new landscape of colors and textures, finding beauty in witnessing decay. The final drawing, done in watercolor, explores the volumes and curves produced as the vegetable peels curl and dry over time.

Living Room
MARI KROIN

This series of drawings comprise a cumulative composition describing the transformation of my living space over the course of the semester. The project explores the tension between objects and how they coexist, forming from critical observations of object characteristics and usage. The position of a cup of tea, for example, is determined by other objects in the table-scape and vice versa. The final drawing, a 360 degree study of the room, is constructed through twenty-eight 24" × 36" newsprint panels.

Mechanical Artifact: Ultra Space

The Space Vase

TYLER KREBS

The preliminary proposal for the Zero-G Project is to create an object that rethinks the presentation of plant life in space. My proposal will allow plants to accommodate the two drastically different conditions of gravity that will be experienced on the flight, including the vertical pull of gravity that is intensified during hypergravity, while remaining absent during microgravity.

A Visual Zero-G Experience

PAUL MEUSER, YANG TIAN

This project was an attempt at a camera-mapping apparatus, freely rotating in a zero-G environment. The idea is to blur our embedded concept of up-down and document a subject's relationship to its background through 2D video as a medium. The performance device creates a new third space that sits in between the object and background. The interaction between the rotating object and the rotating environment would form this third space.

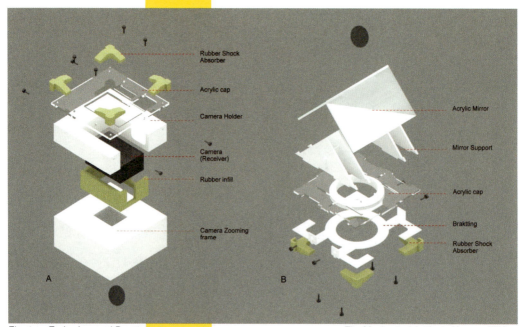

Space-Time-Form

Masking Estrangement
CHARIS ARMSTRONG

Masking has presented us with new considerations on the topic of making. From one perspective, we create deeper connections to material and craftsmanship through the production of homemade and improvised face coverings. On another we are completely disconnected from the manufacturing and material source of the commercially produced mask. Inspired by the writings of Anni Albers, this object is presented as an exercise in the close consideration of a relationship between material and manufacture.

Back To The Basics
BOBBY KA MING CHUN

Typography has been an inalienable part of textual communication ever since humans started writing. Using Wassily Kandinsky's basic color theory as a basis, this exploration seeks to deconstruct and understand type in its fundamental geometry and color. The alphabet is reduced to its strangely familiar shapes to force the reader to slow down and rethink the basics of type that are often overlooked.

Structures II

Pasta Bridge

NOAH SANNES

After constructing the bridge, it was clear that the initial failure occurred at the diagonal end member on the left side of the bridge. The member was bowing and bending substantially prior to failure, snapping at the midpoint. The failure did not occur at a joint. Alas, the relative strength of the bridge could have been increased by reinforcing or thickening the diagonal end members of the bridge. Instead of using single-strand members, pieces of pasta could have been bundled and glued together to increase the bridge's strength. The overall height of the bridge could have been changed from 5" to 6" to increase the strength as well. It's worth noting however, that each of these revisions would increase the weight of the bridge. Such is life.

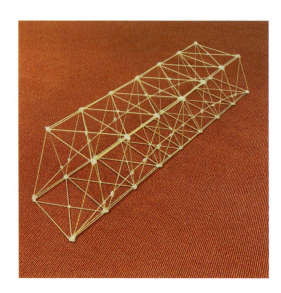

Pasta Bridge

ETHAN CHIANG

The model tests the vertical compression and diagonal tension of a tapered pratt truss. Several design considerations improved the overall performance of the bridge, including strengthening the top and bottom chords of the truss, adapting material thickness in relation to tension/compression members, maintaining a deep cross section proportion, using X-bracing for lateral stiffness, and tapering the profile of the bridge.

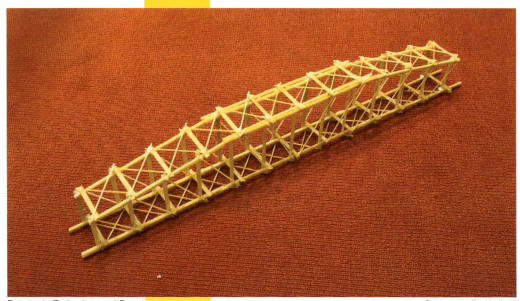

Structures I

Polarity
GRANT DOKKEN

A pavilion with two faces: neither being the normative condition, but both of equal importance to the project's persona. Beneath the pavilion's roof is a series of vertical panels arrayed across five parabolic arcs. On one side of each panel is a portion of John Fery's Iceberg Lake mapped to the surface, while on the other, a portion of a photograph by Vladimir Milivojevich. As each arc travels from the exterior inward, and back out again, the panels slowly turn and reveal a new face.

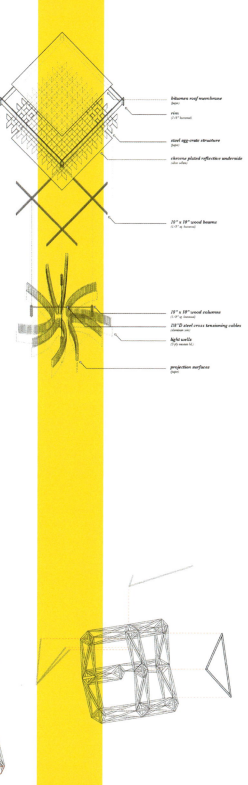

A Room For A Lighthouse Keeper
HARRY HOOPER

Select images are mapped onto a fractal geometry to create a tilted ground plane that blends into the wall, plays between real and false shadows, rises through steps that lead to nothing and nowhere the list goes on. However, any departure from Vitruvian principles which once governed architectural design must still abide by structural logic. This assignment takes a speculative project and reevaluates it through principles of load, stress, tensile, and compressive forces.

Graphic Inquiry

LUKE BULMAN

This seminar explores how architects might use a wider array of communication processes— from text to image, from moving image to network and beyond—to describe, develop, and release their ideas strategically. The inquiry includes, but goes beyond, graphic tools to explore alternate models of knowledge creation. This seminar is structured in three parts, each one looking at a different communication medium and its effects: moving image, printed pamphlet, and a single surface/function web graphic. Each of these media implies different ideas of duration, attention, audience, and distribution and is explored through a series of activities: illustrated talks, readings, precedent studies, and three projects developed by each student. [1243B]

DESIGN AND VISUALIZATION

Architectural Writing and Journalism

AJ ARTEMEL

This seminar is based on three major areas in the practice of writing: voice, craft, and platform. Students learn from examples of some of the architecture profession's most common forms of written communication including the personal statement, project statement, press release, article, and essay. Rather than delving into the history of architectural journalism and criticism, this course seeks inspiration in recent and contemporary writings from adjacent cultural fields. [2207B]

TECHNOLOGY AND PRACTICE

Technology and Design of Tall Buildings

KYOUNG SUN MOON

This course provides an introduction to the analysis and design of building structural systems and the evolution and impact of these systems on architectural form. Students learn about structural classification, fundamental principles of mechanics, computational methods, and the behavior and case studies of truss, cable, arch, and simple framework systems. Applications of structural theory to the design of wood and steel systems is taught through a series of laboratory and computational exercises and design projects. [2211A]

TECHNOLOGY AND PRACTICE

Composition and Form

PETER DE BRETTEVILLE

This seminar addresses issues of architectural composition and form in four, three-week exercises titled Form, Partis, Structure and Section, and Elevation. Leaving aside demands of program and site in order to concentrate on formal relationships at multiple scales, these exercises are intended to develop strategies by which words, briefs, written descriptions, or requirements can be translated into three dimensions. The medium is both physical and 3-D digital models. Multiple iterations emerging from the first week sketches and finalized in the following week are the basis for the generation of multiple, radically differing strategies, each with its own unique possibilities and consequences. [1233A]

DESIGN AND VISUALIZATION

The Mechanical Eye

DANA KARWAS

Despite the displacement of direct human observation, mechanical eyes present in remote sensing, LiDAR scanning, trail-cams, metagenomic sequencing, urban informatics, and hyperspectral imaging have become fundamental to spatial analysis. Mechanical eyes give us unprecedented access to nonhuman views into known and unknown environments. In this seminar, students investigate the impact of the mechanical eye on cultural and aesthetic inquiry; they conceptually consider their role as interpreter for the machine, and create a series of site analysis experiments across a range of mediums. [2222A]

TECHNOLOGY AND PRACTICE

Color in Architecture

SARA CAPLES

This seminar has several objectives. One is to offer each student greater mastery over the creation/selection/juxtaposition of color, allowing the creator to experiment more knowingly and intentionally. Another is to examine a broad range of examples of color in architecture, cutting across time and cultural histories to examine its sensory and cultural impacts. Students will be required to explore color through readings in color theory, a series of paint and paper exercises, and an existing example of color in architecture for class presentation and written paper. [1245B]

DESIGN AND VISUALIZATION

Ruins and Ruination

MARK FOSTER GAGE

Acts against architecture can oftentimes be far more impactful than the creation of the buildings themselves. And yet architecture is rarely discussed in these terms—as a framework of human reality that itself can be damaged or destroyed, thereby producing significant psychological effects on individuals, communities, and nations. Rarely do we consider the buildings that we propose as architects or those that surround us as citizens through decay, destruction, or their end-of-life, or afterlife. This is a course about such ruination in physical terms, but also philosophical ones that will help us determine new relationships between architecture, meaning, cultural value and the act of building. [1228B]

DESIGN AND VISUALIZATION

Building Disasters

JOHN D. JACOBSON

This seminar explores accidents, failures, and catastrophes, large and small, in buildings and—whether caused by bad luck, bad design, bad management, or miscalculation—how such incidents have impacted users, owners, and designers. [2241B]

TECHNOLOGY AND PRACTICE

Structures I

KYOUNG SUN MOON

This course provides an introduction to the analysis and design of building structural systems and the evolution and impact of these systems on architectural form. Students learn about structural classification, fundamental principles of mechanics, computational methods, and the behavior and case studies of truss, cable, arch, and simple framework systems. Applications of structural theory to the design of wood and steel systems is taught through a series of laboratory and computational exercises and design projects. [2011A]

TECHNOLOGY AND PRACTICE (REQUIRED)

Structures II

ERLEEN HATFIELD

This course is a continuation of introductory analysis and design of building structural systems. The course introduces materials and design methods of timber, steel, and reinforced concrete. Structural behavior, ductility concepts, movement, and failure modes are emphasized. Geometric properties of structural shapes, resistances to stresses, serviceability, column analysis, stability, seismic, wind load, and lateral force resisting systems are presented. [2012B]

TECHNOLOGY AND PRACTICE (REQUIRED)

Space-Time-Form

EEVA-LIISA PELKONEN

This seminar aims to develop a particular type of disciplinary knowledge by crossing experience and action with historical and theoretical engagement. The class foregrounds reciprocity of practice and context, an invaluable tool for understanding the origin of ideas. Each class is organized around a single concept (form, structure, space, time); technique (drawing, material, color); or media (typography, photography, weaving). Sessions require both a visual/material exercise and close reading of seminal texts. [1289A]

DESIGN AND VISUALIZATION (REQUIRED)

The Mechanical Artifact: Ultra Space

DANA KARWAS, ARIEL EKBLAW

This course is designed to engage students with our unfolding sci-fi space future. Students design, build, test, and deploy a space artifact of their own. The final object was included in a project slot on a parabolic research flight, and one student from the course will be selected as a flier on the zero-G flight. The final project serves as a mechanism, device, lesson, story, or experience for creatively designing for the zero-G environment. [2238B]

TECHNOLOGY AND PRACTICE

Drawing Projects

TURNER BROOKS

In this course, each student prepares a particular subject that is investigated through the media of drawing for the entire term. Drawing sessions are accompanied by weekly evening pin-ups with group discussion of the work in progress. [1227B]

DESIGN AND VISUALIZATION

Design Computation

MICHAEL SZIVOS

Just as geometry is fundamental to drawing, computation affords a fundamental understanding of how data works, which is essential to advance the development of BIM, performative design, and other emerging methodologies. This seminar introduces design computation as a means to enable architects to operate exempt from limitations of generalized commercial software; to devise problem-specific tools, techniques, and workflows; to control the growing complexities of contemporary architectural design; and to explore forms generated only by computation itself. [2226B]

TECHNOLOGY AND PRACTICE

Design and Visualization
Technology and Practice

XIS

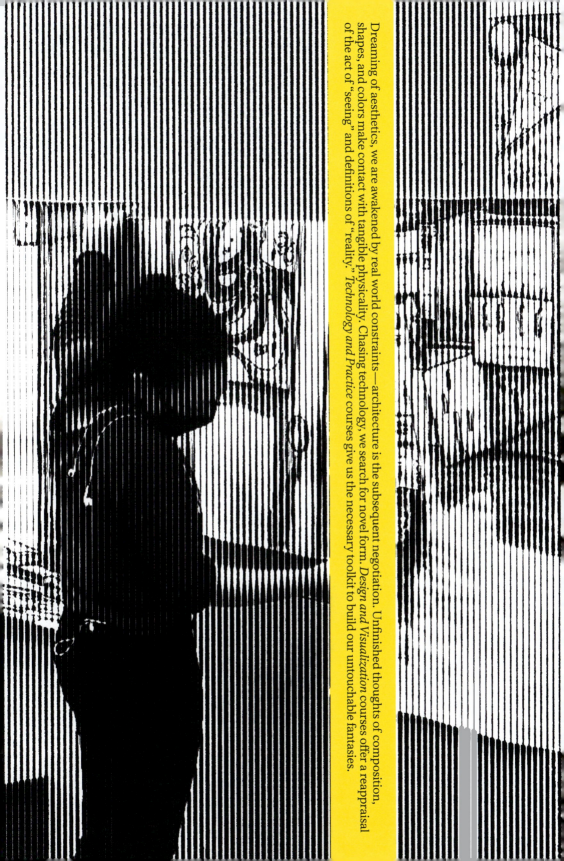

Dreaming of aesthetics, we are awakened by real world constraints—architecture is the subsequent negotiation. Unfinished thoughts of composition, shapes, and colors make contact with tangible physicality. Chasing technology, we search for novel form. *Design and Visualization* courses offer a reappraisal of the act of "seeing" and definitions of "reality." *Technology and Practice* courses give us the necessary toolkit to build our untouchable fantasies.

Christina Zhang

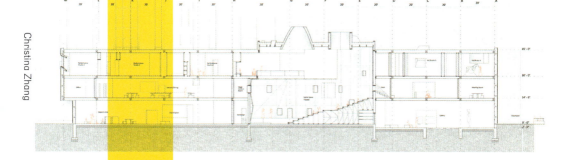

MEANDERING ME
Christina Chi Zhang

The development of this project follows two main points. The first point is about teenagers. Identity development during adolescence always takes on a meandering manner, as constant exposure to different types of stimulus shape development. Rather than subjecting teenagers to any defined path, the project offers resources and stimulus for them to meander through and find their own path. The second point addresses at-risk teenagers. On top of the generalized analysis of juvenile delinquency, homelessness, domestic violence, and teenage pregnancy, we must also recognize the unique voice of individual teenagers. This project consists of special moments generated through conversations with 71 teenagers from New Haven, and 112 teenagers on Reddit. Discussions focused on problems like safe space, independence, and comfort with expressing one's true identity. Hidden and personalized nooks exist in the thick walls between programmed spaces, tailored to the specific needs voiced by teenagers as they pursue independence.

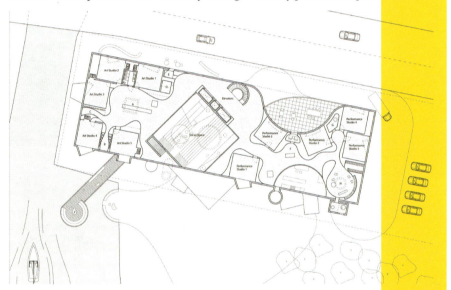

Christina Zhang

Paul Meuser

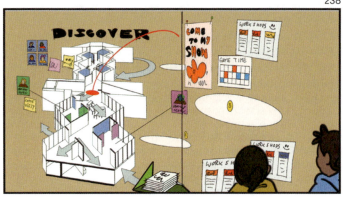

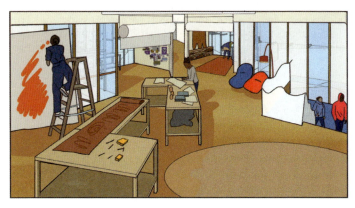

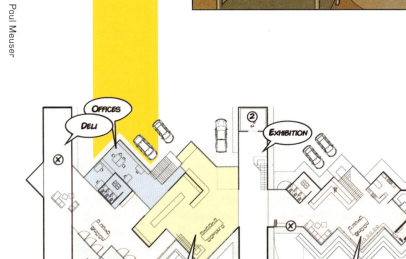

NXTHVN BALL ISLAND
Paul Meuser

The NXTHVN initiative revolves around art and youth; therefore, it was important to create an architecture that offers a relatable program while also fostering new unforeseen opportunities. This project provided an opportunity to design through an exploration of storytelling. A short story was used to develop both the program and the architecture. The final product is a mashup of sport, art, comic and architecture.

Lily Agutu

TERRA PRETA
Lillian Agutu

This project imagines a remediation of Ball Island, a site of industrial use since its inception and one that consequently suffers from highly toxic pollution that isn't constrained only to the island. Rain leaks the toxicity into the Mill River, which connects to the Quinnipiac and affects the ecosystems in between. Introducing mushrooms to the island and its interior spaces is a way to start remediation. The project negotiates the needs of the fungal and human inhabitants as they navigate and claim the same space. While the exterior grounds provide a hidden network of underground roots constantly at work, the interior spaces will be ever-changing, with walls and corners that host and cultivate mushrooms.

Lily Agutu

RUINS AROUND US
AND FUTURES YET
Sean Ming Jue Yang

The project explores the urban economic revitalization project that begins before architecture. The project's approach to regional sustainability is founded upon the "provision for all of an adequate livelihood base." Two-thirds of New London's population currently lives paycheck to paycheck. In order to raise the capital and expertise necessary to spur new economic development in the region, the project recommends the consolidation of disparate community development corporations across New London, Groton, and Fishers Island into a single Joint Organizational Enterprise (JOE). The new JOE will be responsible for purchasing and renovating vacant buildings scattered throughout downtown New London. The visible change agent will be a new urban corridor connecting the city with its waterfront. Along this corridor lies opportunities for an addition to the existing Customs House Museum, a new Maritime Research Center, as well as the introduction of a series of new public realms to service the Greater Thames River Region.

Sean Ming Jue Yang

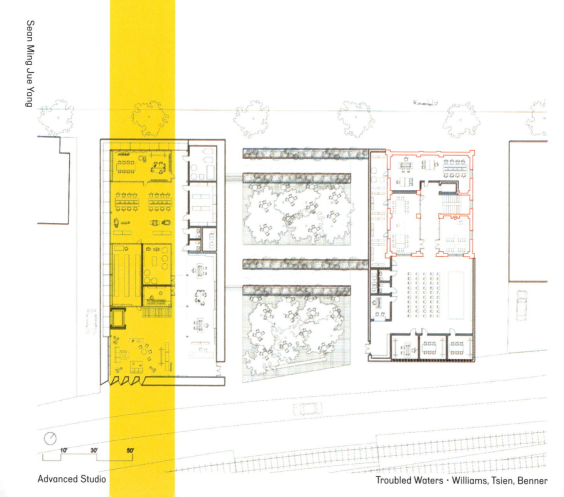

10'   30'   50'

Marlon Blackwell It's all architecture in a way because if you can do it with one planter, instead of five or six planters, you are already a hit. The idea is the space, and I think that is what we are all after. Get the space, so it can be really optimized for what the life of the city can provide for, and the future.

Sean Ming Jue Yang

Troubled Waters · Williams, Tsien, Benner

BETWEEN TIDE AND SOIL:
A NEW INTERFACE
Liang Hu

New London's existing industrial waterfront, once a maritime icon of the region, is now out of date. The concrete piers became impenetrable barriers to support a much-needed robust interface between land and water. The project focuses on defining its new identity by reshaping it into an eco-friendly, storm-resilient park and transforming the existing Customs pier—the formal keystone of maritime New London—into an aquatic museum that addresses both its industrial past and sustainable future. The museum quietly sits among the proposed landscape, illustrating a new interface between land and water, human and nature.

Liang Hu

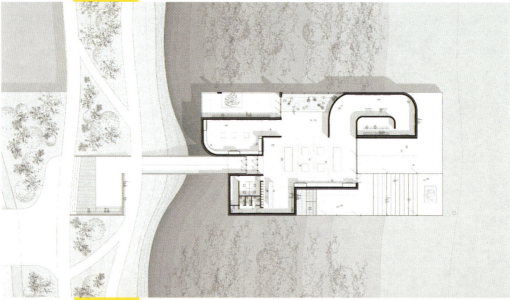

Dana Tang You hit on a fundamental problem of our city planning. The idea that you will convert this to an occupiable park that would solve the flooding issues, create more habitat, and bring more people down to the water is fantastic.

Liang Hu

Troubled Waters · Williams, Tsien, Benner   Advanced Studio

Liang Hu

ove these sectional ideas
e, the roofs, the apertures,
that have the steps that bring
ttery. It is much bigger than
a lot of engagements with the
in a very interesting way.

THE SEA LAB
Araceli Lopez

The Sea Lab is a building that incorporates the earth and landscape to celebrate the past, land, and ecology of Fishers Island. It is meant to connect to both its natural and man-made landscapes. The building is an elongated embedded structure that bridges between the Island's natural landscape and its forgotten and stoic military ruins. This project replaces the current waste management facility that has neglected Fishers Island's past. The building therefore hopes to revive and revisit this part of the Island's history and land. The program combines an open hatchery with public education and meeting spaces. This diverse programming tackles the Island's concerns of declining employment and population by providing revenue generation that builds on the existing economy of oyster farming. The building therefore celebrates an important ecological characteristic particular to the island while anchoring an institution that fosters environmental awareness and a stronger community.

Araceli Lopez · Feldman Prize

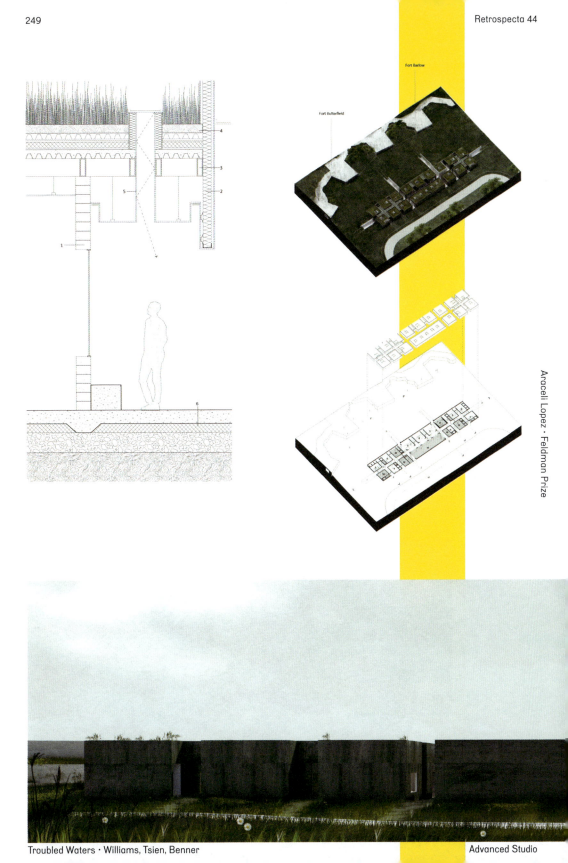

Araceli Lopez · Feldman Prize

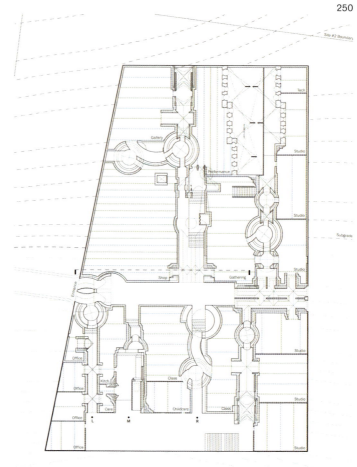

Janelle Schmidt

ARTIST RESIDENCY
Janelle Schmidt

This project's principles emerge from site observation and Leon Krier's Drawing for Architecture. Krier illustrates the ideal city as a neutral box with a collection of monuments that poke out and pathways that carve. Situated on a site where hidden walking paths are necessarily forged through thick vegetation, this building's hallways similarly carve interior spaces and moments that are largely illegible to the exterior view. The programmed spaces act as the neutral fabric with their borders shaped by paths, and classical forms aid in objectifying the circulation; domes and arches are scaled to that of a human, allowing visitors to be hugged by monuments of hyper-architecture. In making destinations out of circulation and scaling giant details to a touchable size, the building coaxes artists to look for things in places they'd normally pass through and expect access to information historically out of reach.

Janelle Schmidt

Tianyue Wang

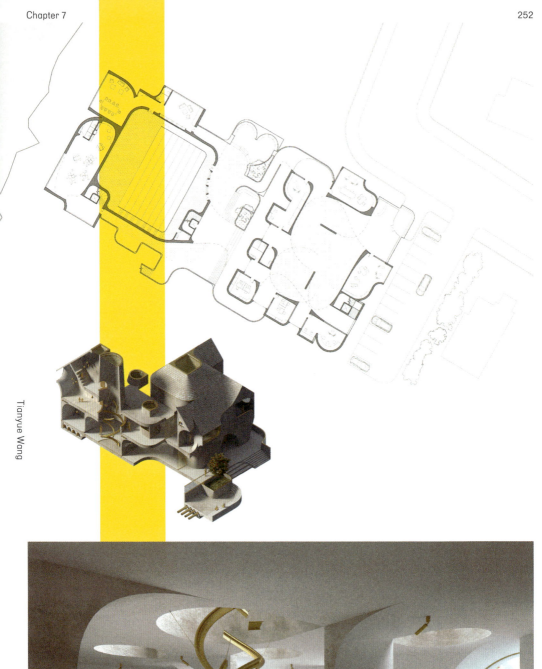

NXTHVN COMMUNITY ARTS CENTER
Tianyue Wang

The project explores the clean and precise fusion of geometries to try and create accurate and controlled organic forms. The project is designed to serve the community, and the building does this by granting visitors the feeling of familiarity. The familiar signals welcoming and access. Initially stripping the decoration and cladding off the adjacent residential houses, the design then plays with basic yet abstract domestic elements. Moments of deformation and fusion are applied sequentially onto these domestic elements. These different treatments can be discrete as well as integrated, depending on their programmatic relationships with one another.

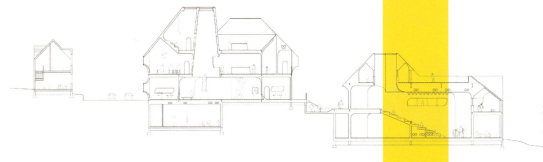

Tianyue Wang

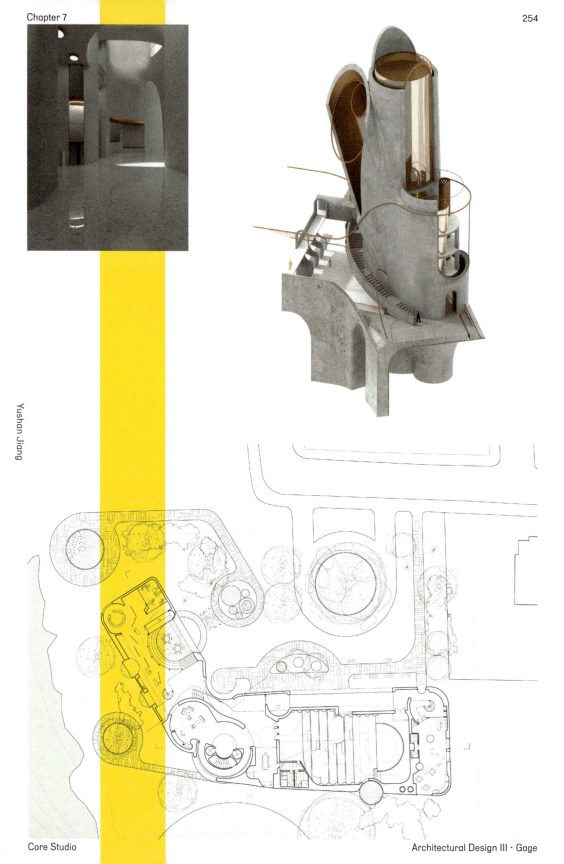

Yushan Jiang

DIVIDED UNITY
Yushan Jiang

This project addresses the transition between horizontal and vertical surfaces at multiple scales to showcase the different but cohesive identities of both. The towers become the symbol of the site and the pivot of the community. Here, artists are granted custom spaces: diverse studios with varying heights and shapes. Here, artists obtain a level of privacy that is not easy to achieve in a common art center. The artist chooses whether they are seen or unseen. Conversely, the public spaces lie humbly on the ground. The experience in the building becomes an adventure for visitors, as they circulate between the inside and the outside through unexpected transitions. This is a place where fluid transitions are built to not only link the artists and the visitors, but to link the vertical and the horizontal.

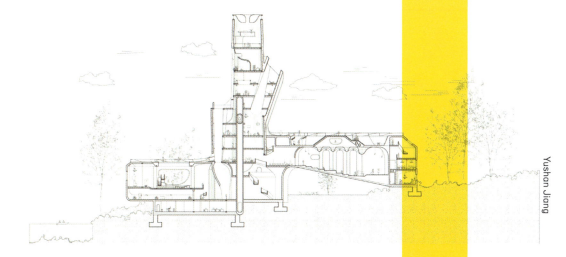

Yushan Jiang

PLAY & PLAY
Leyi Zhang

In this project, the theatre is composed of two parts: the "solid" containing all the theatrical functions, and the "void" around it that creates opportunities for other events. Lingering on the floating platforms, people gather and enjoy a drink while looking at downtown New Haven through the front facade. A restaurant sits on top of the theatre while a playground with a bouncy floor and climbing wall sit below, offering attractions for all generations. Inspired by the brick material dominant in the city and the arch element used in many adjacent buildings, the "solid" employs red brick columns and walls with perforations and openings. In contrast with the "solid," all elements in the "void" have a light and translucent appearance: the foyers, the playscape under the theatre, and the envelope. The design welcomes everyone by opening up the ground floor to the street and making the "void" space available to operate all day throughout the seasons.

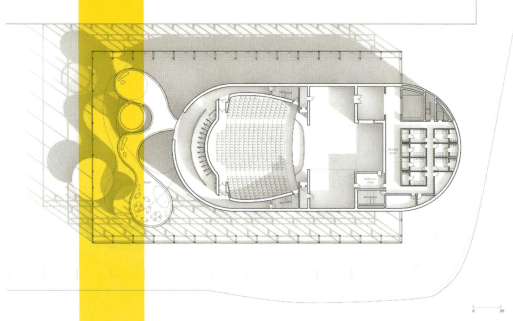

Ruth Palmon This project operates simultaneously.
At one point, it's a traditional theater with a very solid,
enclosed brick volume at its center. Yet it's also
embracing change by enclosing itself with a very big,
modern contemporary glass box. And in between
these two envelopes, new things are going to happen.
It creates a space that is open, even if the theater
is closed.

Leyi Zhang · Feldman Nominee

Intersectional Theater · Caples, Jefferson, Knight   Advanced Studio

THEATER OF INTIMACY AND INDETERMINACY
Shuchen Dong

Shuchen Dong

To compete with the prevalence of movies and television, the modern theater is programmed around experience more so than content, in comparison to classical theaters within prosceniums. Following this direction, the design focuses on the two key concepts: intimacy and indeterminacy. To create a sense of place, rather than an object in the city, the building forms a courtyard that works as both a venue for city life and the core of the theater, ultimately functioning as a mediator that simplifies circulation and brings the auditoriums closer to the city. Around this courtyard, a long continuous ramp makes the building accessible and invites the public in. The building features sliding acoustic gates and operable curtain walls to accommodate both indoor and outdoor theaters and allow the building to be adaptable. When the courtyard is engaged as the center of the performing space, the panels can be lifted to accommodate various performances and public events.

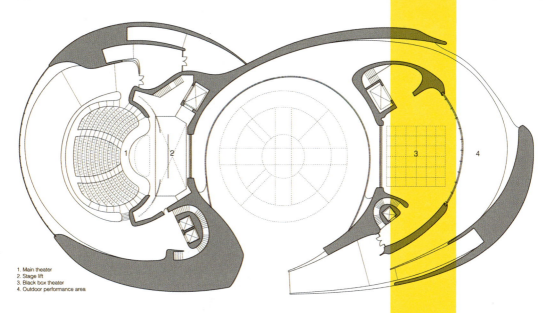

1. Main theater
2. Stage lift
3. Black box theater
4. Outdoor performance area

Ruth Palmon What you provide is a very dramatic monument, which in itself is beautiful. It is kind of free flowing, and there is sort of an interior space. It is very surprising. It is not like a traditional courtyard, it is sort of like you are sneaking into the building, but you are still outside.

Shuchen Dong

Intersectional Theater · Caples, Jefferson, Knight

Shuchen Dong

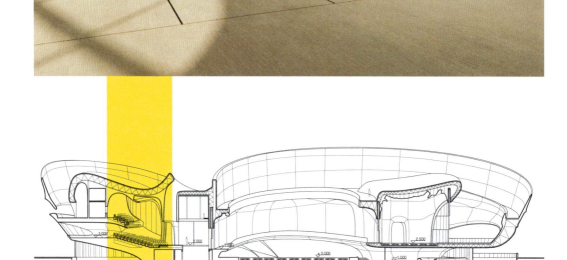

Pat Pinnell It is as though you were recovering that early twentieth century sense of glass as a kind of magical material. That just the simple employment of it was guaranteed to expose truth in things, and to show you things that you never thought about before just by dint of their visibility.

NEW HAVEN CUBE
Araceli Lopez

The theater floats above a sunken courtyard, monumentally anchoring itself as a new civic feature that acts as a cultural center for the city of New Haven. The theater itself has the ability to maintain a formal presence while maneuvering different activities and programming of the building and its site. The Cube also hopes to reclaim the nine-square grid by creating a public space that transforms urban features into performing elements. An internal routine of activity, acoustics, and visibility occur within the building throughout the day by both the audience and performers. The building therefore intends to have the act of people performing throughout the building promote the building itself to be a performative element. The roof's space-frame truss, along with the facade's fixed-point system, dramatize the interior space while a translucent glass facade allows for plays in shadow and light from the exterior.

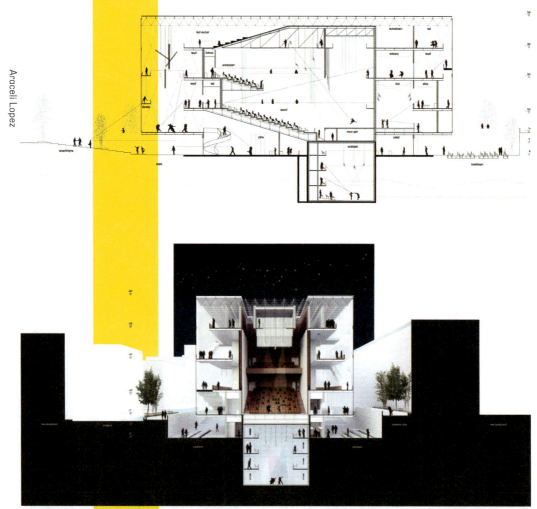

Araceli Lopez

Intersectional Theater · Caples, Jefferson, Knight   Advanced Studio

Joshua Tan

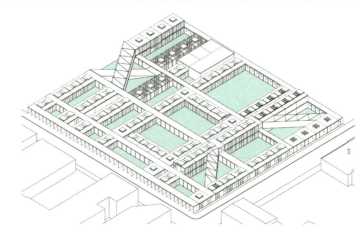

WHAT CAN BE COMMON
Joshua Tan

The project is imagined as a commons of production, representation, and reproduction. Referencing Hannah Arendt's The Human Condition, it proposes that work, action, and labor are all necessary in the construction of a commons. The proposal formally interprets the commoning principles of Elinor Ostrom. Architecture provides the basis for the social organization of commoning by highlighting formal boundaries, allocating space for expansion, creating a graduated organization, and emphasizing interconnectedness. Programs are contained within linear strips of volumetrically similar modules that change according to spatial, programmatic, and daylighting requirements. They are linked by horizontal passages that thereafter define courtyard spaces of various scales. The project is phased: beginning with essential art programs, followed by supportive and collaborative spaces, and ending with more costly fabrication and performative spaces. Concrete and timber are used diametrically, complementing one another and providing solid and permeable readings as one moves along and across the project.

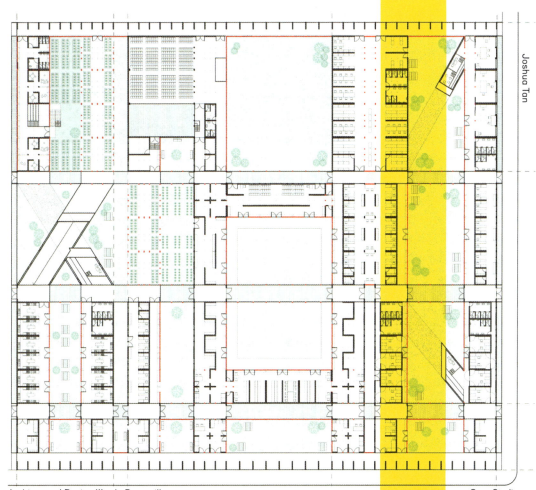

Joshua Tan

RIVER STREET SCHOOL
Adare Brown

Located on a filled site along the Quinnipiac River's flood-zone in the Mill River District, the project addresses the significant industrial waste remaining from the demolition of the Kilborn Factory in 2017. The site is not empty—although "degraded," it hosts a diverse ecology of insect and plant life easily rivaling nearby designated "critical habitats." The architecture wants to foster space for conversation: a long airy porch links classrooms, studios, shops, and an auditorium where ideas are played out. The tower wants to hold on to an ongoing history, hosting an archive of student work and a critique pit where work is tested. The program is lifted with respect to the floodplain and lively ground plane. Landscaping is lightly directed with a regrading of the river bank, the redistribution of young trees at the North corner, and the removal of remaining walls and fences.

Adare Brown

Architectural Design III · de Bretteville

Core Studio

Anjiang Xu

INTER-
Anjiang Xu

This project is a piece of conceptual canvas, where nature and its inhabitants work collaboratively to perform an artwork in the name of NXTHVN. A gradient terrain invites the natural elements to encroach by accumulating the land on the roadside and returning it to the river. It is interpolated with a rhythmic series of spaces, carved from earth or grown through the air. Through spatial respiration between the inside and outside, positivity and negativity is achieved through a three-dimensional grid in plan and in section. This provides inherent chances of interface between niches and stages, while preserving the flexibility for artists to make and keep the earthiness and airiness of their places. In terms of urban geography, the profile of this project engages in both the urban and environmental settings, as the materiality of substrate allows for vulnerability, recognizability, and adaptability to transient dynamics, indifferently representing the will in situ.

Anjiang Xu

DREAM OPERATOR /
TOGETHER TAKES PRACTICE
Sean Ming Jue Yang,
Leanne Nagata

This project has two linked goals: to de-commodify homeownership and provide more space to the practice of living collectively. An initial set of programmed spaces act as prompts on how to use unfamiliar collective space; self-governance, conflict mediation, cooperative agriculture, and shared maintenance shops are then learned from, manipulated, and replaced as desired. In the private units, generic, non-hierarchical rooms are meant to be altered by users. The smaller communities in-between share space and programs that can support dreams and act as resources to the city. In this housing project, one returns home to a group of people and a set of relationships, rather than an investment vehicle. Life may be more challenging, due to the negotiation of more intimate relationships, but it is our belief that this friction is what brings color and worthwhile, meaningful interactions into our lives, encouraging a sense of communal responsibility.

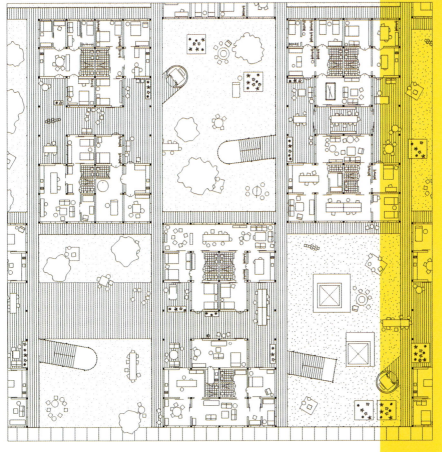

Sean Ming Jue Yang, Leanne Nagata

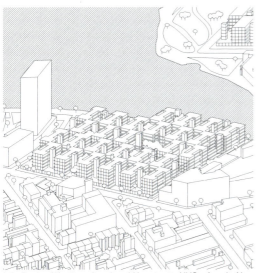

Elisa Iturbe I wonder if this can become a disturbance to our existing notion of urban fabric, where urban form is reliant on the first gesture being the laying down of the road... But what your project puts forward is an inversion of that, where these interstitial spaces are proposing a new kind of mobility from one space to another.

Sean Ming Jue Yang, Leanne Nagata

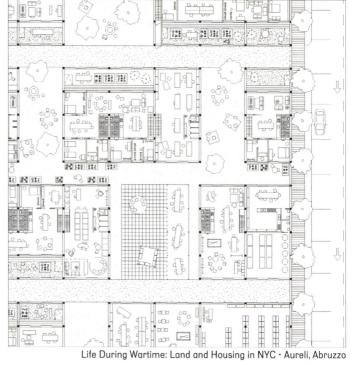

Angela Lufkin, Martin Carrillo Bueno · Feldman Nominees

Life During Wartime: Land and Housing in NYC · Aureli, Abruzzo

Advanced Studio

STAY UP LATE: REFRAMING THE LODGER IN COLLECTIVE HOUSING
Angela Lufkin,
Martin Carrillo Bueno

This project claims a series of parking lots across lower Manhattan as sites for an interconnected network of housing which offers an alternative to the hegemony of profit-driven developments that favor the nuclear family. A new dwelling paradigm is proposed, predicated on an assumption of diverse needs, including various lengths of stay. The new subject of this typology, the "lodger," is inspired by the temporary dwellers of historic tenement houses and residential hotels—bygone typologies that once offered a wide range of dwelling options based on housing infrastructure and the professionalization of domestic labor. This project invokes the diversity of these domestic arrangements as a means to translate the collective ownership of land into an inclusive and cooperative way of living.

Angela Lufkin, Martin Carrillo Bueno · Feldman Nominees

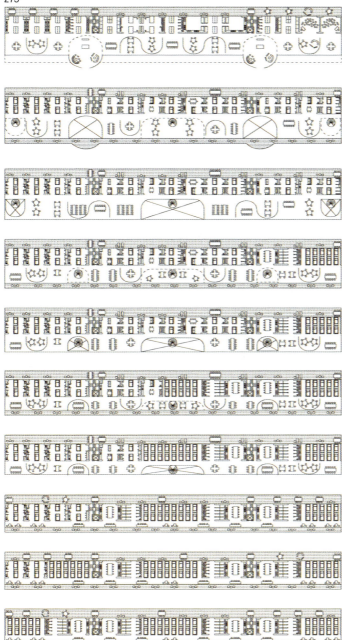

Angela Lufkin, Martin Carrillo Bueno · Feldman Nominees

Tatiana Bilbao   The appropriation of the facade, in the kind of differences in the curtains, signs, and these things, shows an appropriation that is more linked to the individual units. Whereas here, all that out in this facade, is the collective buried white space.

Sangji Han

DESIGN CIRCULAR: BUILD LESS, SHARE MORE, INVITE MORE
Sangji Han

Starting with a close observation of the program in two neighboring buildings—the public school and the library—the project reimagines the future of this site as an extension of existing programs. Based on the ethos of circular design, the project denies that architecture can consist as a singular object in a vacuum. Instead, it encourages the dynamic between the school and the library, inviting more community participation over the course of extended hours. Although it begins by latching onto existing programs, the project then offers a chance for expansion; a transition from existing to new. The project not only shares in terms of physical condition, but also at the scale of the life span of the building. This synergetic approach denies the singularity of the building in favor of dynamic functionality when connecting different parts of the site into a network.

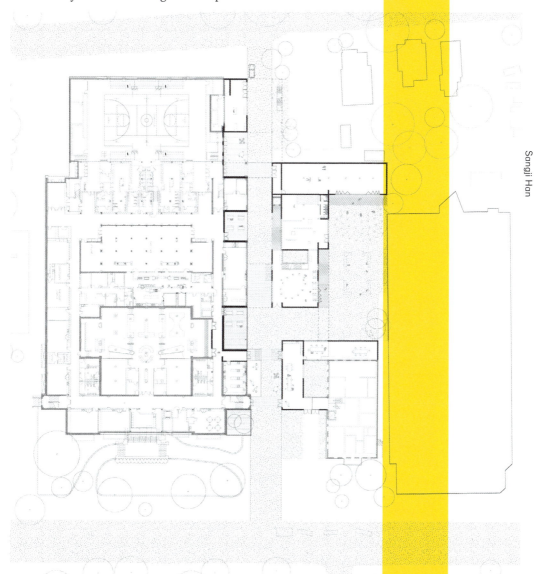

Sangji Han

Audrey Hughes

SCALE NEGOTIATION
THROUGH AGGREGATION
Audrey Hughes

This project builds upon existing community gardens and educational programs in Fair Haven through art studios organized around greenery and the textural qualities of light. A public space sprinkled with community gardens slides between volumes of arts space to connect commercial Grand Avenue to residential Exchange Street. Fluid circulation between the neighborhood and the K–8 school, public library, and new arts center encourages a sense of local ownership over the space. A central void through the arts building floods each level with sunlight and fosters visual interaction between disciplines. From open art studios to intimate study nooks, spaces are assembled sectionally to locate roof garden planters and double-height light wells, drawing in dappled light from the shadows of trees above. An undulating perforated aluminum wraps the crenelated massing, layering another texture of shadow over both the interior spaces and the exterior cladding.

Audrey Hughes

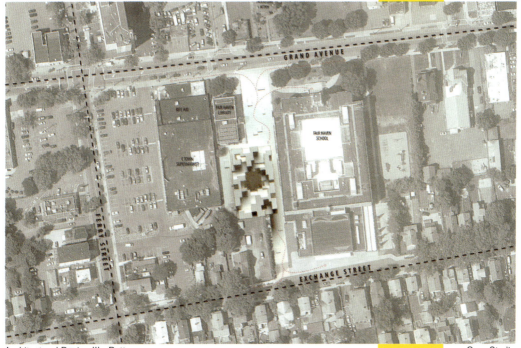

Gustav Nielsen

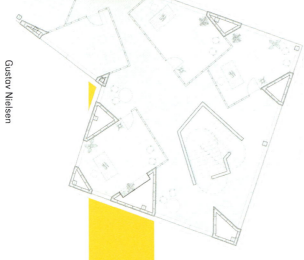

TOWARD AN ASSEMBLED SPACE
Gustav Nielsen

This project explores practices of assemblage in art and the possibility of an
assembled space through the design of a Youth Arts Center. Still suffering from the
effects of the 1930s redlining policies, Fairhaven has lost many of its communal
centers in recent years and become the battleground of violent crime activity. Its
social geography reveals the territorial discrepancies of land-use zoning, gang
territories and ethnic enclaves as an urban assemblage. This project explores the
subversive potential of the assemblage as a means to co-create, pool resources,
learn and re-establish community and citizenry. Here an assembled space becomes
an environment of multiples, a "space of spaces" loosely fit to direct the gaze
and the body in multiple directions at once; a space of simultaneity and synergy.
It is hyper-specific yet open-ended—it spills and coalesces into "cadavre exquis"
sculpted in the image of its community.

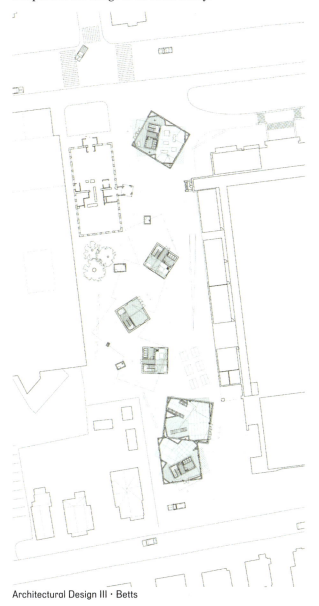

Gustav Nielsen

THE URBAN FOOD HUB
Stella Xu

The Urban Food Hub at Brooklyn Navy Yard introduces a new model of food production and retail; the project reflects the reality of e-commerce and post-covid urban food production, consumption, and research while supporting Brooklyn's employment needs by adding new industrial, service, and laboratory jobs. The result will be an experiential, publicly engaging, environmentally sustainable food hub and dietary research center for New York City, concentrating the cycle of food production on-site to include farming, manufacturing, processing, cooking, distribution, and retail. The design negotiates the opposite spatial qualities of the artificial vertical farming shafts towards Kent Ave (production & work) and the buildinglessness towards the Barge Basin (communal, leisure, landscape), testing the co-programming of urban farming space and urban workspace. From the most vertical—the 4-story vertical farm—to the most horizontal—the landscape and community gardens adjacent to the waterfront—the building slopes down to embrace the public life happening outside, while the interior programs connect back and forth to these two farming spaces.

Stella Xu · Feldman Nominee

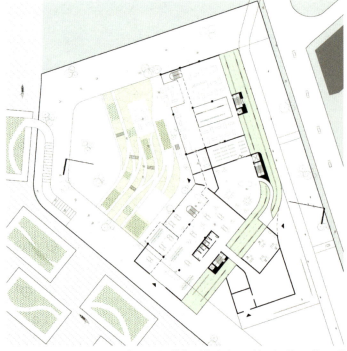

Andrei Harwell Through a smartly constructed program of growing, R&D, and manufacture, this concept was clearly articulated through the project design; an emphasis on entrepreneurial making gave it a relationship to the Brooklyn Navy Yard's mission, while also making it a hinge to the adjacent neighborhood and city.

Stella Xu · Feldman Nominee

Innovative Urban Workplace · Hamlin, Tang, Harwell

Advanced Studio

BROOKLYN NAVY YARD INNOVATION CENTRE
Hyun Jae Jung

Work-space design responds to many factors: rapidly changing technologies, the blockchain, and security and mobility. These spatial, cultural, technological, and systemic changes have and will continue to evolve post-COVID. Thus, the next generation of commercial developments must consider whether previous trends will continue to be in demand. Building upon in-depth research studies of two folds in parallel—the historical and global paradigm shift of workspaces and workstyles—the project considers context and process when redesigning and reimagining the definition of innovation in the workplace model. Will the new model of the urban workplace be composed of small linkages and cultivate interactions between ideas, investments, education, culture, and people? How can those in public and private sectors create spaces and cities that provoke ways to enhance and improve our work styles and spaces in the coming future?

Hyun Jae Jung

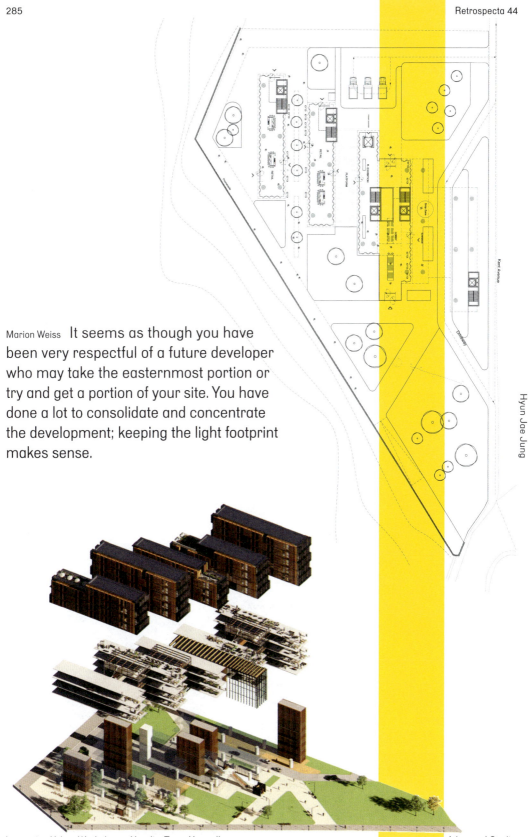

Marion Weiss It seems as though you have been very respectful of a future developer who may take the easternmost portion or try and get a portion of your site. You have done a lot to consolidate and concentrate the development; keeping the light footprint makes sense.

Hyun Jae Jung

BROOKLYN'S INNOVATION HUB
Niema Jafari

Kent Avenue's lack of resources for the immediate community was highlighted in the recent pandemic, exposing an inequity of access to parks and workspaces, particularly for the impoverished neighborhood. The project seeks to blur the boundaries between public and private space by creating an accessible landscape in the form of a communal makerspace, flexible tenant suites, and local business developments that will educate aspiring residents of Williamsburg to serve all sectors of society. The center will become a public interface and strengthen Brooklyn Navy Yard's position in connecting the yard to the public, offering resources and training as well as rentable suites to the immediate community and greater Williamsburg. The site is on the brink of the Brooklyn Navy Yard's master plan and provides an opportunity to engage with the community and connect visitors along the proposed Williamsburg esplanade.

David Ehrenberg So I think the push and pull here is the functionality of the upper floors, particularly as companies begin to scale up and need more space. That's when they start adding not only more jobs, but typically, the more accessible jobs... Finding that balance between design and function is something that is, for us, extraordinarily important.

Niema Jafari

Innovative Urban Workplace · Hamlin, Tang, Harwell   Advanced Studio

Jack Rusk

DIXWELL'S COMMUNITY THEATRE
Jack Rusk

The theatre is conceived as a site within which the neighborhood's social life encounters itself as art. The quiet exterior of the theater complex is counterposed to the messy life it frames. The building acts as an armature to support the performance and teaching of theater, while supporting the community's shared life. The interior spaces are connected through an active enfilade, freely shifting from AA meetings to improv classes, from sewing costumes to mending wedding dresses. "The Revolutionary Theater," writes Amiri Baraka in an essay of the same name, is not peopled with "weak Hamlets debating" but with "men and women digging out from under a thousand years of 'high art,'" whose performances "treat human life as if it is actually happening." Along Dixwell, the show has already begun.

Jack Rusk

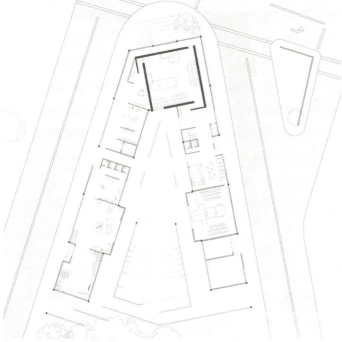

Caroline Kraska

NEXTUS
Caroline Kraska

This project presents itself as a mediation for an integrated community arts program; a place for the artist, guest, or member to feel inspired and in turn create inspiring work. Diagrammatically, the building is a series of enfilade walls running the direction of the main street, creating a linear momentum which is then punctuated and rippled by more tightly-programmed spaces. Zones of compatible elements are adjacent to optimize square footage, while interstitial spaces offer flexibility for blended activity. Service facilities are grouped to allow the central atrium to host a multitude of events. A reduction of enclosed rooms emphasizes the continuous ground plane, which is articulated through monolithic stone walls, concrete fins, and terrazzo floors. As an offset to this weight, the roof is expressed as a white cloud-scape of faceted ceiling planes, allowing for diffused sunlight to be folded in.

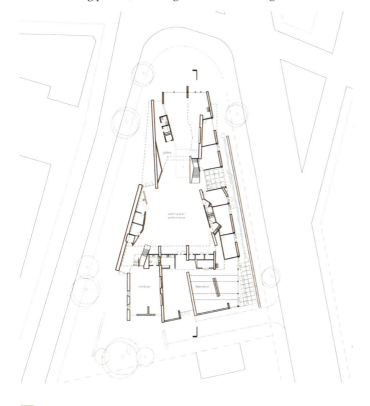

Caroline Kraska

Jessica Jie Zhou

THROUGH INTERSTICES
Jessica Jie Zhou

The project celebrates relationship-building on both individual and community scales; it gives agency back to local users and addresses the youth from the Dixwell neighborhood in New Haven who are disproportionately affected by a lack of educational resources. This youth center explores the potential of interstitial spaces, and how they might encourage spontaneous collaboration. The project investigates the idea of a "productive liminal" through the undulation, entanglement, and thickening across and between elements. From the oscillating roof planes to the studio spaces, the project provides articulations of interstices that address different scales, group sizes, and degrees of openness. The experience is designed around the act of approaching without overlapping. By leaving spaces indeterminate, simply travelling from A to B becomes engaging and accommodating.

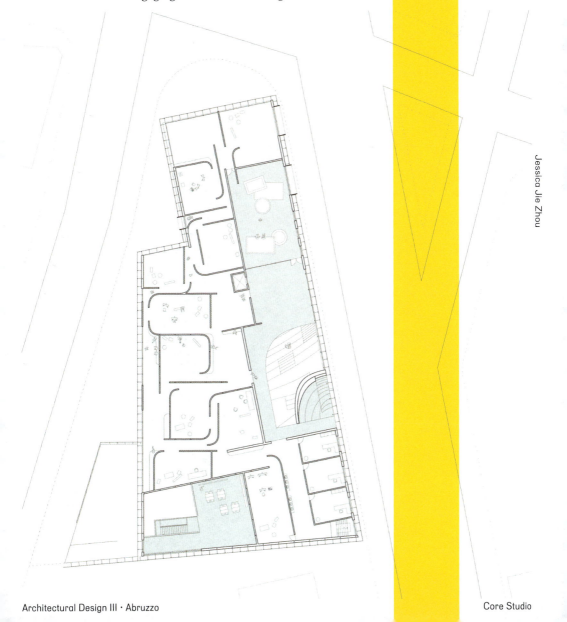

Jessica Jie Zhou

TROUBLED WATERS

Our studio will explore the spatial and programmatic dimensions of striking a new balance and compact for cohabitation with the oysters. A key model for us is the Billion Oyster Project, which is restoring oyster reefs in the New York Harbor. Their goal is to reestablish a sustainable oyster presence and habitat, along with protection from the storm surges that come with it. The Billion Oyster Project is an outgrowth of an aquaculture program at the Harbor School on Governor's Island. The project was founded by Murray Fisher and Pete Malinowski. The Malinowski family has been cultivating oysters on Fishers Island, at the other end of the Sound, for over forty years. Our project will build upon their work, focusing on the oyster's capacity to provide abundant and healthy food along with opportunities for work and education. [1107A]

FACULTY — Tod Williams, Billie Tsien, Andrew Benner

STUDENTS — Ruchi Dattani, Jiachen Deng, *Liang Hu*, Hiuki Lam, Ingrid Liu, *Araceli Lopez*, Sydney Maubert, Sarah Weiss, *Sean Ming Jue Yang*

JURY — Marlon Blackwell, Mary Burnham, Andrew Freear, Jonathan Jackson, Walter Hood, Janet Marie Smith, Beka Sturges, Dana Tang

INTERSECTIONAL THEATER

As this virus hiatus makes us seek more ways to experience "live" contacts, it's a good time to reconsider a building for performance. What are the boundaries and bonds between performers and audience, both in-person and virtual? Should a theatre provide a "fixed" environment or a more flexible one, opening up possibilities for blurring boundaries between physical and virtual presence, between indoor and outdoor performance, between seated and moving audiences, between fixed and movable performance elements? How does the theatre engage and impact its urban environment, offering access at both neighborhood and regional levels? How can the building and its exterior performance areas continuously contribute to the civic experience of park or other public outdoor space, cultural information, and public engagement? And what physical components of the building can extend that experience? And how might all these layers conspire to attract a broad range of cultural engagements, signaling access to people of many backgrounds and incomes and ages. [1118B]

FACULTY   Sara Caples, Everardo Jefferson, George Knight

STUDENTS   Christopher Cambio, *Shuchen Dong*, Lillian Hao, April Liu, *Araceli Lopez*, Alex Olivier, Steven Sculco, Yuyi Shen, Qizhen Tang, *Leyi Zhang*

JURY   Sandra Barclay, Vladimir Belogovsky, Joan Channick, Xiahong Hua, Ruth Palmon, Pat Pinnell, Jonathan F.P. Rose

LIFE DURING WARTIME: LAND AND HOUSING IN NYC

We tend to associate the idea of "home" with "domesticity." Yet the "domestic" is a specific mode of housing that is very different from the way many cultures around have produced their home. "Domestic" addresses a space of inhabitation organized around a vector of command embodied by the household's property. Within the history of domestic space, from antiquity to the present household, property was centered on the paterfamilias, the landlord, the homeowner and, more recently, on the real estate of the rarefied yet extremely powerful rule of hedge funds. Within the evolution of domestic space, architecture has played a fundamental role in both representing and naturalizing domesticity and property as something "normal" and thus "acceptable" as the only way in which people can live within society. This studio asks students to rethink the idea of the house beyond domestic space and the concept of private property. This entails rethinking not just the architecture and politics of the house, but also the latter's relationship to land tenure as the fundamental precondition for inhabitation. [1114B]

FACULTY	Pier Vittorio Aureli, Emily Abruzzo
STUDENTS	*Martin Carrillo Bueno*, Jiachen Deng, Stav Dror, Gordon Jiang, Hiuki Lam, Dreama Simeng Lin, *Angela Lufkin*, *Leanne Nagata*, Serge Saab, Stella Xu, Jiaxing Yan, *Sean Ming Jue Yang*
JURY	Neeraj Bhatia, Tatiana Bilbao, Michael Robinson Cohen, Maria Sheherazade Giudici, Elisa Iturbe, Marc Norman

INNOVATIVE URBAN WORKPLACE

Even before COVID-19 upended the national economy and shifted our work and travel patterns, significant forces of change were influencing four dimensions of urban work: the work itself, who does the work, the location of work, and the design of workspaces. Traditional manufacturing that once provided jobs in cities like New York has relocated to suburban and exurban settings, and offshore, or been eliminated through automation. Small scale urban manufacturers remain, and innovative industrial and office uses in the "TAMI" sectors (technology, advertising, media, and information), as well as biotechnology, healthcare, arts, and cultural creation, hold significant promise for the future of urban economies, like New York's. This shift in the profile of urban business has had a profound impact on individuals as well as cities. New York currently faces a large and growing disparity in economic opportunity for different segments of its population. Fueled by the booming technology sector, college-educated, professionally-trained individuals are thriving here, while many immigrants and those who lack college degrees, especially individuals of color, struggle to get by with more limited educational and economic opportunities. [1103A]

FACULTY Abby Hamlin, Dana Tang, Andrei Harwell

STUDENTS Ives Brown, Xuefeng Du, Kevin Gao, *Niema Jafari*, *Hyun Jae Jung*, Dreama Simeng Lin, *Stella Xu*, Yong Joon Yun, Yuhan Zhang

JURY Anna Dyson, David Ehrenberg, Richard Gluckman, Johanna Greenbaum, Shani Leibowitz, Nina Rappaport, Michael Samuelian, Marion Weiss, Claire Weisz, Tod Williams

ARCHITECTURAL DESIGN III

The third core studio asks students to develop their comprehensive design skills by defining a civic building. By focusing on a program relevant to the New Haven area, the class offers a larger look into who (and what) forms our communities, and how architects may work to serve their neighbors. The program is an arts facility for an educational, mentor-based, diversionary art program for New Haven youth. The course looked at New Haven's NXTHVN, "a new national arts model that empowers emerging artists and curators of color through education and access," as an architectural precedent and model. Each critic defined the site for their group's projects, setting up unique responses from studio to studio, as well as between the individual students. [1012B]

FACULTY

STUDENTS

Emily Abruzzo, Coordinator

Claudia Carle, Sarah Kim, Zhanna Kitbalyan, *Caroline Kraska*, Zishi Li, Abraham Mora-Valle, Dominiq Oti, *Jack Rusk*, Levi Shaw-Faber, Rachael Tsai, *Jessica Jie Zhou*

Stella Betts

Lauren Carmona, *Sangji Han*, Claire Hicks, *Audrey Hughes*, Jessica Kim, *Gustav Nielsen*, Brian Orser, Jun Shi, Kevin Steffes, Hao Xu, Tian Xu, Iris You

Peter de Bretteville

Adare Brown, Audrey Tseng Fischer, Chocho Hu, Calvin Liang, Meghna Mudaliar, Yikai Qiao, Jingyuan Qiu, Diana Smiljković, *Joshua Tan*, Yang Tian, Timothy Wong, *Anjiang Xu*

Mark Foster Gage

Brandon Brooks, *Yushan Jiang*, Morgan Anna Kerber, Perihan MacDonald, Hannah Mayer Baydoun, Veronica Nicholson, Michelle Qu, Taku Samejima, *Janelle Schmidt*, Andrew Spiller, *Tianyue Wang*, Alex Mingda Zhang

Bika Rebek

Lillian Agutu, Katie Colford, Lindsay Duddy, Sam Golini, *Jingfei He*, Suhyun Jang, *Paul Meuser*, Abby Sandler, Wenzhu Shentu, Hao Tang, Calvin Yang Yue, *Christina Chi Zhang*

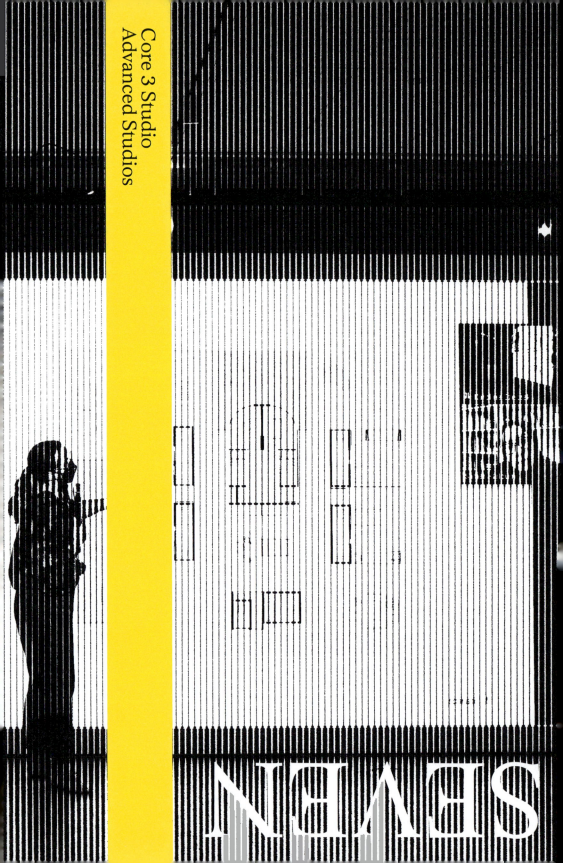

Core 3 Studio
Advanced Studios

SEVEN

Architecture undulates across public and private realms, constantly negotiating how we inhabit "real" or "imagined" space, be it civic or domestic. *Core 3 Studios* interrogate the familiarity of our immediate surroundings, generating a bank of communal knowledge for living; *Advanced Studios* dissect contextual binaries at a global scale, reinventing our language of cohabitation and syntax of development for greater resilience against instability.

Approaches to Contemporary Architectural Theory

HYBRIDSCAPES
ALAN ALANIZ

Whether we acknowledge it or not, we are all people of border. Borders permeate and influence nearly every aspect of our lived experience: they provide definition by demarcating the bounds of "us," they are sites of engagement where this and that side are both conceptualized and dissolved, and they activate our imaginations, materializing another world just beyond. Whether soft or hard, state or self imposed, real or imaginary, borders create architectures that are catalyzed by the tensions of fluidity, territoriality, and hybridity.

    This course seeks to analyze the form borders take throughout our contemporary contexts and understand the influence these material and immaterial boundaries place upon the built environment and our interpersonal relationships. Focusing on both the "outer" and "inner" border relations that define the United States, this seminar encourages an interdisciplinary perspective to deconstruct and eventually reconstruct the role borders play in American socio-political discourse and architecture at large. Sessions will be organized in thematic groupings of theory, cartography, migration, subjectivity, security, and resistance in order to provide both a far-reaching interpretation of border studies and multiple points of engagement with the goal of facilitating cross-disciplinary discussion. In this course, borders prompt questions: "What role does the built environment play in contexts of hybridity?" "How is architecture or its absence weaponized?" "How are borders performed?"

Whether soft or hard, state or self imposed, real or imaginary, borders create architectures that are catalyzed by the tensions of fluidity, territoriality, and hybridity.

BAM! Bodies, Affect, Materiality
M.C. OVERHOLT

Architecture, and our experience of architecture, is inextricably bound to categories of identity. Our gender, sexuality, race, ethnicity, and (dis)ability shape our affective relationship to space and the material world, and generate a multiplicity of partial perspectives regarding architecture and our inhabitation of the built environment. Yet architecture has long been a white, straight, cis-gendered profession that, beyond supporting individuals that fit squarely within those identity categories, naturalizes the white, straight, cis-gendered subject as a universal subject. From Vitruvius to Le Corbusier, architects have taken this universal subject as a unit of measure from which rooms, buildings, and cities have been imagined and created. The historical centrality of the universal subject has also informed centuries of philosophical hypotheses on how we, as humans, are to know, experience, inhabit, and interact with the world around us. In this course, students will think with cultural theorists, historians, architects, and artists working at the nexus of architectural, feminist, queer, and critical race theories to interrogate, deconstruct, and contest the role of the universal subject in shaping spatial discourse and practice. The course is divided into three thematic areas: Body, Affect, and Materiality. As we will see in the course, the boundaries between thematic areas (bodies, affect, materiality), theories (feminist, queer, critical race, architectural), and modes of production (theory, pedagogy, practice) are porous. BAM! is designed to be cross-listed between an Architecture department, Art History department, and a Women's, Gender & Sexuality Studies department. The intention of the course is to build interdisciplinary dialogue and to think broadly about the relationship between design, dwelling, and embodiment.

Architecture has long been a white, straight, cis-gendered profession that, beyond supporting individuals that fit squarely within those identity categories, naturalizes the white, straight, cis-gendered subject as a universal subject.

The City Before and After Tubewell

Lakes Revenge: Land Subsidence in Mexico City

CLAUDIA CARLE

Mexico City, supporting a population of over 20 million residents, faces a great water paradox—cyclical flooding and water shortages. In order to reveal patterns pertaining to Mexico City's contemporary water crisis, a layer analysis of eight 1-by-1-kilometer samples of land subsidence varying from "hot" to "cool" are examined. This collection of samples of various degrees of land subsidence comprise a patchwork ethnography, providing fragmentary glimpses into the cyclical crises of drought, flooding, and sinking in Mexico City.

POVERTY	POP. DENSITY	GEOLOGY	AVG. DAILY WATER CONSUMPTION	FLASH FLOODING FREQUENCY
LOW	8,000 - 16,999 sq/km	LAHAR + ASHES	> 600 L PER CAPITA	7 EVENTS PER YEAR

The Power of Steam

YANG TIAN

This project investigates two interrelated yet hidden economies in contemporary Indonesia. The goal is to trace marginal workers in a unique setting and understand how their livelihood entangles with local geology and policies. A landscape's spectacularism connotes not only its unique geomorphology but also its capacity for commodification and consumption, qualities dependent on geoheritage and geotourism.

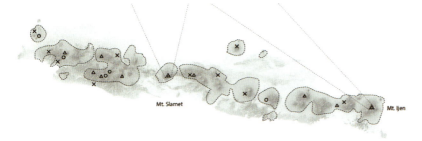

△ Volcanic Geothermal System
o Liquid-Vapour Dominated System
✕ Unspecified High-Temp System

Mt. Slamet

Mt. Ijen

Out of Date: Expired Patents and Unrealized Histories

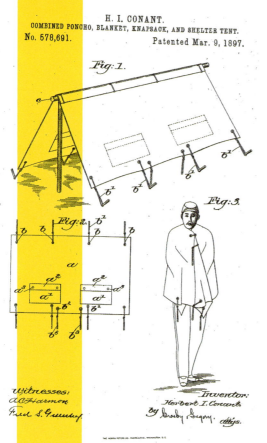

H. I. CONANT.
COMBINED PONCHO, BLANKET, KNAPSACK, AND SHELTER TENT.
No. 578,691.
Patented Mar. 9, 1897.

Fig: 1.

Fig: 2.

Fig: 3.

Witnesses:
A.C.Harmon
Fred S. Greenleaf

Inventor:
Herbert I. Conant.
By Crosby Gregory. Attys.

How We Shelter. Realities of Contemporary Placement and Security.

GUILLERMO ACOSTA NAVARRETE

This exhibition and accompanying publication narrates the counterfactual history of the inventions that could have potentially changed the way of living in a contemporary, nomadic, and fictional New America. It takes a look back at the different situational shelters that could be inhabited, not with a sentiment of retaliation, but with one of ever-preparedness, asking the questions: how is displacement shaping our virtual ties to one another? How can we critically address the effects of temporary receptacles?

The Vermin and Bug Shield

BEN THOMSON, MARTIN CARRILLO BUENO

The project traces the possible effects of the Vermin and Bug Shield on the timber industry as though it would compress the rings of the tree as it grew. This was tracked to a moment when the material capacity of timber was tested—the Howard Hughes flight of the Spruce Goose. The resulting forged history has the Spruce Goose breaking apart on its maiden voyage, tracing its failure back to weakened wood as a result of the Barry Brothers' invention.

Exhibitionism: Politics of Display

Wellness Fountains

SZE WAI JUSTIN KONG, IVY LI (UNDERGRAD), CRISTOBAL GARCIA (SCHOOL OF ART)

Addressing the challenge of hygiene for visitors of Corona Park and the Queens Museum, this project focuses on creating multipurpose water infrastructure stations that will provide for hand washing, drinking fountains, sprinkler systems, and drainage. The design taps into the existing fountain infrastructure in Flushing Corona Park. Part functional and part sculptural, the water stations will orchestrate movement of the body in relationship to water while also framing the surrounding park views.

Gateway: A Multi-Generational Maker's Space at the Queens Museum

NATALIE BROTON, MARTIN CARRILLO BUENO, ALEX OLIVIER, LEYI ZHANG

Given the end user and stakeholder feedback gathered, our team proposes the insertion of a building that will serve as an intergenerational maker's space meant to disrupt the predominance of the museum as an exclusive space for viewing art. Our proposal aims to be an inclusive space that supports the making and learning of art for the museum's community, understanding that the museum can be a space for people of all backgrounds, conditions, and ages to come together for community building.

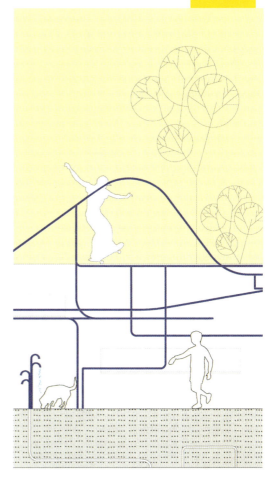

Topics in the History of Architecture Education

OBJECT LESSONS / OBJECTS OF DISPLAY / OBJECTS OF DESIRE: Model collecting at the Yale School of Architecture

LUKA PAJOVIC

The Yale School of Architecture occupies a special position among its peer institutions in the United States and further afield in that its architectural container is as well, if not better-known than the institution it houses. Designed by Paul Rudolph and built between 1961 and 1963, it stands as one of the world's most famous examples of Brutalist architecture, and indeed total design. The material presence and influence exuded by such a building on the institution housed within has already been remarked on, as has its conception as a pedagogical tool on an architectural scale. Essential to the latter, alongside the material and spatial lessons integral to its fabric, are the numerous objects permanently displayed in its halls. Perhaps the most famous among these are the plaster casts famously salvaged by Rudolph after their banishment from the University Gallery by Josef Albers. These monumental works were mounted on the building's bush-hammered walls, in a way that still defies ready classification despite several scholarly attempts.

However, there is another class of objects, of an even more complicated extraction and standing within the YSoA's material culture, namely, the collection of architectural models on display in its halls. Strewn across the building's eight levels, and concentrated in its most representative spaces in and around the main stair-tower, these objects bear all the hallmarks of a carefully designed and institutionally concerted display. It is the history and the evolving role of these objects the present paper seeks to examine, touching in the process on the pedagogies that inspired them, and problematizing their present position within the YSoA's wider material culture.

Shifting Pedagogy at Yale School of Architecture: from "Exclusive" to "Inclusive" (1951–1970)

STEVEN SCULCO

In the late 1960s, Yale School of Architecture shifted away from an emphasis on the master architect's total expression of power over society to a different kind of pedagogy: an eclectic, Pop-inspired approach under the direction of Charles Moore. Breaking out of Yale's 1950s period of repression, Moore's bold curricular changes—including the introduction of the First-Year Building Project in 1967, and the replacement of the master's thesis with instructor themed, advanced studios in 1968—served to rectify the school's emphasis on individual authorship, while enabling students to expand notions of a wider architectural language and occupation. Under Moore's direction from 1965 to 1970, Yale's architecture school came closer to achieving a sense of plurality somewhat reminiscent of George Howe's initial intent for Perspecta in 1952, as it finally broke with the singularity that actually was promoted by Howe, Henry-Russell Hitchcock, Paul Rudolph, and others throughout the 1950s and early 1960s. However, prominent Yale figures, including Charles Moore, Robert Venturi, and Denise Scott Brown, failed to confront immediate urban issues during the social unrest of the late 1960s, focusing instead on rural Appalachia, sprawling suburbs, and institutional polemics. As a result, the school remained unable to incorporate a truly diverse accumulation of "attitudes and experiences," and Moore's adventitious leadership would face criticism for allowing the school to "spin out of control." Nonetheless, Moore provided a more open learning environment at Yale that, at the very least, began to permit students the freedom to learn cultural frameworks outside of their own and discover a sense of collective agency within and beyond the sanctum of the design studio.

Topics in the History of Architecture since 1945

Giancarlo de Carlo: Architecture Dematerialised

LUKA PAJOVIC

When discussing the work of Giancarlo de Carlo (1919–2005), any mention of dematerializing tendencies risks negating the importance of his built oeuvre in favour of a familiar discussion of its social content and aspirations, often invoked under the heading of "Architecture of Participation." Not least among the reasons for this is the fact that the architect himself consistently prioritized "the critical potentialities of the social body" afforded by his designs (of which he did not consider himself the sole author), rarely dwelling on their material and technical aspects in his public lectures and extensive writings. As the ideator of the so-called "Architecture of Participation," as well as one of the most articulate and influential champions of the rights of non-architects in the design process during a period of increasing professionalisation, Giancarlo de Carlo left an extensive framework for the interpretation of his built work in terms that transcend, if not neutralize its material expression. What this paper seeks to do is to look at a selection of his designs, both built and unexecuted, and attempt to identify some of the ways in which de Carlo—a passionate designer and consummate engineer—transmogrified this anti-materialist understanding of architecture into often compelling physical artifacts.

In the process of doing so, the paper will focus on a selection of projects, mainly interventions in historic areas, executed over a period of almost four decades between 1968 and the architect's death in 2005. These include the celebrated Magistero, designed for the University of Urbino inside a former convent (1968–1976), Palazzo Battiferri in Urbino (1986–1999), a new power station for the Convento di San Nicolo in Catania (1986–1992), and finally, the unbuilt Lift Tower for Palazzo degli Anziani in Ancona (1998–2002). What unites them, in addition to their public character and situation in some of the most architecturally complex and, at the time, endangered historic environments, is a certain material sensibility, expressed primarily in the extensive and unconventional use of reflective glass.

However, the idiosyncratic details at play in these delicate interventions, largely overlooked in past studies of de Carlo's work, seem to find their fullest expression in a conceptual screen-project formulated at the very end of the architect's career, and published as a Domus article two days after his passing. In this article, de Carlo questions contemporary architecture's very right to visibility in the face of historic preservation, proposing a universal facade model which would dematerialise the insertion, screen from view all situations deemed incompatible with their context and reflect the surrounding panorama like a kaleidoscope. The striking detail is illustrated with a series of model photographs which show it to be not unlike the entropic curtain walls employed in the projects mentioned above, going back as far as 1968.

Taking these exercises in dematerialisation as a point of departure for our understanding of de Carlo's attitude to construction, this paper seeks to relate them to the architect's ideas on history, material production, and participation in the context of late twentieth-century Italy, as well as interrogate their critical potential within the historic environments they reflect.

History of British Landscape Architecture: 1600 to 1900

7 *Ways to Defend: British Military Landscapes*

NAOMI JEMIMA NG

Military landscapes have been an integral part in the historical development of landscapes in Britain since the Middle Ages, from initially serving a functional role to being appropriated for recreational purposes. This project presents a series of seven landscape elements, like a kit of parts, that are characteristic of British defensive landscapes. These include: the rampart, the covertway/ditch, the glacis, the angled bastion, the grid, the motte-and-bailey, and the hillfort/mound.

The Sequence of Castle Howard Garden

SHUCHEN DONG

This drawing is a collection of narrative sequences based on the gardens of Castle Howard, starting from the bottom left of the drawing and moving clockwise around the site plan. The principal entrance is on Lime Avenue, where Hawksmoor's "Medieval" Carmirre Gate, Vanbrugh's Roman Pyramid Gate, and the obelisk line up in order. The Temple stands at the head of a valley and has views to the Mausoleum and the bridge over the New River.

History of Landscape Architecture: Antiquity to 1700 in Western Europe

When Tillage Begins, Other Arts Follow

ELISE LIMON

The project interrogates the qualities of the Roman centuriation system—a grid-based method of land subdivision used to impose control and define limits of territory—and its relationship to Palladio's Villa Emo. The assimilation of agricultural elements with the ambition of the Venetian patrician class is embodied in the character of the two facades —the sober yet dignified front facade and the looser back facade.

The Edge of Forestscapes: 5 projects

NAOMI JEMIMA NG

Formal gardens like the Vaux-le-Vicomte distinguish themselves from the surrounding forest through the sharp edge of its clearing, separating "first nature" from "third nature" in a landscape. This project looks at the edge conditions of five vastly different forest landscapes, and explores how these edges promote certain ideologies of such landscapes: French formal garden's preference for the hard-edge; Halpin's gradual blurring edge into the naturalist forest; and the 9/11 memorial's democratic urban forest where trees arranged in a grid are accessible to all.

Introduction to Islamic Architecture

Islamic Architectural Influences in Sterling Memorial Library

MICHELLE TONG (UNDERGRAD)

Sterling Memorial Library serves as the focal point of Yale University. Upon a closer look at the building, often described as Collegiate Gothic, one can see influences of Islamic Architecture. This essay explores several of the Islamic Architectural elements that are appropriated by James Gamble Rogers in the design of Sterling Memorial Library, and the way it was used to help situate Yale as a renowned academic institution.

Upon closer inspection, many architectural details beyond collegiate gothic attribute to various cultures spanning both time and location. When viewing Sterling through the lens of Islamic Architectural influences, one can see the variety of elements tied to these origins: inscriptions, relief carvings, and structural components.

Appropriation of Geometric Pattern in Scroll and Key

MEHER HANS (UNDERGRAD)

The design of Scroll and Key, a building on Yale's campus, is one that appropriates heavily from Islamic Architecture. This essay explores the geometric patterns that Scroll and Key exhibits and compares them to those of the "originals" studied in class, such as the Dome of the Rock and the Great Mosque of Cordoba. An interesting pattern emerges from these comparisons: Scroll and Key patterns consistently invert traditional geometric pattern principles, effectively drawing the viewer's attention to the building's materiality and the unit level of each pattern.

If the purpose of grids and geometric patterns in Islamic architecture is manifold, from serving as manifestations of divine, empirical, or ideological worlds to reflections of "textile mentality", it is thus interesting to think about what the Scroll and Key simplified grid accomplishes, with its repeated unit or generator of pattern being undecorated and plain.

Lightness and Modernity: Architecture, Design, Energy

Amassing Lightness in the Japanese House

LEANNE NAGATA

Our current conception of "Japanese architecture" is just that, a conception. The dominating image, light and white, glossy and clean, outshines a layered history of oppositions, off shoots, alignments, and undercurrents. Through the private home, "lightness" is perceived actively, conscious or unconscious, to continually reconstruct our preconceived notion of Japanese architecture as minimal, as simple, rooted in Western modernism, seeded by Bruno Taut.

With a lack of familiarity, it is tempting to simplify constellations into points, points aligned or opposed to those you already know. There is much lost in this translation. As uncomfortable as it might be to feel unsure, unknowing, it could be the place you learn the most. To inquire while withholding an agenda feels difficult in a place where certainty and argument are prized, in a world that weaponizes knowledge as authority. I hope to offer my own unresolved first step in this inquiry as part of a movement towards working, learning, and interacting more vulnerably.

How to Define a Synagogue

SARAH WEISS

Jewish history is punctuated by cataclysms: destructive moments of displacement and re-orientation that often require rapid and profound adaptation. Informed by this tumultuous history, Jewish religious spaces have always been highly mutable. Such structures are subject to change, often through the appropriation of contextual influences. Unlike Christian space, which requires well defined components to facilitate elaborate processions and ceremonies, the demands of synagogues are simple and general: a Bima (a platform from which to lead the congregation) and an Ark (a place to store the Torah). In fact, descriptions of the synagogue do not appear until the New Testament, documented by Christians. Hence, throughout history the space constructed around these components has been subject to influence and context, its form indeterminate. It is the synagogue's mysterious and under-defined origins coupled with its relatively unsubstantial programmatic requirements that render it mercurial and absorptive—light in its lack of formal rigidity and stability—imbuing it with the agility required to endure periods of anti-semitism and instability.

Territorial Cities of Pre-Colonial America

Dynamic Model Observed in Ruins of Maya Region

TAKU SAMEJIMA

This project explores the spatial conception of Copan and Tikal ruins in the Maya region. These two cities were formed through a continuous fluctuation between both centralizing and de-centralizing force. They were identified as an adaptive urban tissue, consistently evolving, changing in formal structure through the dialectical conflict between these two forces. This idea of an "adaptive city" gives us a crucial perspective when criticizing our contemporary cities, which are far less ecological, and environmentally unsustainable. The series of drawing were developed to express such fluctuation in both cities, through an experimentation on the method of "Hieroglyphic Drawing," inspired by the knowledge system of these two cities.

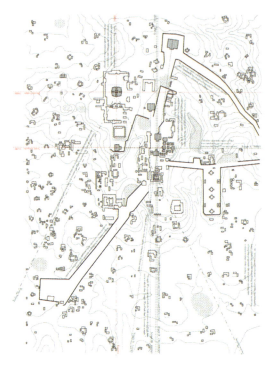

The Productive Urbanism of Tenochtitlán

JOSHUA TAN, ARACELI LOPEZ,
AUDREY TSENG FISCHER

The ancient city of Tenochtitlán that lies beneath present-day Mexico City is evidence of the intelligent indigenous management of water. Situated in the Valley of Mexico, Tenochtitlán faced seasonal and, at times, catastrophic flooding. Water infrastructure had to be carefully developed to manage flooding and provide potable water. The resulting solutions of dams, dikes and causeways revealed a high level of co-dependence between the state and the local communities. Tenochtitlán was also extremely productive and sustainable through its urban agriculture and hunter-gathering practices, forming productive landscapes within and around the city. This essay primarily investigates the Aztecs' relationship with water, arguing that water is inextricably tied to the urbanism of Tenochtitlán.

New York as Incubator of Twentieth-Century Urbanism: Four Urban Thinkers and the City They Envisioned

The BQE: Urgent Fixes for a Maligned Motorway

LEVI-SHAW FABER

In the same way that the early days of the COVID-19 pandemic caused New Yorkers to question the city's role in the national economic landscape, urban traffic congestion in the early to mid-twentieth century was so bad that, in an effort to maintain the city's economic superiority, municipal leaders poured huge amounts of money into multi-lane motorways that connected the metropolitan area to the growing nation. In the last few months, Biden administration's Transportation Secretary, Pete Buttigieg, has increased his attacks on the nation's mid-century, urban, multi-lane motorways that he claims to be discriminatory and destructive to the urban fabric. In New York City, no other road needs more urgent intervention than the Brooklyn-Queens Expressway (BQE). The BQE, a section of I-278, trenches under, passes over, and cuts through residential, commercial, and industrial neighborhoods from Red Hook in Brooklyn to the Calvary Cemetery in Queens. Its most iconic feature, a Roberto Moses-design triple-cantilever that saved the tiny neighborhood of Brooklyn Heights from the destruction that the expressway caused other less affluent areas, is on the verge of failing. Corroding steel members supporting the cantilevered section of the BQE and its iconic promenade are losing strength so quickly that, if nothing is done by 2026, trucks will have to be rerouted onto local roads, and by 2036, if not sooner, the cantilever will have to be closed altogether. The New York City Department of Transportation and organizations of private citizens have put forward multiple proposals to renovate, or even decommission, the BQE, but as of right now, the city has yet to decide what to do with New York's most maligned motorway.

An Observation on the Organic Narrative of Skyscrapers

TAKU SAMEJIMA

New York provides a rich source of material in examining the transition of architectural conception within the United States, specifically composing skyscrapers, the one and only building typology originated from the context of the country. Through examination, one could associate a relationship between this building typology and the term "organic," which remains an ambivalent term defined by varying interpretations. While the term "organic" was originally put forth by Horatio Greenough as a pure expression of architecture in the United States, the term was later inherited, re-interpreted, and re-defined by three successive architects: Louis Sullivan, Frank Lloyd Wright, and Frank Gehry, each of them playing a major role in the development of architectural discourse in the country. Interestingly enough, all three architects come together later in the context of New York through the design of a skyscraper, often read as monumental manifestations of each of their architectural conceptions: organic architecture, organic space, and organic form, respectively. This paper hypothesizes and argues the lineage of the "organic narrative" as what makes the skyscraper typology a pure invention of American architecture through the close reading of three skyscraper proposals in New York: Bayard-Condict Building (1899), St. Mark's Tower Project (1931), and 8 Spruce Street (2010).

Globalization Space: International Infrastructure and Extrastatecraft

Mapping Grounds for Reparations in Jaraguá Peak

LAURA PAPPALARDO, NICK MASSARELLI (SCHOOL OF ART), MIGUEL GAYDOSH (SCHOOL OF ART)

This project maps the history of infrastructural expansion in Jaraguá Peak. It represents the history of each infrastructural layer in sectional maps that expose long-term changes on the ground. Each map accompanies a set of case studies that received reparations for infrastructural harm. They are organized as appendix-tools, which can serve as detachable documents from the larger body of the thesis. Each appendix-tool (infrastructural reparations cases for reference, activist mapping, and public engagement strategies) aspires to contribute to Guarani activism.

Infrastructure Space and Boundaries of Sovereignty

MEGHNA MUDALIAR, ZHANNA KITBALYAN

Global networks of trade, broadband, and energy supplies have a difficult relationship with the notion of sovereignty, given that the infrastructural landscape of a territory may be controlled by its neighbors or occupiers. We seek to explore extensions of sovereign rights within the infrastructural stratum, and their conflict with geographic boundaries. Specifically, we are looking at how autonomous and semi-autonomous territories and bodies struggle for agency over their node of the global network. Our research focuses on three case studies. Firstly, the Armenian energy crisis of 1991–1995 presents an example of a newly independent territory's lack of infrastructural autonomy, complicated by a regional military conflict. Secondly, Indian-administered Kashmir's internet suspension provides a new paradigm of the harms, costs and consequences of the digital siege. Finally, the vaccine rollout in Palestine demonstrates that its semi-autonomous status, as determined by Israel, grants Israel the ability to block international vaccine deliveries to the region, while not bearing responsibility for the low vaccination rates there. An exploration of these three crises shows the fragility of the autonomy of nodes within global networks, indifferent to the self-determination of geopolitical territories.

Global networks of trade, broadband, and energy supplies have a difficult relationship with the notion of sovereignty, given that the infrastructural landscape of a territory may be controlled by its neighbors or occupiers.

From Shigeru Ban to IKEA: Designing Refugee Camps

Refugee Camp Analysis: Amplify Resilience

VICKY ACHNANI, ALPER TURAN, MAX WIRSING, RACHEL MULDER

This project consists of a document that offers a series of questions and categories we asked in conversation with each other as well as generated by larger discussions we had throughout the course of this semester. We felt the need to emphasize the importance of full and in-depth inquiry of refugee camps prior to offering any designs or suggestions of our own. These questions are meant to offer a foundation for analysis, one that might be the starting point for other investigations. We as a team curated these questions to center the occupants of the camp and produce specificity and highlight latent resiliencies. It is not a complete list—it could never be complete. It is only a place to start.

We felt the need to emphasize the importance of full and in-depth inquiry of refugee camps prior to offering any designs or suggestions of our own. These questions are meant to offer a foundation for analysis, one that might be the starting point for other investigations.

Articles of Agency and Resistance in the Global Refugee Crisis

SAMAR HALLOUM, ANGELA LUFKIN, ALEX KLEIN, SARAH KIM

A field guide that attempts to catalogue select examples of refugee agency as moments of disruption to the status quo. An open-ended living document, it is organized to be expanded upon and revised as the body of research and critical analyses of the polemic of permanence, impermanence, and sustainability within the context of refugee camps as they grow and shift over time. This body of work looks at two seemingly disparate experiences: Palestinian and Syrian refugee camps in the Levant region, and detention centers for refugees along the US-Mexico border in Arizona. It is in this juxtaposition that the challenges of designing for and with refugee sites emerge. Their comparison reveals critical moments of rising collective resistance by refugees against the oppression of nation states, the restriction of movement, and the denial of self-hood and self-determination, evidenced by revisions made to these camps from the scale of the body, building, block, and region beyond. While it is essential that the specificity of each context serve as the primary lens through which each camp is analyzed, refugee resistance in both case studies show that the resilience of the human spirit and reclamation of human dignity are universal ambitions and rights disobedient of any borders or boundaries.

Critical History of Domestication:
Environments of Subsistence

The Transformation of Rural England Landscape after Enclosure

WENZHU SHENTU

Rural England landscape is now well known for its geometric order, where large fields are divided into small plots of land by hedgerows or fence walls. This countryside aesthetic has a history of being romanticized as a place of "nobility," "purity," and "abundance," in dichotomy with the town. However, behind the peaceful iconic image of the rural England landscape, enclosure played an historically pivotal role. Enclosure happened over a long period of time, ranging from the fourteenth century to the nineteenth century. This tactic progressed from piecemeal enclosure to general enclosure, superseded eventually by parliamentary enclosure beginning from the eighteenth century. While the chronology of the three types differed from region to region, they all fall into the same story of power and space. Historic writing for land improvements regarded common fields as "wasted," directing them to be enclosed and cultivated. Enclosure transformed the notion of land from "the concepts of right" to that of "property," which enabled a landscape of boundaries and severity, a land demarcated by hedges, walls, and fences which replaced a landscape of openness. This dismantled the supporting system of customary rights to the commons. The rural landscape, no less than the urban context, is constructed by human activities.

Enclosure transformed the notion of land from "the concepts of right" to that of "property," which enabled a landscape of boundaries and severity.

The Inca Civilization: How a Distinct Ecology Informed Subsistence Practices, Settlement Patterns and Social Structure in the Andes

ABBY SANDLER

This paper explores the effect of the distinct Andean ecology on the everyday life, settlement patterns, and subsistence practices of Inca and Pre-Inca civilizations. Emerging out of one of the world's harshest landscapes, the Inca and Pre-inca civilizations found unique ways to not only subsist off this landscape, but thrive within it. In a conversation around early sedentary groups the Inca provide a unique case study insofar as they developed a very specific form of sedentism within the Andean ecology that was largely predicated on mobility. Such mobility was not so much necessary as mandatory given the verticality of the landscape that these villages and eventually cities inhabited. Using John Murra's notion of the "vertical archipelago" as a point of departure for this discussion, this paper unpacks some of the nuances of Pre-Columbian Andean life, and the adaptive measures taken by these peoples to thrive in such an extreme environment, without resorting to or striving toward domination over that environment. The subsistence practices, settlement formations, and even power structures of the Inca, are inextricable from the ecological conditions of their surroundings. This paper offers an investigation into the complex and dynamic relationship between the Inca and their environment.

0   1m   2m

0   1m   2m

Critical History of Domestication: The House

There is a Light that Never Goes Out

JACK RUSK

The monumental ruins of Chaco Canyon in present-day New Mexico, the story goes, are a testament to the hubris of the Pre-Colombian peoples who overran the carrying capacity of the land and whose fractious nature prevented social cohesion. This narrative describes a city collapsing on the precipice of its transition to a complex society. A synthesis of recent scholarship, however, allows us to reinterpret this alleged collapse as a transition from one form of complexity to another. This transition was indexed by the reoccupation and reuse of great houses as residential structures by inhabitants in the twelfth century CE. This reoccupation is notable in two ways: It is exceptional to the teleology assumed by the idea of house society, and it runs opposite the narrative of collapse. At Chaco Canyon, we see the canonical pattern in reverse: Attending the rise of Kachina ceremonialism, we observe the conversion of the great house to domestic spaces occupied by residents of no special standing. This paper seeks to understand the context of this reoccupation in both the history of the region and within late twentieth and early twenty-first century archeological discourse on the house.

At Chaco Canyon, we see the canonical pattern in reverse: attending the rise of Kachina ceremonialism, we observe the conversion of the great house to domestic spaces occupied by residents of no special standing.

The Studiolo: Ideological Origins of Private Space

CLAUDIA CARLE

The studiolo ("study-room") is a manifestation of the compartmentalized domestic architecture of the Italian Renaissance. Originally used by learned clerics, it can be considered a descendant of the monk's cell. The studiolo generally consisted of a small room featuring a built-in desk, seat, and cupboard, but the typology varies and evolves across space and time. Primary sources have often led scholars to identify the studiolo as a patriarchal space in which the male owner displayed his individuality, wealth, intellect, and sovereignty over the household. The boudoir has been interpreted as the female version of the studiolo, but these definitions deserve further examination. These conceptions overlook differences in rulership in which under some sovereigns women could hold political positions, receive a humanist education and maintain studioli, such as Eleonora d'Aragona and Isabella d'Este. The history of the studiolo requires a reexamination in its relationship to gendered division of labor, differing political systems, primitive accumulation and the rise of capitalism.

This paper uses several case studies to explore the location and evolution of the studiolo within the domestic architecture of the Renaissance. Floor plans are used to analyze the studiolo's role in reinforcing, reflecting, and perpetuating the division of labor manifested in political and economic systems. If the studiolo is a paradox in which public and private intersect, it's history will be explored not only as a space of solitude and intellectual pursuit, but also as a space representing the power and sovereignty of its owner.

Introduction to Urban Design

Cape Town

BRANDON BROOKS, HANNAH MAYER
BAYDOUN, AUDREY TSENG FISHER,
SARAH KIM

Cape Town presents a dramatic landscape
of radical fragmentation, the interaction of
geography and patterns of human settlement
reflecting hidden and overt continuities of the
legacy of South African apartheid and European
colonialism. Our collective analysis of select
contemporary, urban projects reveals the city
to be a collage of conflicting cultural forces.
Poorly maintained sanitation infrastructural
systems in the Khayelitsha township underscore
the post-apartheid persistence of state-level
violence against impoverished Black communities. Historically fraught beaches remain
underutilized as transportation inequities
preclude equal access for all Capetonians. The
winelands, a bastion of white privilege and
the city's most popular tourist destination, remain
caught between the preservation of natural
resources and South Africa's status as a global
wine exporter. The mixed-used revitalization
of the Victoria and Albert Waterfront's Silo District
operates in terms of both global capital and
consumerism and as a lively platform for public
life in a city otherwise plagued by a dearth of
safe, well-planned urban spaces.

Urban Analysis: Rio de Janeiro

VERONICA NICHOLSON, MORGAN ANNA
KERBER, BRIAN ORSER, RACHAEL TSAI

The historic Centro of Rio de Janeiro is laced
with a network of historic roads integrating
commercial and residential fabric, and registering the city's role as a colonial capital. Located
along a central East-to-West axis from interior
farmland and forests to the Atlantic harbor, the
historic city is built upon years of colonial history
and an Afro-Brazilian culture which has shaped
its physical and cultural identity.

Architectural Theory

Decoloniality, Demateriality? How Decolonial Praxes Shape Architectural Outcomes

CLARE FENTRESS

Recent discourse around decolonizing architecture has tended to focus on institutional reform rather than specific propositions for the built environment. This reform often manifests as calls for excision: ridding curricula of Eurocentrism, removing carceral buildings from the field's purview, erasing the names of racist oppressors from our schools and museums. Such actions are critical components of the decolonial project; however, an excision-focused interpretation leaves open the question of how the application of decolonial theories and method to architectural practice itself shapes the resulting built environment. That is, what are the actual material consequences of architecture produced through a commitment to the nonhierarchical, the anticapitalist, the collective, the hyperlocal?

This paper explores how one branch of decolonial theory—the concept of decoloniality as developed by Aníbal Quijano, Walter D. Mignolo, and Catherine E. Walsh, within a South American context—affects built outcomes when employed by architects. An overview of this reading of decoloniality is followed by analyses of two case studies: the Palestine-based Decolonizing Architecture Art Residency, led by Sandi Hilal, Alessandro Petti, and Eyal Weizman, and the UK architectural collective Assemble. I conclude by proposing that the material consequences of these decolonial praxes are an architecture that is slight, light, furtive, and transient in comparison to architecture produced in traditional environments.

Dividing by Zero: Nature, Neutrality, and Subservience

COLE SUMMERSELL

The extent of architecture's ambitions with respect to nature seems to be neutrality: reducing energy consumption during a building's construction and use, as well as minimizing the embodied carbon energy in its materials, with the goal of achieving a sort of detached homeostasis where energy systems become closed loops. How did humanity arrive here? This paper suggests that the demands of the market shifted architecture's focus from ecology and ecosystems to a commodified marketplace of energy and material flows, obfuscating the tangible impacts of development on the natural world. Ian McHarg's seminal 1969 book, Design With Nature, anticipates our current civilization's dance between ecological imperatives and market forces.

50 years later, architecture's relationship with nature is still influenced by his hatred of, but ultimate subservience to, the mechanisms of development; and his protectionist view of nature, aimed at inflicting the least harm on existing natural and cultural resources. McHarg's fatalistic neutrality has led designers to a primary conclusion: we must reduce the rate at which things get worse. But moving to a new paradigm, where the business of constructing buildings and cities becomes productively intertwined with natural processes, requires a complete reimagining of current practices and our aloof, analytical relationship to those processes.

Exhibitionism: Politics of Display

JOEL SANDERS

Since their inception in the eighteenth century, art museums—prestigious buildings commissioned by those who wield power and influence—have behaved like cultural barometers registering changing attitudes about the role cultural institutions play in society. Looking at museum buildings from the inside out, this seminar traces the evolution of this building type through an in-depth analysis of its key architectural elements: gallery, interstitial and infrastructure spaces, and site. This seminar explores how the spatial and material development of these tectonic components both mirrors and perpetuates changing cultural attitudes about aesthetics, class, power, wealth, nature, leisure, gender, body, and the senses as seen through the eyes of artists, architects, critics, collectors, and politicians. [3272B]

HISTORY AND THEORY

Out of Date: Expired Patents and Unrealized Histories

ANTHONY ACCIAVATTI

What if the U.S. Army Corps of Engineers had developed "soft infrastructures" and "living systems" for dealing with the changing flows of the Mississippi in and around New Orleans? What if Henry Ford had used soy protein for automotive parts and synthetic meats in the 1940s? What do these seemingly disparate examples all have in common? Each is based on a patent or series of patents that were never adopted for one reason or another. Rather than shy away from such counterfactuals, we will explore and seek to visualize these historical what-ifs by taking a comparative, global perspective on the history of patents as visual and textual artifacts. [4224A]

URBANISM AND LANDSCAPE

The City Before and After Tubewell

ANTHONY ACCIAVATTI

The course will proceed chronologically from the nineteenth century to the present. While global in scope, we focus most of our attention on South and Southeast Asia. In particular, the seminar centers on the evolution of pump technologies and how they have changed life in cities and their hinterlands. If, as historian Swati Chattopadhyay argues, "Urban forms have a direct correlation with infrastructural norms," then what can the shift to decentralized water infrastructure tell us about the form and life of cities? [4245B]

URBANISM AND LANDSCAPE

Approaches to Contemporary Architectural Theory

JOAN OCKMAN

Architectural theory is back. Having fallen out of favor for a couple decades, it is once again generating discourse, but in new and arguably more interesting and important ways. In previous periods, theory offered architects a doctrine, a set of justifications for their work, and a canon of essential texts and authors. Today the very idea of a canon is contested, as are the disciplinary definition and scope of architecture itself. Architectural theories—now inescapably plural and transdisciplinary—today function more as a mode of thought, a platform for debate, and an array of intellectual and critical strategies. Meanwhile the need for theoretical reflection and renovation has perhaps never been greater. The transformative events that have taken place over the last quarter century—including those of 2020—make it imperative to reassess our received architectural ideas. [551A]

HISTORY AND THEORY

History of Landscape Architecture: Antiquity to 1700 in Western Europe

BRYAN FUERMANN

This course presents an introductory survey of the history of gardens and the interrelationship of architecture and landscape architecture in Western Europe from antiquity to 1700, focusing primarily on Italy. The course examines chronologically the evolution of several key elements in landscape design: architectural and garden typologies; the boundaries between inside and outside; issues of topography and geography; various uses of water; organization of plant materials; and matters of garden decoration, including sculptural tropes. Specific gardens or representations of landscape in each of the four periods under discussion—Ancient Roman, medieval, early and late Renaissance, and Baroque—are examined and situated within their own cultural context. [4222A]

URBANISM AND LANDSCAPE

History of British Landscape Architecture: 1600 to 1900

BRYAN FUERMANN

This seminar examines chronologically the history of landscape architecture and country-house architecture in Britain from 1500 to 1900. Topics of discussion include the history of the castle in British architecture and landscape architecture; Italian and French influences on the seventeenth-century British garden; military landscaping; the Palladian country house and British agricultural landscape; Capability Brown's landscape parks; theories of the picturesque and of the landscape sublime; Romanticism and the psychology of nature; the creation of the public park system; arts and crafts landscape design; and the beginnings of landscape modernism. Comparisons of historical material with contemporary landscape design, where appropriate, are made throughout the term. [4223B]

URBANISM AND LANDSCAPE

Topics in the History of Architecture since 1945

JOAN OCKMAN

The past two decades have seen a burgeoning of scholarship on the culture and practice of global architecture from World War II to the millennium, but much remains to be investigated and rethought with regard to this recent period, especially in light of the crises we are facing today. This research seminar focuses on the impact of ideological conflicts, political and economic upheavals, technological and environmental changes, social, cultural, and intellectual paradigm shifts on postwar architecture and cities around the world. Members of the seminar will carry out a semester-long research project on a topic of their choosing, leading to a substantial term paper. [3102A]

HISTORY AND THEORY

Topics in the History of Architecture Education

JOAN OCKMAN

This seminar takes up a series of topics in the evolution of modern architecture education, addressing historical, institutional, and ideological formations and transformations that have taken place over the last two centuries. How have the changing norms and values of the profession, of higher education, and of modern society shaped attitudes and approaches to the architect's training? Reciprocally, what kind of impact have architecture schools had on architects' subsequent careers and on architectural practice and culture at large? This seminar will endeavor to bring a sharp critical-historical lens to questions concerning architecture education past, present, and future. [3298B]

HISTORY AND THEORY

Globalization Space: International Infrastructure and Extrastatecraft

KELLER EASTERLING

This course studies networks of trade, transportation, resources, communication, labor, tourism, energy, commerce and finance from the late nineteenth century to the present. Focused on the special political powers of large spatial/technical systems, lectures visit free zones and automated ports; hydrological, oil, and solar landscapes; satellite, broadband, and mobile telephony; high-speed rail; the internet; networks of labor and migration; international organizations; offshore financial centers; highways and airports; and the circulation of repeatable spatial products, standards and management platforms. [4216B]

URBANISM AND LANDSCAPE

New York as Incubator of Twentieth-Century Urbanism: Four Urban Thinkers and the City They Envisioned

JOAN OCKMAN

The seminar is constructed as a debate among the ideas of four urban thinkers whose influential contributions to the discourse of the modern city were shaped by their divergent responses to New York City's urban and architectural development: Lewis Mumford, Robert Moses, Jane Jacobs, and Rem Koolhaas. In counterposing their respective arguments, the seminar addresses issues of civic representation and environmentalism, infrastructure development and urban renewal policy, community and complexity, and the role of architecture in the urban imaginary. [3301B]

HISTORY AND THEORY

Territorial Cities of Pre-Colonial America

ANA MARÍA DURÁN CALISTO

The main purpose of this research seminar is to contribute toward a growing study of architectural typologies and urban constellations characteristic of ancient pre-Columbian civilizations. The central premise of this seminar, to be examined and questioned, is that the characteristic urban model or settlement system that evolved in the Americas was profoundly territorial, intertwining agriculture, settlement, infrastructure, and landscape. [4209A]

URBANISM AND LANDSCAPE

Lightness and Modernity: Architecture, Design, Energy

CRAIG BUCKLEY

The course probes the significance of lighness as a condition of architectural modernity. In the nineteenth and twentieth centuries the ancient requirement that architecture embody solidity was fundamentally transformed by new materials in which strength and stability could be achieved with relatively light and slender materials. Such material transformations were culturally ambivalent. Lightness was linked to ideas of dematerialization, taking to the air, and a new culture of transparency. Yet it was also associated with the loss of gravity, derealization, and rootlessness. While the elimination of extraneous weight has been associated with efficiency, nimbleness, and a judicious use of resources, it has also been mobilized in designs for warfare and colonization over the last two centuries. Students will consider some of the major positions around the conception of "light modernity," learn about key buildings and projects since the nineteenth century that have been defined by the problem of lightness, and critically examine differing historical claims about lightness. [3314B]

HISTORY AND THEORY

Introduction to Islamic Architecture

KISHWAR RIZVI

The course is an introduction to the architecture of the Islamic world from the seventh century to the present, encompassing regions of Asia, North Africa, and Europe. A variety of sources and media, from architecture to urbanism and from travelogues to paintings, are used in an attempt to understand the diversity and richness of Islamic architecture. [3103B]

HISTORY AND THEORY

Architectural Theory

MARTA CALDEIRA

This course explores the history of Western architectural theory, from 1750 to the present, through the close reading of primary texts. Lectures place the readings in the context of architectural history, and texts are discussed in required discussion sections. Topics include theories of origin, type and character, the picturesque, questions of style and ornament, standardization and functionalism, critiques of modernism, as well as more contemporary debates on historicism, technology, and environmentalism. [3012B]

HISTORY AND THEORY (REQUIRED)

Introduction to Urban Design

ALAN PLATTUS, ANDREI HARWELL

This course offers an introduction to the history, analysis, and design of the urban landscape. Emphasis is placed on understanding the principles, processes, and contemporary theories of urban design, and the relations between individual buildings, groups of buildings, and the larger physical and cultural contexts in which they are created and with which they interact. Case studies are drawn from cities around the world and throughout history and focus on the role of public space and public art in shaping the form, use, and identity of cities and regions. [4011A]

URBANISM AND LANDSCAPE (REQUIRED)

Critical History of Domestication: The House

PIER VITTORIO AURELI, ELISA ITURBE

The premise of this joint-seminar is to interrogate the human settlement through a critical genealogy of domestication and its corresponding architectures and ecologies. The logic of the house as primary enclosure initiated a transformation of the whole environment, with the domestication of crops and animals becoming an irreversible ecological turning point and an origin point for the patriarchal premises of both capitalism and colonialism. By studying the evolution of the household alongside changing practices of subsistence, this joint-seminar locates the house and the environment as two fundamental sites of transformation. [3313B]

HISTORY AND THEORY

Critical History of Domestication: Environments of Subsistence

ELISA ITURBE, PIER VITTORIO AURELI

The premise of this joint-seminar is to interrogate the human settlement through a critical genealogy of domestication and its corresponding architectures and ecologies. The logic of the house as primary enclosure initiated a transformation of the whole environment, with the domestication of crops and animals becoming an irreversible ecological turning point and an origin point for the patriarchal premises of both capitalism and colonialism. By studying the evolution of the household alongside changing practices of subsistence, this joint-seminar locates the house and the environment as two fundamental sites of transformation. [4250B]

URBANISM AND LANDSCAPE

From Shigeru Ban to IKEA: Designing Refugee Camps

ESTHER DA COSTA MEYER

This seminar analyzes refugee camps and detention centers from a transnational perspective, probing the limits and problems evident in different cases, as well as the state of exception and extraterritoriality that applies to all of them. It will also study disaster relief housing around the globe sometimes built with the help of refugees. What metrics should we use to judge successful design? Faced with the need to scale up response, it is imperative to address the housing problems faced by a growing number of displaced people. [3297B]

HISTORY AND THEORY

EIGHT

Breaking from generalized narratives in architecture catalyzes agency-centered, interdisciplinary discourse. *History and Theory* courses offer the past as a rich field of play for investigations in subsistence and domestication, where counterfactual studies underscore the importance of pluralistic thinking, and close readings of primary sources—patents, paintings, and texts—obfuscate traditional premises presented through *Landscape and Urbanism* courses.

Claudia Ansorena

Joseph Zeal-Henry Is it always the right thing to do to keep people living somewhere with the precariousness of what they might face and are there institutions and structures in place to help them navigate that? [...] The responsibilities of the civic and ethics—the role of civic space—suddenly become interested in all of this.

LEARNING FROM PRECARITY
Claudia Ansorena

Given the speculative and theoretical framework that ultimately disillusions recent architecture school graduates, how can students of architecture become better prepared to design for the unknown while simultaneously engaging the challenges of their time? The architecture student should be taught to exist and design in various time zones—that is, the past, the present, the future—in order to best frame their role in ever-changing societies. Relying on memory, observation, and data as tools for learning, this alternate model provides architects-to-be with hands-on experience from an interdisciplinary perspective. Four key actors—government, community, designers, and researchers—will help to realize intervention-based attachments to existing infrastructure and introduce new typologies that will be integral to the survival of our cities. Situating itself in a near future of drastic sea-level rise and seasonal coastal flooding, the project envisions a possible reality where Miami becomes a host to climate adaptation experimentation and agile learning in precarity.

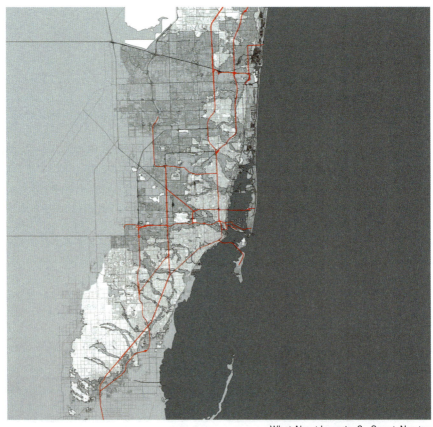

Claudia Ansorena

Claudia Ansorena

What About Learning? · Saunt, Newton

Advanced Studio

THE PARASITE
Ashton Harrell

Ashton Harrell

In the world of the artist and the creator lies inequalities of racial and gender representation in both education and exhibition. Additionally, creators like artists, architects, and builders traditionally have been taught in isolated studios and workshops, removed from the outside world, subjected to constrained mechanisms of learning, interaction, and exhibition. Thus organically, these creators view the city as a massive grand exhibition hall. Feeding off the city, The Parasitic School infests the urban landscape with the common utility of creative experimentation and exhibition, presenting itself as a chain of diverse spaces. Crossing the island of Manhattan from the Hudson to the East River, the project attaches to the city's derelict infrastructure to create a new home for creators to learn, experiment, and display; this free, communal, and social environment is able to provide creators with everything from housing to study, exhibition, and performance spaces. Over six years, these disciplines will transform diverse sites to challenge the conventions of social interaction within architecture.

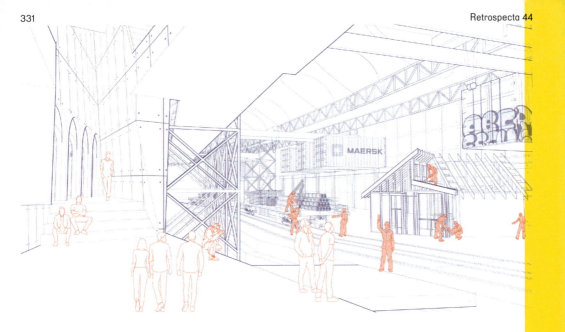

Gavin Hogben I was particularly intrigued by the world below, and the idea that it wasn't just simply stations, but a kind of continuous metabolism that moved along its length of different educational possibilities and different kinds of memberships of this parasitical community.

Ashton Harrell

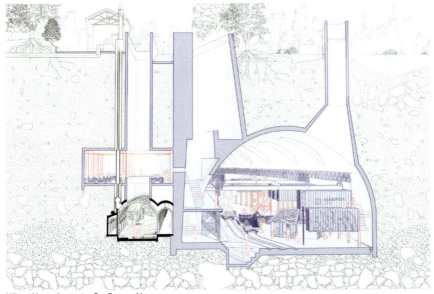

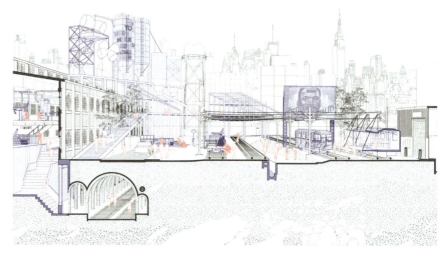

Tyler Krebs · Feldman Nominee

Seth Scafe-Smith The site that you've identified and the way that the school has almost learned from the history of the river in its adaptability is really strong, and posing that at the center and future of the project—how you might learn from other industries and disciplines in order to shape the future of the institution—could really help push the proposal forward.

ADAPTIVE RIVER USE
Tyler Krebs

Tyler Krebs · Feldman Nominee

The studio brief asked students to critically analyze architectural education and speculate new ways of learning about the built environment. It also asked how learning can address critical contemporary issues in our cities. By considering learning to be an essential ingredient to urban design, my proposal turns a series of abandoned industrial structures along the Cuyahoga River in Cleveland, Ohio into a dispersed network of education. The school ultimately becomes a network of site-specific learning interventions that embrace the whole of the circular building economy. As the school grows or its needs change, it can leave sites or take over new ones. New businesses and industries along the river mean new opportunities for the school to adapt and engage. Regardless of the future structure of the school, the lasting impact will be a new public core of the city where people from the East and West sides can come together and learn about the built environment.

Tyler Krebs · Feldman Nominee

Wenzhu Shentu, Abby Sandler

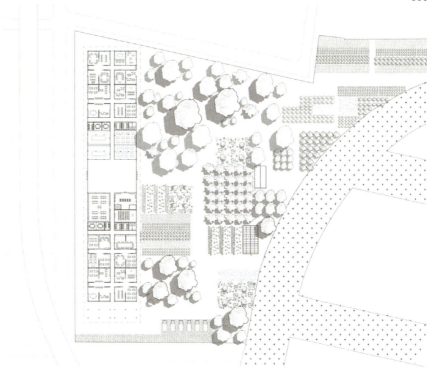

BROOKLYN FOREST GARDEN
Wenzhu Shentu, Abby Sandler

This project introduces a forest garden into the Brooklyn landscape, prioritizing sectional biodiversity and regeneration, and offering a different approach to achieving food sovereignty and security. This differs from a conventional community garden system by acknowledging the changing need and capacity across different sites throughout the borough. The Garden School bridges the gap between the District 15 school system, community, and the rest of the city. The remainder of the site operates as a tree nursery and garden that the students help maintain over time. Trees are then distributed throughout the city to a number of satellite gardens. What begins as a patchwork on a single site proliferates into a patchwork across the city. This transforms the urban fabric into a series of biodiverse ecological havens that, at different stages, provide habitats for various species, shade and occupiable space for its residents, and food during its periods of short term cultivation.

Wenzhu Shentu, Abby Sandler

GROUNDS OF INTEREST

Rebecca Commissaris,
Steven Sculco,
Gabriel Gutierrez Huerta

Rebecca Commissaris, Steven Sculco, Gabriel Gutierrez Huerta · Feldman Nominees

Land allotment, the system of private property imposed by the Dawes Act of 1887, diminishes the collective and individual benefits from the oil industry for Mandan, Hidatsa, and Arikara (MHA) Nation today, and further compounds environmental harm. Lost revenues, excessive venting, flaring of natural gas, and the scattering of well pads are all directly related to convoluted lease negotiations on allotted land. However, Fort Berthold has another valuable resource: The high wind speeds covering vast portions of its terrain carry tremendous energy potential—enough to create a utility-scale wind farm that, if Tribal-owned, could match if not exceed the collective economic benefits from oil. The spatial potentials of land consolidation could empower MHA Nation to leverage the resources of the oil industry to create a path for an energy transition while enticing oil companies to pursue their own interests. Land consolidation would eliminate the obstacles that allotment creates for oil extraction, essentially lifting the Dawes Act and creating space for MHA Nation to develop collective agency through energy development, environmental protection, and economic independence.

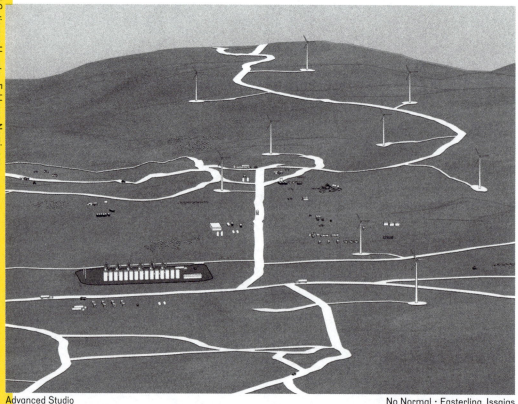

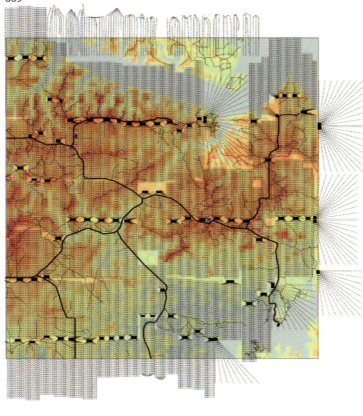

Rebecca Commissaris, Steven Sculco, Gabriel Gutierrez Huerta · Feldman Nominees

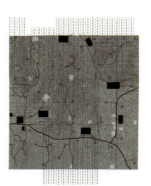

Elsa Hoover You've stacked up an excellent set of points about how the boom economy and the infrastructuralization of the space in a very specific context has given rise to the physical, lower-case "a" architectural form.

EAST PHILLIPS COMMUNITY LAND TRUST

Samar Halloum, Jiaxing Yan, Scott Simpson

Acknowledging the fundamental mutualism between urban and rural spaces, the project, East Phillips Community Land Trust, unites them into a symbiotic relationship through an innovative land trust, which engages police-defund protocols and remixes them with existing government funds to create spatial assets in the East Phillips neighborhood of Minneapolis. The land trust model is a useful tool to decommoditize assets that the open market has forced outside the reach of those who need it most. Our land trust is unique in that it prioritizes visibility in space. We seek to translate the idea of a land trust from a ledger of discontinuous properties to a concrete, contiguous urban territory. Further, we propose the acquisition of both urban and rural lands by the same entity. Understanding that there is precarity at both ends of the urban-rural spectrum, we believe that pairing the diverse spaces, loosening the boundaries of municipal budgets, and ultimately refracting them through the East Phillips Community Land Trust can catalyze a chain reaction that generates new value through interdependency.

Samar Halloum, Jiaxing Yan, Scott Simpson

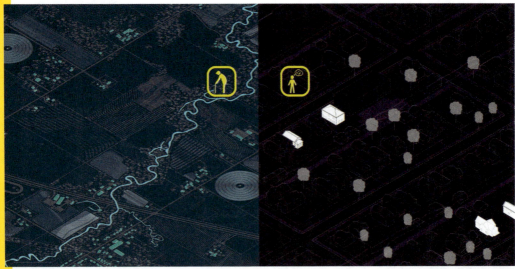

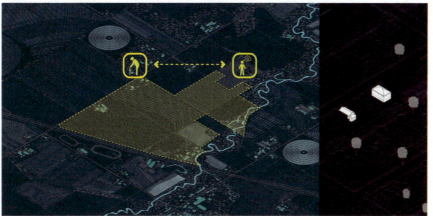

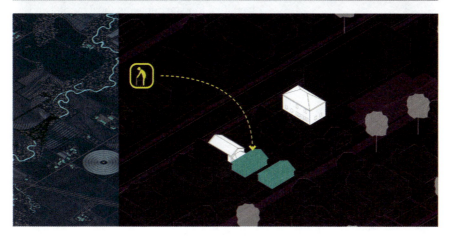

Samar Halloum, Jiaxing Yan, Scott Simpson

No Normal · Easterling, Issaias

OKFOODLANDFUTURE
Sasha Zwiebel, Rachel Mulder,
Leanne Nagata

Oklahoma is a place of fields, faith, and football. Built on a palimpsest of past and current failure, violence, and disaster, it is home to the forcibly removed, the end of the Trail of Tears, the Dust Bowl, racial discrimination, and terrorism, including the Tulsa Race Massacre. Where there is failure and funding, there is opportunity. Opportunity to face the violence in our shared past and confront their new forms by working to end continued harm; to restore, repay, and redistribute that what is owed, reparations and land. Our first interplay aims to facilitate food sovereignty and small farming by shifting USDA resources to support community-based, diversified food farming and local market and food processing initiatives. Our second interplay utilizes the power of collective ownership and stewardship by changing the terms of the State trust lands, adapting USDA subsidies, and enforcing the power of tribal jurisdictions, to redress the stolen land, wealth, and sovereignty from Black, Brown, and Indigenous folks in Oklahoma.

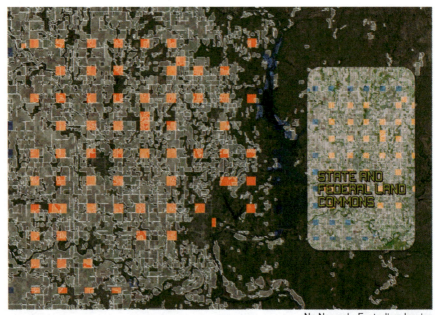

Sasha Zwiebel, Rachel Mulder, Leanne Nagata

Elsa Hoover There is real strength and a lot of depth in how those margins and distributive calculations of state management or federal control of lands that, as you're arguing, have more potential to serve locality and to serve the land itself, can actually be turned on their heads and used as a reparative framework for return of all different sorts, and different kinds of healing.

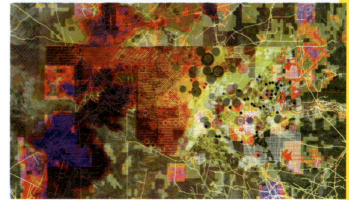

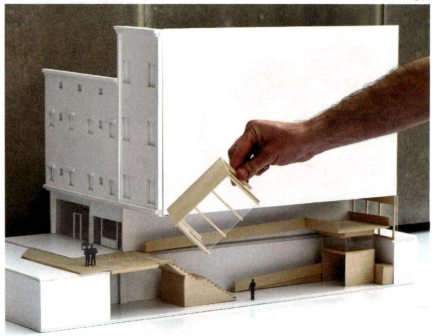

Sangji Han, Jack Rusk, Paul Meuser

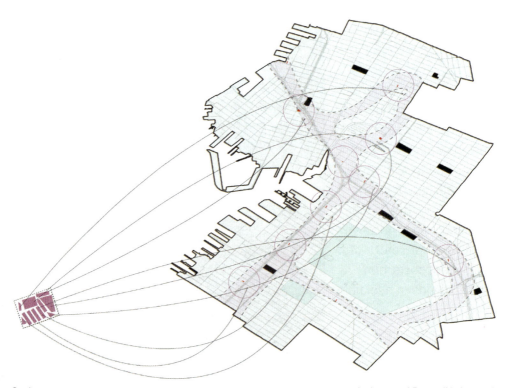

A NEW SCHOOL FOR DISTRICT 15
Sangji Han, Jack Rusk, Paul Meuser

This project addresses inequities in District 15—a New York district without the ability to directly redistribute resources between its privileged and dispossessed communities. We seek to expand the district's middle ground, allowing students autonomy in their education and a place in the urban realm. The middle ground is made up of a network of Home Rooms in disused retail spaces, connected by a micromobility system, and a pedagogical model based on social learning. This project roots a vision of urban vitality in middle schoolers, who have grown accustomed to loitering without any place to be, shooed from people's stoops, and profiled by the police. By giving over part of the urban realm to people in a transitional period in their lives, we demarcate a more radical transition in District 15. This is a vision of a vital city that places people, not commerce or development, at the center of urban life.

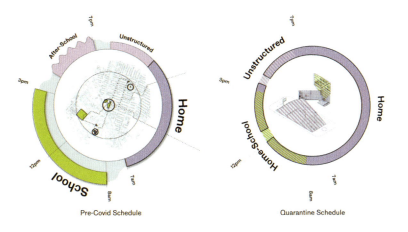

Pre-Covid Schedule   Quarantine Schedule

Sangji Han, Jack Rusk, Paul Meuser

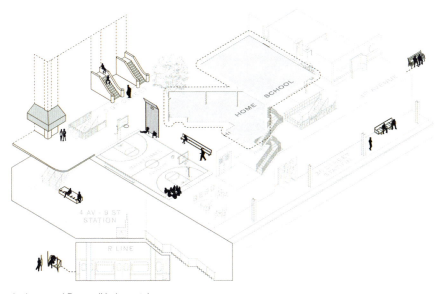

CONCEAL/REVEAL
Hongyu Wang

This project aims to highlight the coexisting human nature of self-concealment and self-disclosure through architecture. Within public spaces, users wish to be part of a communal atmosphere yet desire a sense of privacy both physically and mentally. This nature instigates a constant back-and-forth relationship between people, space, and their varying interactions. To provide dynamic experiences and movements, the project designates various degrees of privacy and publicity throughout the building. The architectural elements are sculpted by the guiding principle: inhabitable and accessible spaces are not always obvious to the eye. In doing so, users can decide whether to move through or linger within various spaces of the building. Therefore, the project creates an implicit ambiguity and the phenomenon of presence within absence; users are constantly negotiating between privacy and the curiosity of further exploration.

Hongyu Wang

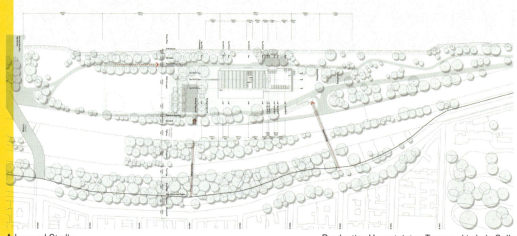

Kim Yao You have this incredibly thoughtful building that nestles into the topography within the site. It feels quiet—it doesn't announce itself, it integrates into the landscape.

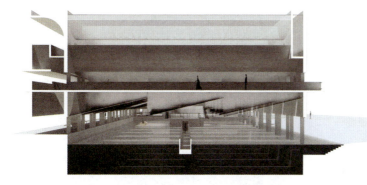

LIVING SOILS
Vicky Achnani

Vicky Achnani

Productive Uncertainty, the central theme of the studio, is addressed through various transformations achieved using systems of suspension and deployable assembly at local and regional scales. Each of these devised systems are further detailed in terms of material assembly, both informing the brief while testing its effectiveness. The combination and detailing of steel, CLT, and bamboo in various building systems at both unit and site scales allow for flexibility and play as the response to the growing uncertainty of crop culture. The design proposal operates in the Brownsville neighbourhood of Brooklyn, aiming to transform the area into a productive site of supported relationships and larger partnerships between the intervention and the community. Farming takes place on the site at an individual and collective level, while the design proposal—through terrace farming, compost collection, and a portable food market—reaches out to the immediate and larger neighborhood.

Ariane Lourie Harrison There's an argument here, not just of reusing waste, but also creating food systems that distribute less waste. As you were talking, I had fantasies of families coming to pick their meal—no bags, no packaging, just pick what you need. There's a nutritional aspect; there's a public education aspect; there's a waste reduction aspect.

Vicky Achnani

Productive Uncertainty · Tsurumaki, de la Selle   Advanced Studio

Vicky Achnani

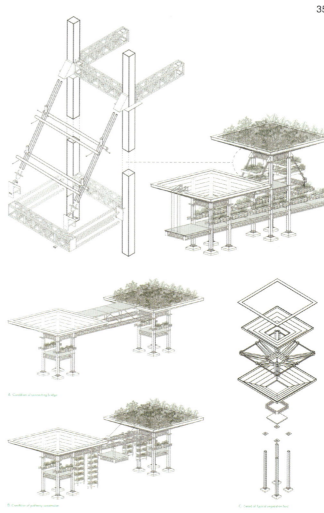

A. Condition of connecting bridge

B. Condition of pathway connection

C. Detail of typical vegetation bed

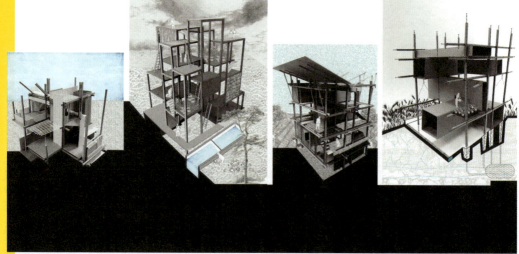

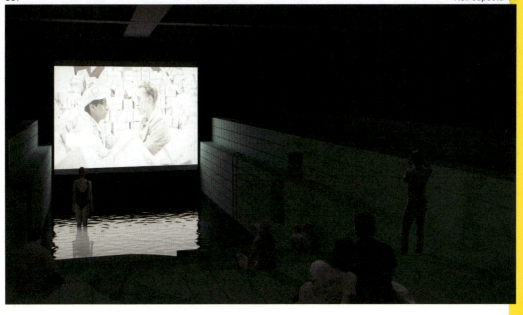

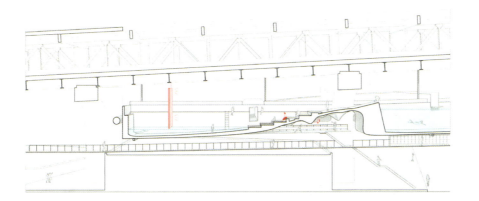

Leyi Zhang · Feldman Nominee

Jerome Haferd   The promise of the big section is that you almost start to transcend the pool as the program; It starts to read more as a different type of infrastructure or urban section that might apply across any number of possible futures that we are headed toward.

LEISURE IN THE AIR
Leyi Zhang

Leyi Zhang · Feldman Nominee

The question of uncertainty has led this project to focus on a certain type of space in New York City, titled "by-products" for the purposes of this investigation. "By-products" are surplus spaces created by urban infrastructures, often generated unintentionally and not serving any design purpose. This proposal selects one district around the Manhattan Bridge as a starting point and focuses on the space underneath the bridge as the site for experimentation. Instead of proposing program traditional to urban development, the project considers surplus space as an opportunity for new urban activities and suggests an intervention within the densely-populated urban environment. Thus, the proposal's main design features a pool and hot bath structure hanging under the Manhattan Bridge, intermixed with additional programmatic elements of a performance venue, climbing club, bowling alley, and more.

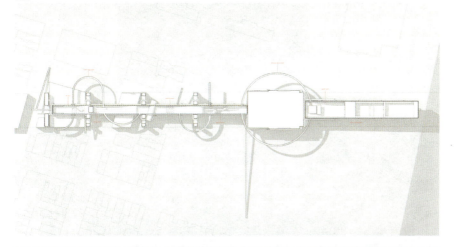

Leyi Zhang · Feldman Nominee

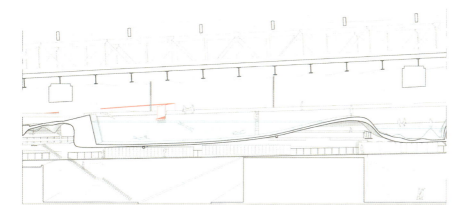

Productive Uncertainty · Tsurumaki, de la Selle   Advanced Studio

Morgan Anna Kerber, Yushan Jiang

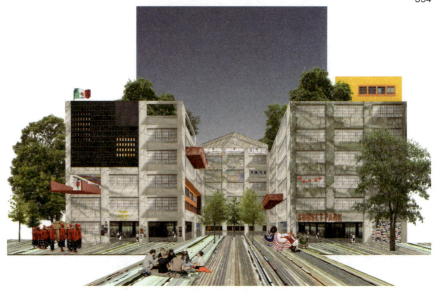

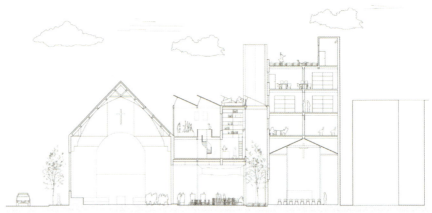

SPLICE CITY
Morgan Anna Kerber, Yushan Jiang

Our project seeks to splice racial segregation through event organizing; specifically, we define a new ownership model for the community of sunset park, which prioritizes local-based decision making. This urban plan focuses on establishing space for events to occur at three scales distributed along with a slice of Sunset Park Community; allowing for rhizomatic growth of the community from the existing rigorous grid and typology of the area; encouraging the layers of life to gather and becoming interaction points for the community members to engage and learn from each other. This urban infrastructure focuses on small built interventions in partnership with a large injection of vegetation into the material pallet. Building an internal cycle of material appropriation, reducing the pace of living, focusing on communal transportation, and creating space for happenstance, are all strategies that become the tools for memory and tradition to be mapped upon.

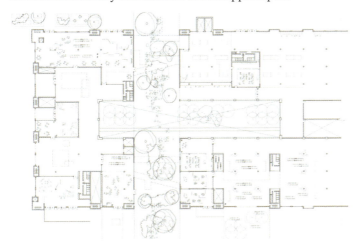

THE TOWER AND THE TABLE
Tyler Krebs

Sacred monuments, or huacas, once dominated Lima's Pre-Columbian landscape. These huacas were carefully organized in relation to the sun, moon, stars, and other important natural features like the mountains and ocean. This urban constellation would have played an important role in the daily lives of Indigenous populations—it tracked farming seasons, acted as a calendar for sacred events, and enforced a sacred connectivity between humans and nature. This proposal is composed of two elements: the tower and the table. The towers act as both plant-growing structures and observatories. They offer a privileged view of the huacas, providing a presence throughout the city that reestablishes the urban constellation; they also act as pedagogical tools to display altitude-related distributions of plants in the Andes. The tables define gathering spaces and provide the infrastructure for programs such as housing, gardens, and kitchens. Together, these elements give the heritage sites visibility and turn them into meaningful public spaces throughout the city.

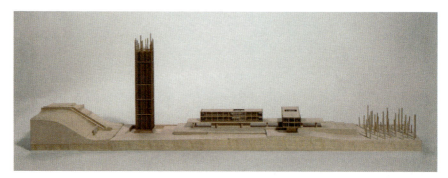

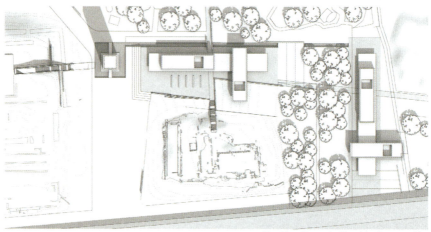

Tyler Krebs

Tyler Krebs

Billie Tsien The tower is beautiful. I love this idea of these markers that are green that tell you where the huacas are as you look across the city. It's like you are actually in a site where there are pyramids that haven't been uncovered and you look across and you get up to the one that's been uncovered and you see the mounds and you get a sense of a greater deeper history.

Qiyuan Liu · Feldman Nominee

Adine Gavazzi Through this project, you are generating a green buffer zone where agroforestry is not just a square or an enclosed area; it is part of the landscape and has certain characteristics. There is an absence of straight divisions and separation between the two- instead, they slowly buffer and morph into another organization of space.

INVERTED HUACA: CREATING NEW OASIS IN THE CITY OF LIMA
Qiyuan Liu

This project focuses on highlighting and celebrating the presence of huacas while providing habitable and lively living space. Instead of superimposing a new system, which would compete with existing huacas visually and spatially, the proposal follows methods of subtraction over construction, thus extending space into the ground and leaving the lower level to the huacas. The original architectural language of the huaca is reconstructed in an inverted manner, and a new ground below the existing is created. This new sacred—the inverted huaca—would work mutually with existing ones to reinforce the cultural identity already existing on the site. Rearticulation of the huacas also happens on an urban level—Incan culture is represented with the constellation of both original and inverted huacas. By being formless, simple in geometry, and blending with its surroundings, this project gives the space back to the huacas and the local people.

Qiyuan Liu · Feldman Nominee

The New Sacred · Barclay, Crousse, Bui

Qiyuan Liu · Feldman Nominee

Zishi Li, Michelle Qu, Calvin Yang Yue

COMMON GROUNDS
Zishi Li, Michelle Qu, Calvin Yang Yue

The intention of the project is to increase mixed-income housing and access
to recreational amenities and infrastructure in New York City's District 15.
In particular, we propose a new urban model that incorporates new forms
of domesticity and play in New York City.

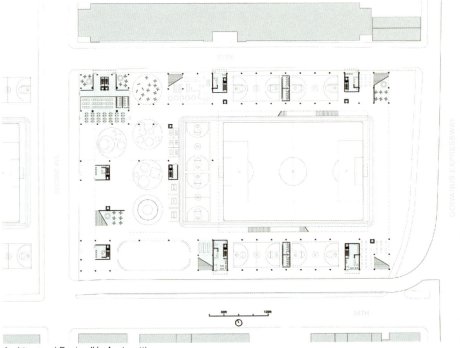

Zishi Li, Michelle Qu, Calvin Yang Yue

SEEING CHARTREUSE
Elise Limon,
Rebecca Commissaris

Rebecca Commissaris, Elise Limon · Feldman Nominees

Seeing Chartreuse is an attempt to rethink adaptation on an island facing the challenge of sea level rise, through one of the region's most pervasive yet overlooked landscapes: the salt marsh.

The project excavates the deep history of the salt marsh, its cultural use and ecological potential. It addresses the challenge of sea level rise at three scales: at the scale of island-wide planning and land-ownership, the scale of public space, and the scale of the individual highly-fertilised garden lawn. The salt marsh is used as both a strategic ecological protective buffer to storm surge, as well as a guiding metaphor for living with—instead of fighting against—more watery landscapes.

As architects who believe in fostering a deeper disciplinary awareness outside of the red lines of the traditional "site" and into the complex and important landscapes that support human and non human habitation, the salt marsh was an important tool through which to question the current mode of dwelling on Nantucket island and coastal sites throughout New England.

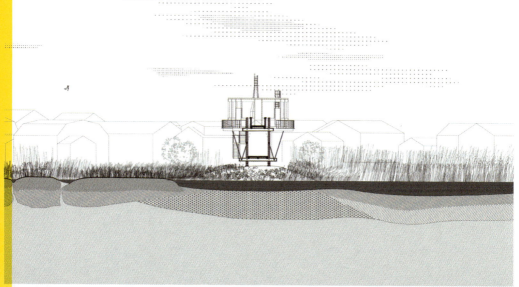

Lynnette Widder I really appreciated your incredible attention to the nature of the salt marsh, specifically to its coloration and its role as an imaginary in fiction, in popular imagination, and in fact.

NANTUCKET'S WORKING WATERFRONT
Niema Jafari,
Yangwei Kevin Gao,
Xuefeng Du

Nantucket's new working waterfront seeks to transition away from obsolete gray infrastructure towards a renewable and resilient future. The new working waterfront uses shipbuilding and whaling as a precedent to move towards new forms of mobility and energy—making room for fishermen and real economic activities that will advocate local renewable energy. With rising sea levels and the advancement of new technologies in energy and vessel transit, future piers will have to adapt. These new piers may become working waterfront islands that connect to a new ecological shoreline, allowing water to penetrate between. By cutting into vacant spaces, which contain obsolete infrastructure in historical towns such as Harbor Place, landfill can be used to raise the datum of the new ecological shoreline along New Washington Street and Edge Pier.

Niema Jafari, Yangwei Kevin Gao, Xuefeng Du

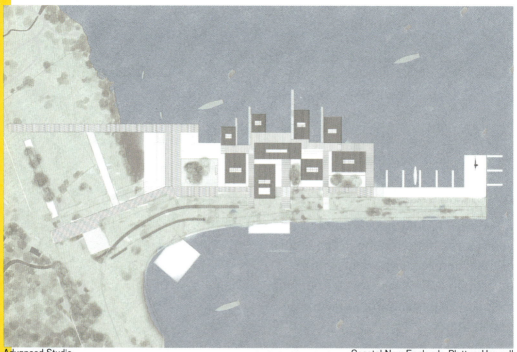

Anne Tate This project has a lot of different interesting pieces, and one of them is the way in which the pier itself acts as an emblem for different ideas about the shore line. I find it quite interesting; the soft and the hard; the active and the passive; the natural and the built.

Niema Jafari, Yangwei Kevin Gao, Xuefeng Du

Coastal New England · Plattus, Harwell   Advanced Studio

Jessica Kim, Caroline Kroska

A NEW SCHOOL MEAL
Jessica Kim, Caroline Kraska

The school lunch menu consists of more than just food; it contains state contracts, agricultural lobbies, and income brackets. This project seeks to explore food infrastructure and subsequently disrupt, decentralize, and disaggregate the existing food system within D15. It proposes an integrated network that connects students more directly to the foods they are eating: how it is grown, transported, prepared, and advertised. It also opens opportunities for necessary after-school programs at reduced travel and cost to the student. Red Hook is used as the preliminary location for large-scale retrofitting of warehouse buildings into agricultural hubs, with localized expansion as school kitchens, test kitchens or community dining. More mutable programs would be created through partnerships between the schools and nearby bodegas, buses, bike shares, and distributors. The ambition is to allow students to be agents in the system that feeds them.

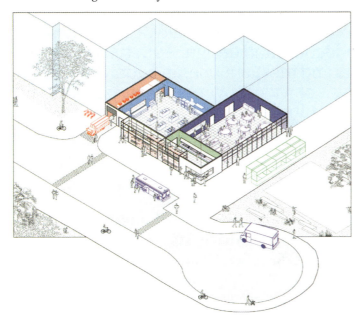

Jessica Kim, Caroline Kraska

WHAT ABOUT LEARNING?

Published in May 1968, at a no less tumultuous time in history, Cedric Price's Architectural Digest issue "What about Learning?" is a poignant critique of the strictures of education and institutional learning at large. Today's ongoing crises and protest movements have created a new impetus to question the ethical and spatial relationships of educational institutions to diversity, the climate, and the pandemic. With the campus now extended out from Rudolph Hall to the geographically-dispersed living rooms of students and professors, there are radical questions of communication, mobility, and participation in knowledge production, and design. As a studio, we will look beyond just bricks and mortar alone, and apply spatial intelligence to the analysis of wider environmental, political, and socio-economic relationships in learning and their different manifestations in urban and virtual environments. [1109A]

FACULTY   Deborah Saunt, Timothy Newton

STUDENTS   *Claudia Ansorena*, Shuang Chen, Vignesh Harikrishnan, *Ashton Harrell*, Gordon Yuhao Jiang, Sze Wai Justin Kong, *Tyler Krebs*, Saba Salekfard, Ben Thompson

JURY   Pooja Agrawal, Shumi Bose, Joel De Mowbray, Christopher Pierce, Akil Scafe-Smith, Seth Scafe-Smith, Joseph Zeal-Henry

NO NORMAL

While many may long for this semester to be like any other, No Normal projects plans for a semester like no other. The ticking time bombs of WHITENESS, pandemic, and climate catastrophe are in our hands—all during an US election year with global consequences. The modern Enlightenment mind that is still so dominant in culture addresses these problems and failures with the myth of solutions—solutions that often give authority to new technologies, econometrics, law, and other technical languages in the absence of spatial knowledge. Constraints on studio processes cause energies to balloon out into long overdue experiments and rehearsals of skills that are necessary now more than ever. We will design conventional forms—objects, details, and buildings. But we will also design forms for the interplay between those forms—interplay that adds power and relevance to those forms. The search for solutions and master plans may lead to the most dangerous outcome of this moment—a "new normal." The studio's experiments with site, form, representation, pedagogy, and authorship are instead looking for No Normal. [1102A]

FACULTY   Keller Easterling, Theodossis Issaias

STUDENTS   *Rebecca Commissaris, Gabriel Gutierrez Huerta, Samar Halloum, Rachel Mulder, Leanne Nagata, Steven Sculco, Scott Simpson, Jiaxing Yan, Sasha Zwiebel*

JURY   Aristide Antonas, Ana María Durán Calisto, Billy Fleming, Elsa Hoover, Laura Kurgan, Philip V. McHarris, Gabrielle Printz, Joel Sanders, Jeff Washburne

PRODUCTIVE UNCERTAINTY

As we navigate a global pandemic emerging in the context of an existential climate crisis, exacerbating long standing systemic inequities of race and class, it is easy to feel that we are living through a time of unprecedented volatility and radical instability. This fundamental paradox of uncertainty for a discipline based on projection, of impermanence for a practice predicated on permanence, will define the studio. We will ask how the material conditions of architecture might engage with the increasing volatility that characterizes our collective relationship to emergent environmental, climatological, biological, political, and social conditions. Each student or student group will examine these broader concerns in relation to an architectural territory: membrane/envelope, structure, environmental systems and thermal performance, program and interior organizations. The studio will encourage an imaginative engagement with uncertainty. Rather than seeking the elimination of uncertainty, we will embrace it as a catalyst for productive possibilities, navigating between the anxieties of the present moment and the projection of an unknowable but still possible future. [1105A]

FACULTY   Marc Tsurumaki, Violette de la Selle

STUDENTS   *Vicky Achnani*, Elaine ZiYi Cui, Janet Dong, Anjelica Gallegos, Alex Olivier, Serge Saab, Yuyi Shen, *Hongyu Wang*, *Leyi Zhang*

JURY   Emily Abruzzo, AJ Artemel, Sunil Bald, David Benjamin, Renaud Haerlingen, Jerome Haferd, Nahyun Hwang, K. Brandt Knapp, Ariane Lourie Harrison, Nick Pacula, Peter Pelsinski, Joel Sanders, Kim Yao

THE NEW SACRED: TRIGGERING COMMONS IN HERITAGE SITES

In times of confinement, individualism, and climate change, we should explore how to transform traditional public spaces into twenty-first century commons through intensifying city life, designing innovative, hybrid-urban architectural spaces, and ensuring food and water security in our ever-growing megacities. From a design point of view, the studio will investigate how to define spaces for the contemporary "new sacred" in ancient heritage sites by combining innovative mixed housing and a food-hub system with educational and cultural programs. The project will be located in an abandoned heritage site with residual areas, neighboring two of the most important university campuses in Lima. [1112B]

FACULTY   Sandra Barclay, Jean Pierre Crousse, Can Vu Bui

STUDENTS   Elaine ZiYi Cui, Kate Fritz, Srinivas Narayan Karthikeyan, Sze Wai Justin Kong, *Tyler Krebs*, *Qiyuan Liu*, Rachel Mulder, Louisa Nolte, Alix Pauchet, Taiga Taba, Sarah Weiss, Yuhan Zhang

JURY   Marlon Blackwell, Andrew Benner, Angelo Bucci, Adine Gavazzi, Billie Tsien, Tod Williams

COASTAL NEW ENGLAND: HISTORY, THREAT, AND ADAPTATION

This studio will consider broadly the natural and human landscape of coastal New England, with a specific focus on the island of Nantucket and related coastal sites. We will consider the ongoing evolution of this unique region in light of the impacts of climate change and sea level rise along with changing environmental, economic, and cultural conditions. Projects in the studio will propose strategies that support coastal adaptation at the scale of the region, illustrated through specific architectural and landscape interventions on Nantucket and in other coastal cities and towns. [1111B]

FACULTY   Alan Plattus, Andrei Harwell

STUDENTS   *Rebecca Commissaris*, *Xuefeng Du*, Anjelica Gallegos, *Yangwei Kevin Gao*, Gabriel Gutierrez Huerta, *Niema Jafari*, Mari Kroin, *Elise Limon*, Daoru Wang, Hengyuan Yang

JURY   Harrison Fraker, Ed Mitchell, Andy Sternad, Anne Tate, David Waggonner, Lynnette Widder

ARCHITECTURAL DESIGN IV

The site and problem for the Core 4 studio is District 15 in Brooklyn. One of 32 public school districts in New York City, it overlaps and conflicts with physical, administrative, political, social and cultural urban boundaries. It is a microcosm of the clashing values and interests that make a city vibrant, yet often segregated and unequal. The design of a school system is inextricably linked to the design of other urban systems such as housing, transportation, commerce, health, and ecology. Through the design of buildings, neighborhoods, and communities, students explore—for better or worse—ideas about how we, as citizens, should educate children. [1022B]

FACULTY

STUDENTS

Aniket Shahane, Coordinator

Jessica Kim, Levi Shaw-Faber, Kevin Steffes, *Caroline Kraska*, Brandon Brooks, Tian Xu, Joshua Tan, Yikai Qiao, Chocho Hu, Suhyun Jang, Jessica Jie Zhou

Peggy Deamer

Lillian Agutu, Yuan Iris You, Claire Hicks, Lauren Carmona, Meghna Mudaliar, Jingyuan Qiu, *Yushan Jiang*, *Morgan Anna Kerber*, Gustav Nielsen, Diana Smiljković, Audrey Hughes, Claudia Carle

Alicia Imperiale

Hannah Mayer Baydoun, *Sangji Han*, *Jack Rusk*, Veronica Nicholson, Sam Golini, Calvin Liang, Jun Shi, Yang Tian, Katie Colford, *Paul Meuser*, Audrey Tseng Fischer

Elisa Iturbe

Rachael Tsai, Timothy Wong, Taku Samejima, Janelle Schmidt, Zhanna Kitbalyan, Tianyue Wang, *Abby Sandler*, Anjiang Xu, Andrew Spiller, Sarah Kim, Alex Mingda Zhang, *Wenzhu Shentu*

Anthony Acciavatti

Perihan MacDonald, Adare Brown, *Michelle Qu*, Abraham Mora-Valle, Lindsay Duddy, Christina Chi Zhang, *Zishi Li*, Brian Orser, Dominiq Oti, Hao Tang, *Calvin Yang Yue*

NINE

systems, regional climatic responses, and urban interventions. Complementary to this scale, *Advanced Studios* use uncertainty as a generative tool; trade normality for productive ambiguity; and celebrate hybridism in its belonging to the values of the past and present.

Preface

The 2020–2021 academic year was complex. Students overcame remarkable difficulties to research, study, learn, and do their creative work. Faculty and staff put in enormous hours across global time zone differences to teach, provide support, exchange ideas, and help shape a community with members both in Rudolph Hall and around the world. As such, this issue of *Retrospecta* is truly celebratory. In it you will find the design studio and course work of the '20–'21 academic year—the year of the pandemic. You will also notice a new format for *Retrospecta*, which we are celebrating as well.

COVID-19 forced us to rethink our fundamental conception of community and urban life, and the work of our students—architects, designers, spatial and sustainable visionaries—now has an urgency and an applicability that would have been unimaginable a year ago.

Despite the many challenges, this was a productive academic year. The crisis further emphasized the need to tackle global problems as they relate to architecture and the built environment. Our students have always been passionate about design driving positive change; this attachment to tangible problems enhances their interest in form-making, technology, materiality, and beauty.

Whether teaching via Zoom or in Rudolph Hall our faculty is committed to helping our students broaden and enhance their knowledge, enrich and expand their passions and become architects who will change the world. Our goal is that they have both an individual voice and a commitment to the greater good. We also expect a strong philosophical position in their creative work that includes respecting the creative motivations of others, from all disciplines.

It is impossible now to know the long-term impact of this past year, but there is no doubt that it will be historically significant. In that context, this volume of *Retrospecta* captures new voices in architecture at a unique moment of shared crises across the planet. The work displays critical insight, exciting new forms and approaches to design and invention, along with the rigor necessary to meet today's obstacles and plan for a better future. In pushing architecture, in practice and as a field of study and research, toward design justice and environmental sustainability, we stand to improve the discipline and practice of architecture, as well as the world we build together.

—Deborah Berke, Dean

Contents

Contents

Contents

Contents

RETROSPECTA 44
Yale School of Architecture
2020–21

yaleretrospecta.org